ONE OF THE BEST BOOKS OF THE YEAR:
PopSugar, Kirkus Reviews

"Riveting. . . . [Carmen Rita Wong] tells her story in vivid conversational prose that will make readers feel they're listening to a master storyteller on a long car trip. . . . Hers is a hero's journey."
— *The New York Times Book Review*

"A stunner about race, culture and the deeper meaning of family."
— *People*

"One of 2022's most captivating books about race relations in America."
— *Reader's Digest*

"Vivid . . . a propulsive pursuit of the truth and the way it's shaped this writer's life."
— *Literary Hub*

"This is a vivid and surprising memoir, bracing and bright. Wong drives, without swerving, straight into the thicket of daughters and mothers and (a lot of) fathers; of racism and sexism and the ways in which inequity seeps into every corner of the American narrative. It is, among other things, an incredible story."
— REBECCA TRAISTER, *New York Times* bestselling author of *Good and Mad*

"This is the Carmen Rita Wong I know—fierce and true. Her story broke my heart and filled it up at the same time."
— SUNNY HOSTIN, three-time Emmy Award–winning co-host of ABC's *The View* and *New York Times* bestselling author of *I Am These Truths*

WHY DIDN'T YOU
TELL ME?

Why Didn't You Tell Me?

A MEMOIR

CARMEN RITA WONG

CROWN
NEW YORK

Published in the United States by Crown, a division of
Penguin Random House LLC, New York.

Crown and the Crown colophon are registered trademarks
of Penguin Random House LLC.

Originally published in hardcover in the
United States by Crown, an imprint of Random House,
a division of Penguin Random House LLC, in 2022.

All photographs are courtesy of the author.

Library of Congress Cataloging-in-Publication Data
Names: Wong, Carmen Rita, author.
Title: Why didn't you tell me? : a memoir / Carmen Rita Wong.
Description: New York: Crown, 2022.
Identifiers: LCCN 2021054234 (print) | LCCN 2021054235 (ebook) |
ISBN 9780593240274 (trade paperback) | ISBN 9780593240267 (ebook)
Subjects: LCSH: Wong, Carmen Rita. | Authors, American—
20th century—Biography. | Television personalities—United States—
Biography. | Internet personalities—United States—Biography. |
LCGFT: Autobiographies.
Classification: LCC PS3623.O597485 Z46 2022 (print) |
LCC PS3623.O597485 (ebook) | DDC 818/.5209—dc23/eng/20211116
LC record available at https://lccn.loc.gov/2021054234
LC ebook record available at https://lccn.loc.gov/2021054235

Printed in the United States of America on acid-free paper

crownpublishing.com

2 4 6 8 9 7 5 3 1

Book design by Barbara M. Bachman

For my brother,
Alex "Aldodado" Wong

When you bury the truth,
you bury it alive.

CONTENTS

A NOTE TO
READERS

———

This is my story as I best remember it and as it has shaped me. This is not *the* truth but my truth. I've changed names and characteristics to protect some and to not give satisfaction to others. This is by no means a full account of my life or the lives of the people in it. There are hundreds more memories where these come from. But you'll get the gist.

WHY DIDN'T YOU
TELL ME?

Prologue

MY YOUNGEST SISTER ONLY RECENTLY GAVE ME A PHOTO-
graph that she had found in our dad's closet. If I had seen it at any point
in my first three decades on this earth, it would have burst my life—and
our family's lives—wide open.

It had to have been taken in 1971 because the swaddled baby that my
mother is holding in the photo is me and I am a newborn. The scene is on
the narrow terrace of an apartment in Manhattan. My mother, Lupe,
stands in semi-profile in what looks like the late afternoon sun. To the
left in the photo is the man I knew later in life as my stepfather, Marty,
holding another baby, the son of the tall woman in the middle of the
photo. This woman's arms are open to the friends on each side of her, her
Afro the apex of the photo's staging. I had been told all my life that my
stepfather—the man in the picture—didn't know my mother when I was
born. So why was he in this picture? Why were we—my mother and I—
with his friends? And why was this photo just surfacing now?

Seeing this photograph two years ago was like finding one of the biggest clues in a long-unsolved case. By the time I saw it, I knew only some
of the truths it revealed.

The name on my birth certificate for "Father" is Peter Ting Litt Wong. At the time of the photo, my mother, Guadalupe Altagracia, and Peter, "Papi," were married. I was raised as their child, as a Wong. But there in the photo was my mother, a married woman, standing on a terrace holding me, her Dominican-Chinese baby, with a man who was not her husband and not my father—a white man. This should be a happy photo celebrating two new little humans brought into the world. So why does my mother look like her heart is breaking? As if in her expression I can hear her say to herself, as she looks at me, her new baby girl, "What have I done?"

The truth she held behind her eyes that day would unfold over decades and have repercussions that she never could have imagined.

CHAPTER 1

... Because the Stage Was Set

ONE OF MY FIRST MEMORIES IS BEING DOLLED UP ONE night in a miniature rabbit-fur chubby coat made by my abuela, my mother's mother, whom we called "Mama." She was an elegant, square-faced, handsome Dominican woman who kept her deep-black straight hair in a short, chic cut, never leaving the house without red lipstick. She worked in Midtown Manhattan as a seamstress for Oscar de la Renta, the suave, perpetually tan Dominican American fashion designer with a legacy of dressing First Ladies starting with Jackie Kennedy, and who filled his workshops with immigrant women from his home country. Abuela dressed for work every day in a smart tailored navy or black Oscar skirt suit and a starched white or cream collared blouse. She was divine to me.

My chubby coat was calico in color and uneven. There were variations in the length of the fur pieces, all shades of brown, from light to dark, patchy like a calico cat. It was sewn of remnants from Mama's salon, a manufacturing loft filled with her fellow countrywomen, who were most likely also various shades of brown and Black, speaking to the island's history of enslavement and colonialism as old as Columbus's first landing. I couldn't have been more than three, almost four years old that night, but what I remember most was the feel of that fur, the absolute luxe of it, unspoiled by any knowledge of the carnage that happened to put it on my back. And I remember that in wearing the coat, along with my fancy lace-up go-go boots and emerald-green velvet evening purse—also custom-made for me with a rabbit's fluffy gray tail smack in the middle at the clasp—I felt like the most loved and special thing. I remember it so well because it was a feeling that was rare and would be gone from my life all too soon.

I was dressed up to go out with my older brother, Alexander ("Alex" to everyone except our parents), to Chinatown with our father, Peter "Papi" Wong. He was coming to pick us up from our apartment in Morningside Heights, which at that time, the 1970s, was Harlem. My brother and I lived alone with our young mother, Lupe, a firstborn child in her father's second family. My grandfather, Abuelo, had two families: one with his wife, who was somewhere else in New York City at the time, and one with his longtime—let's call her partner: my grandmother, Mama. It was decades before I'd find out that this was typical of Dominican culture back then (and it's handed down still a bit today), for a man to have a wife, never divorce, but have another family (or more) and even live with this other family, like my grandfather did. Of course, this was never spoken of, and I didn't meet anyone from Abuelo's other, "legitimate" family—our family—until nearly thirty years later.

"Ay, m'ija, que linda eres!" Abuela said to me as she bent down to put the hook into the eye at the top of my coat. She would say this phrase to me like a mantra, that night and every day that I was lucky enough to see her: *Que linda*. Her greeting to me was always this, and what I heard was, *Oh, my child, how lovely you are*. It could never have been said to me enough. But it wasn't about my appearance. When Mama held my face in her hands, she looked into my being and told me, *me,* that I was worthwhile, even with all she could see inside me, just as I was and as all I was to be. No one before or since has done the same. But at three or four, the prime years in which we shape and form ourselves, our personalities and programming, that was all I needed to build a foundation for the adventure and struggle that was to be the rest of my life.

I hear my abuela's voice so clearly in my memories, but I find it a bit strange that I don't remember my mother's voice at all before the age of maybe five or six. Her silence, or my perception of it, is a striking impression from my childhood. I can see her clearly, though. I saw my mother, "Mami," Lupe, that night at the end of the narrow and dimly lit railroad apartment hallway, holding open the door for my brother and me. Both of us kids all gussied up and fresh and clean for a night out on the town with our Chinese father, who didn't live with us. Papi and Mami were still married but separated. Abuela had kissed me on my cheek and turned me around to follow Alex down the hall to the door. My jaunty boots clip-clopped on the linoleum. Mami held the door open to Papi but didn't let him in. He was a bit thin then, and small, maybe five foot five, looking like an Asian Johnny Cash, dressed all in black, a slick fitted jacket (more biker than suit), hair Brylcreemed back into a low, shiny black pompadour.

As Papi spoke, he embraced us each with one arm like we were buddies. He always did that. "Cah-MON! Cah-mon, there's my daughter and here's my son! My son. Okay, okay, let's go. Ready to eat? You hungry?"

I'm sure we got to Chinatown, nine or ten miles downtown, by car, Papi's preferred mode of transportation. Later I would find out why he always had a car or van. Let's just say that it was job related. Our two closest cousins lived on the street that intersected ours in a building we could see from our windows. They also had a father not living with them who was Chinese. *Un Chino.* I remember that he had a car too, one we'd see parked in front of either their building or ours. No one in our Dominican family had a car, though.

The restaurant was overwhelming in size, filled with gold chairs as far as my eyes could see, and red, so much red, and people and chatter everywhere. Eyes were on us. When our father, Peter Wong, entered a space, no matter the expanse, he made sure you heard and saw him coming. Chinese Johnny Cash was a star, you see, in his mind. And he was being followed by his two darker, not very Asian-looking children. But two children who looked very much like each other, big brown eyes, tan-colored skin, black curly hair, though my brother carried a hint of the Asian fold in his eyelids that would grow more pronounced over time, along with enviably lush lashes. We were just two little brown kids who looked like full siblings, Black, white, and gold.

"Aaaaa!" Peter greeted every server, host, male person, standing or not, that he passed. He rattled off in whichever dialect was applicable to whomever he was addressing. Papi was Taiwanese born, of Chinese descent, a former merchant marine who worked as a chef on a Norwegian shipping vessel. One day he stepped off his ship as it docked at a pier in Manhattan, and never looked back. No bags, no belongings, no home or friends or family. You'd better believe that this slick, car-owning-in-the-city man knew how to hustle his way around this town. Or at least this neighborhood. He had little formal education, yet he could speak English, simple Spanish, and multiple Asian dialects. He was also thirty-four years old to my mother's nineteen when he married her, seven years before I was born. He had fourteen or more years in the United States to my mother's four.

I wish I could tell you a loving story, a cross-cultural heart-filled fest of American melting-pot dreams, of how a teenage Dominican immigrant girl ended up married to a thirty-something Chinese immigrant man, but no. The story is instead in two extremely unromantic parts. One leads to the question of the cars, and one to racism.

White supremacy steeped in the history of the enslavement of African peoples is a thing not only in the United States but also in South and Latin America and the Caribbean, particularly in the Dominican Republic. This flavor of oppression meant that when you married off your daughters (and there was no marrying without your father's permission or choice), especially in the "Ju-nited States," you had to marry someone who elevated your racial status and therefore your family.

This was my mother's answer to me when I asked her many years later: "Mom, why did Abuelo have both you and Maria [her sister] marry Chinese?"

Lupe: "Because the Chinese were the closest thing to a white man."

"Oh . . ."

There was another (still racist) story of my grandfather that my mother floated around when she was being more obtuse about it all. She tied it to Abuelo's business in Santiago, Dominican Republic, being next to a Chinese-owned business and "how well they managed the business. They were good people. So, that's what he wanted."

"Ah . . ."

Abuelo was also a Brylcreem man but his hair wasn't straight and black like Papi's or even Mama's. It was a Langston Hughes finger wave, like a 1920s Harlem bandleader. He was a light-skinned Black man who stayed out of the sun and would most likely beat anyone who would dare to call him "negro." In our home, in our Dominican community, we were "Spanish," a common colonial misnomer in the seventies and beyond. Dominicans have a long and tragic history of racism and denial of their African ancestry. As with the United States, it has a colorist caste system that grew out of European conquest and rule. Ideas of anti-Blackness stuck with those who left the island to establish themselves into our Dominican–New York–immigrant–American life. So, even today you'll hear old-school Dominicanos call themselves "Spanish."

For my grandfather, living in the United States, particularly in New York City, meant access and proximity not only to Anglo white Americans but to other groups who came pretty close to them. So he chose an Asian husband for my mother and for my aunt, Maria, too. The next closest thing to white.

Back to the cars and reason number two.

Elevating my mother's and her children's standing via lighter skin was one thing that benefited her, but Peter Wong brought another thing, as did my aunt's husband: immigration status.

Remember, Abuelo, Señor Eugenio, was married to someone else. So when he—along with thousands of others—was granted immigration clearance in an overall deal that the United States government struck with the Dominican Republic—a mea culpa for the CIA's backing of a man who turned out to be a racist, genocidal dictator, Rafael Trujillo—

his wife and his children with her could enter and work in the United States legally. Unfortunately, it was harder for a mistress and her family to join in the same way.

So, he needed another way for his second family, my family, to be able to stay in the United States. He bought it by paying off two Chinese hustlers with green cards to marry his daughters.

These truths were the opposite of the tales told to me and to my brother nearly all our lives. Tales. Not a hint of this monkey business was discovered until family started going six feet under. Selling off daughters. Imagine. Imagine being my mother, in a new foreign country, her formal education over at fifteen years old. She had to learn a new language, get a full-time job to help the family, and my mother was very smart, ambitious even. She was also demanding and independent. Here she is in this land-o'-the-free, but her father pawns her off—pays a man—to marry her to ensure the immigration status of her mother, brother, and sister. Worthy sacrifice, you may say, to be treated like chattel? I mean, look at the legacy she left, no? No. To be nineteen and forced to marry an older man from another culture—the rage and despair, the feeling of entrapment, I can only imagine. It took decades to get this full story out of Papi. And my mother was only Papi's first, maybe.

In the late 1990s, when I was almost ten years older than my mother was when they married, I visited Peter, then in his sixties, in his dank, windowless, illegal apartment in a basement in Brooklyn. He was packing up to go to Hong Kong, telling me of this wonderful young nurse, maybe thirty years old, a single mother he was going there to marry. That this time, "This time, she loves me. I know. She will take care of Papi. And her family is paying me to marry her, but I know she will stay with me and take care of Papi because I get old."

"They're paying you to marry her?" I asked.

"Yes! Yes, and my plane tickets too—look, look at my tickets!"

He was so excited. I admittedly had a bit of hope too because he had been single for so long—at least as far as I knew—and he wasn't getting any younger. Someone was going to have to take care of him in his old age and I genuinely did not want it to be me.

"You wanna know how much they pay me?"

"Ah . . . okay . . . ," I said, though I wasn't sure if I wanted to know any of this.

"Ten thousand dollar!" he said.

"Ten thousand dollars?" I was reminded of a forensic psychology course I took in grad school a few years before that covered the interviewing of immigrants getting married for citizenship. We were warned by the professor that Chinese women in particular had a scoop on marrying Americans and American Chinese for money, then filing for annulment on the grounds of abuse, which allowed them to keep their new immigration status. That lesson didn't sit well with me at the time. It felt racist. Yet here was an example, in my own family.

Papi waved off my shock. "Oh, c'mon . . . Papi's done this before!"

"What? You've done this before? Married someone for money?"

"Oh yeah, yeah. Ten times. Ten thousand each. But no one sent me in a plane to get married in Hong Kong! That's how I know she is going to take care of me. The family says so."

The next time I went to visit him, a few months later, he was alone. The day that they had all landed in New York from Hong Kong—Papi, the nurse who was his newlywed wife (his eleventh counting my mother—I think), and her daughter, they were met by her uncle who came to fetch everyone but my father from the airport. She went with this "uncle," said goodbye to the man she'd just married in Hong Kong in front of her family and friends in a lavish ceremony, and Papi said he never saw her or her daughter again. None of her family members even picked up the phone when he called. He received the annulment papers and signed them, with ten G's, an international trip, a big dinner party, fancy wedding photos, and dashed expectations all under his belt.

I almost felt sorry for him. I still sometimes do. But then I remember my mother telling me that she left him—twenty-plus years before his Hong Kong wedding—because he'd beat her with the butt of his gun. He would gamble away all their money, including the cash for Alex's baby formula. Lupe left him, supposedly when I was two years old, the only "wife" he truly had, and the three of us then lived alone in our apartment on Claremont Avenue, near our grandparents, siblings, and cousins. Her single-parent status is probably why I don't remember my mother's voice or presence in those early years. She had to go to work.

Money came from Peter when it could. That night of the fur coat, like any time we saw him, he peeled off big bills for us from the roll of cash he kept in his front pocket held together by a rubber band. "How much you want? One dollar? Two dollar? One hundred dollar? Okay, one dollar!" he'd tease, then laugh seeing our faces drop at the single before he handed us instead a hundred-dollar bill, huge in those days. We took a moment to gawk at the bills, feel their potential, then handed them to our mother.

Sometimes the roll he had was as thick as a soda can and other times so thin the money was folded, not rolled, no rubber band needed. This night out, though, was surely for some special occasion. Peter, the "businessman," taking his two little kids out for a fancy dinner, slapping backs and shaking hands. Our usual visits to Chinatown were not so special and certainly not in a restaurant like this, covered in gold and red, embroidered dragons and phoenixes filling my eyes. We usually went to restaurants below street level. The ones with hanging roasted ducks and ribs in the window, cloudy-water fish with big, hazy eyes. I loved those restaurants—still do. But the boss wasn't in those restaurants. He was in the red-and-gold one.

"Ay-ya!" My brother and I followed Peter like puppies. Alex sometimes behind me, sometimes in front, depending how we maneuvered between chairs and tables as Papi greeted everyone like a salesman. (He was a salesman, of a sort.) I clearly remember looking down at the black patent toes of my go-go boots, bashful. He was so loud. It was like we three were a mini parade, Papi the bandleader announcing our arrival, as we snaked around the restaurant, me not understanding why it was taking so long to sit down and eat.

One more stop before dinner. The dais. The elevated platform at the far back of the room, reserved for VIPs, like the bridal party after a wedding, or the celebrating couple and their children and grandchildren at a fiftieth-anniversary party. Or, in this case, for the head of whatever gang my father was involved with. The boss, the don, and his crew. I don't remember what this boss looked like. I kept my head down, staring mostly at my shoes, probably blushing as much as my skin allowed. There was a lot of laughing, but softer tones, and a different kind of handshaking than Papi was doing on the restaurant floor. It was slowed down, with purpose and deference.

In the couple of decades that would pass, as Alex and I became adults, and over multiple visits back to Chinatown with our father, we'd participate in the same parade of our childhood: Papi nudging Alex and me in front of the "gang" at the dais. There was only once where I remember looking at the boss's face and standing tall, not shy at all. It would be the last time the "show" happened. I was in my midtwenties, working a salaried, full-time job, living in and paying for my own apartment, and Papi had brought only me with him to the restaurant. Age had made him a bit less boisterous and, just like an older Johnny Cash, he wasn't as thin anymore. There I was again, stepping up that step to be displayed and examined like a show pony. This time, when Peter introduced me as his daughter, the men at the table scoffed. They snickered and sneered.

"Papi," I asked, "what are they saying?"

"Huh? Oh, oh, they silly. They say, 'How can she be your daughter? She not your daughter!'" They all watched me as Papi spoke. I looked at the boss (I assumed) at the table, a rotund man of maybe forty, big, bald, and fat. I caught his eye and in it, a challenge of some sort. ("Whatcha gonna do, little lady?") I registered it in a moment, clenched my jaw, put on a fake smile, and said, "Okay, Papi, I'm going to go to our table." I didn't say goodbye to the group.

A few minutes later as the server poured my tea, Papi sat down. "Oh, they say you not my daughter because you so pretty, that's why they say that! So pretty!"

"Sure. Sure. Thanks." I fake-smiled again, keeping watch on them out of the corner of my eye. I couldn't let them see that they had me dark and steaming, like my tea.

———

A DAIS IS A stage. So was our living room at the apartment on Claremont. A place that some Friday or Saturday nights filled with cousins and friends of my mother, all young women surely letting off steam from long workweeks in clinics or clearing their heads from the sound of sewing machines, fingers flying with fabric quotas. There was music, loud Latin music, glistening straightened black hair, low seventies bouffants, and clip-on ponytails like my mother would sometimes wear. I'd peek into the room and see the clinking glasses the women held and the glass of our fish tank—an important status symbol, as it was unnecessary and expensive—holding the poor tropical pets I'd accidentally kill soon. (I attempted to feed them a whole bottle of fish food all at once. They looked hungry.) My brother would stay in his room and away from all these lady shenanigans. He was maybe eight or nine and probably welcomed the respite from the annoying, cloying attention of his six-years-younger sibling, me.

And then it was my birthday. I must have been four. My mother had given me a dancing doll. Maybe twice the height of a Barbie, though she was very much not a Barbie, more like the anti-Barbie. An Immigrant Uptown Barbie. She had the same hairdo as Lupe and her friends, black and full. A tiny waist, high, round breasts and hips. Hips that were robotically detached from her shape but attached to the flouncy flamenco-style bottom of her dress. When you flipped a switch at the base under her feet, her hips would swing as if she were dancing the merengue. It was incredible to me. My own personal glamorous dancing doll robot. One who looked like my mother, except for her skin, of course, which was snow-white.

As I was lurking in the hallway, staying up late to watch my mother's end-of-week party, I heard a guest laugh and shout over the music in Spanish, my first language, "M'ija, bring us the doll! Show us!" I imagine my heart must have raced to be acknowledged by these beautiful women. I ran to my room and brought to the doorway my birthday treasure.

"Ven, ven!" I heard, as some guests waved me into the room. Come, come!

Stepping over that doorway, welcomed by these women, was like stepping into another dimension. Change was afoot. Change in me. I looked to my mother sitting off to the side of the room, seeking some form of permission to take over her space. I remember a Mona Lisa smile and a nod. Magic.

I held the doll in front of me and stood near the middle of the room, holding it out like a proud offering. The women buzzed and giggled. One woman reached over and flipped the doll's dance switch on, and her hips started to move in time to the music playing, like a bedazzled pendulum. There were squeals and claps. My smile must have been enormous. I'd had her maybe only a day or two so watching her move and sway, all allure and femininity in that moment, eliciting such a reaction, I was awed.

Then, someone took the doll from me, placed her on the floor—I was confused—and put the attention onto me.

"Baila! Baila, Carmencita!" they called at me. Dance, dance.

And so I danced. Tiny me, rotating my hips like the doll, feeling the music and using the genes I'd be so happy to have my whole life, dance genes. The clapping and attention filled me up like nothing before. I wasn't shy. I was proud and reveled in it.

Where was my mother in that room? I may have seen her sitting off to the side, smiling proudly. I may have made up the memory of her approving presence because I only remember other women's faces. I don't know. She was so absent then. Lupe was a twentysomething single mother working many hours; I have no memories before the age of maybe five of her doing anything domestic or maternal, like cooking for me and my brother, tucking me into bed, or reading me a book, until she remarried and had another child. I didn't have a father who did those things either.

Instead, while Lupe was at work or doing other things, my brother and I were shuttled between apartments. At our abuela's when her working hours didn't overlap with Mom's, or at our cousins' sharing a babysitter as their mother worked too. Or the worst, a strange, pale-white, childless older Dominican woman with a high helmet of tar-black hair and an ornate apartment with tasseled drapery in red, gold, and purple and baroque plastic-covered furniture. She didn't speak to or interact much with my brother or me or let us watch television or eat anything more than farina, cream of wheat, in what must have been an eight-or-more-hour day. (She had such beautiful, fancy things in her house yet didn't want to spend more than a dollar feeding us when she was surely being paid?) My brother would do his best to watch over me and keep us quiet so she wouldn't beat us as she threatened to. This place, all laws and deprivation, and the other, our cousins' apartment, lawless, animalistic, sugar and cartoons. Only Abuela filled our bellies with Dominican food and café con leche, and my heart with her unconditional love. Her watchful eye never a burden, nothing to fear.

But oh, that night, the night of my "cuchi-cuchi" doll and all those beautiful women, under the glow of the fish tank, as I danced and danced to applause and cheers. Dancing for my mother and her friends in our living room. Paraded by our father in front of his associates. The stage was set.

Did they look at me like I looked at my new doll? With admiration, but no connection beyond their own projections? And if so, what was to stop them from doing what I did to my doll? Make up a life for her? Make up stories about where she was from, where she was going to go? Who she was?

Maybe it was easier for them that way. Creating their own realities. It was their world. I was conjured from it.

CHAPTER 2

... Because White Is Right

MARTY, MY MOTHER'S HUSBAND NUMBER TWO, WAS an introduction to a third American culture, the dominant one: white. This older, college-educated bachelor lived only thirty blocks downtown from our apartment and brought along with him an abrupt shift in many things, but first I remember the scents. His place held a soft cloud of professorial pipe smoke blended with the musk of beer and rattan chairs. These notes were added to my already dynamic cultural bouquet of soy sauce, boiled plantains, incense, and Oscar de la Renta perfume. My first visit to Marty's apartment—our first meeting as far as I knew and can recall—was seemingly the same year of my chubby fur coat and cuchi-cuchi doll, when I was three or four.

It was a Saturday morning of cartoons when my brother, Alex, and I woke up in a place that wasn't our home. We sat together in silence in front of a TV bigger than any we'd seen yet. There was much more light compared with what we were used to. Our home was a railroad apartment laid out just like it sounds, a narrow but highly decorated and cared-for train car with small windows. But this particular morning, as I sat cross-legged too close to the TV set, the sun was there to warm my neck and back through wide glass window frames. To my right I could see the whole open kitchen and dining table. I'm sure it was a simple enough middle-class 1970s pad in the city, but I took it in as a whole other language. During commercials I would glance a bit too eagerly away from the TV toward the wrought-iron coiled staircase that led up to the bedroom where I assumed my mother was. We were in a stranger's home and in what felt like an even stranger situation. Our father, Papi, had never lived with us while I was around, but as far as we knew, our parents were still married. It was unsettling to wake up somewhere else knowing your mother was upstairs with a man who was not your father, in an unknown neighborhood. My older brother seemed either unbothered or unsettled. I wasn't yet sure.

Our mother and her new paramour eventually came down the winding stairs together, still in their sleepwear.

"You kids want some breakfast?" this new man asked us. Shy and anxious, I probably nodded. I doubt Alex said a word as his eyes stayed glued to the TV screen. I watched our mother hover in the kitchen while Marty started cooking.

A man, cooking for us? A new sight. So was the alien food eventually set down on the table. Runny eggs, soft whites, without a hint of the crispy edges I loved. I can see their nauseating viscosity to this day. Our mother said something to Marty and in a few moments the offensive blobs disappeared and in their place returned eggs closer to how we knew them and liked them, fried hard, Dominican-style. Nothing on them but the hot butter they were cooked in. Next, out came ketchup, a condiment that I don't think I'd ever had but if I knew it, it was from television commercials for McDonald's. I watched Marty pour Heinz on his still-soupy eggs. I impulsively decided that I wanted to do that too. So I did. I did until I was in middle school. It was my first attempt at assimilation in what was to become a painfully long history of pleasing this man and people in general.

I wanted Marty to like me. My mother lavished attention and energy on him and surely at that age, not having her around much, I wanted to make sure that this new beau understood that I was part of the package.

And, I thought, if he liked me, it would make Mom happy. And if I made Mom happy, well, maybe then I'd be more than her doll. Performing for Mami's benefit was part of the deal. Smile and look pretty and stay quiet unless spoken to and don't complain and "por favor" and "gracias" to all those who took care of me and Alex while Mami worked. My big brother had a different attitude toward Marty. He seemed quiet and patient at first, but ten-year-old Alex was the "man" of our house with no desire to be displaced, nor to have our Papi be displaced. My big brother settled into a mode of stern detachment, in contrast to my fawning and grins.

Marty was eight years older than our mother. He was a Detroit-born second-generation Italian American teller at a local bank branch and had come to New York City to attend graduate school at Columbia University, going for a master's in economics. He never got to finish his graduate studies, as he lost his scholarship after getting arrested with the "hippies" who took over the school's administration building in the anti-war protests of 1968. The story went that my godmother, Carmen— whom I was told I was named after, but we called her by her nickname, "Pimpa"—our neighbor down the hall and my mother's best friend, had been taking courses at Columbia too. She met Marty in a class and introduced him to my mother.

There is some math I have never done until now. If Marty was kicked out of grad school in 1968 or '69, and I was born two or three years later, but here we were, meeting Marty for the first time five or six years after our mother first met him, either they had become acquainted long before and didn't get serious until now or they'd been serious and didn't tell us. They had to have met while our mother was married to Peter and only a year or so after Alex was born. Funny, the things we don't want to see once we are grown, even with facts in our hands. Or we don't see because we have zero curiosity to explore things further because we trust the word of others—ones we're supposed to be able to trust. We put our parents on pedestals, in bubbles or boxes; their lives before we were born unexplored land, because going there would mean learning things that could change the stories we've been told. Discovering our trust mislaid.

Papi and Marty could not have been more different as human beings and even more as fathers. But there was one thing they had in common: wheels in the city, though they rode differently. Papi was dressed in all black, looking like a Triad gangster, driving an aggressive boat of a vehicle. Marty was a white self-proclaimed "honky" academic type with glasses, a head of Italian curls and a bushy mustache, driving a tiny AMC Gremlin hatchback. These disparate presentations provoked a different response in 1970s New York City than we'd been used to. People knew to leave Papi alone. Whereas with Marty, Alex and I once watched from the back seat as he got punched in the face in a road rage incident by someone who looked like us, brown, Marty's blood dripping where his glasses had been forced into his skin. Then there were the times he'd come pick us up at our apartment, only to return with us to find some neighborhood "crew" leaning on his car, holding it hostage, making him pay a "fee" to leave so we could drive away. They wouldn't dare do that to Papi.

Despite tensions of actual or implied violence, Marty's car—and his tastes—also meant worldly transportation to places Alex and I had never been before—visits to the Metropolitan Museum of Art and the Museum of Natural History. Places that set my child mind on fire. We'd see Egypt one weekend and dinosaurs another, and on one afternoon, Marty bought me a clay kit from the gift shop to make my own dinosaur as we picnicked in Central Park, just across the street. The sticky, earthy gray clay felt like the future.

I had come from the insides of apartments filled with varying levels of plastic-covered furniture and blue-eyed Jesuses to Chinatown fish markets and steel drums on the subway. Now my view expanded to places that felt like doorways to the rest of the world. My addiction to the new and different was solidified. Even before Marty, my repertoire of cultures was stuffed to the gills more than most American kids', but all this "more" was intoxicating. If this new love of my mother's was trying to impress us, I was sold. Of course, it all came with a price. Because bringing you toward something can steal you away from something else.

We accelerated from overnights at Marty's apartment and Saturdays at the Met to leaving the city for weekend road trips into the woods of upstate New York and Vermont.

"Okay, so what you do here, is pull. Puuuuuull it up high, then . . . push down!" Marty was instructing me on how to pump our own water from a well. We were in the forests of Bear Mountain, New York, about an hour north of Manhattan, the autumn leaves a landscape of yellows above us and below, crunching under our feet.

"Oof!" I grunted as I hoisted my little pre-K frame onto the cold metal of the pump. It was like trying to bring down a seesaw with some- one heavy on the other side. I needed my full weight to get the lever to move a tiny bit. Marty put his hand on the end of it and pushed down, my body falling with the lever, a ride from one realm to another.

"There you go! You did it!" he said. "Feel that."

I hopped off and touched the water. It was frigid.

"Go ahead, taste it! Watch," Marty said as he put his face directly into the stream as if it were a water fountain in Central Park. My turn. It took my breath away. It tasted like the cleanest ice. It tasted like cleanliness itself.

Do you blame me for being enthralled? I was a Chinese-tea-sipping, Abuela-cafecito-drinking "China-Latina" city girl now pumping water from a well in the middle of the woods and popping popcorn in a pan over a campfire. And the eggs again. This time, I was served them scram- bled and cooked well in a wad of butter over a fire of chopped wood. There is nothing in the world like it. It was a wonder. I was so focused on Marty, and out of my right eye, my big brother, who was like my guard- ian angel at that age, soaking in every sight and scent, that I can't remem- ber much of my mother then, again. It hurts my heart to search for her in these memories. Was she withdrawn, as she'd seemingly always been by that point, or in this case was I the one withdrawing, jumping too quickly and hard into this man's world? Or were we both?

Several weekend trips to the mountains later, it was time to pay that "new world" price. During one Vermont weekend when we stayed in a cabin in the woods, they made it official. Mom and Marty eloped. I don't remember it, but my brother told me he remembered that someone came to the cabin and married them while we just sat and watched. And with that done, our lives as we knew them were gone. My mother, brother, and I no longer lived on Claremont Avenue, off the 1 and 9 subway at 125th Street in Harlem, among our cousins and grandparents and uncle and aunt and Papi—among our whole family and the Dominican, Chinese, and Black uptown cultures we knew. Over what felt like one night, we suddenly lived in Hudson, New Hampshire. Might as well have been Mars. But in 1970s New England, we brown folks were the Martians.

IT WAS JUST AFTER dinnertime, dark out already, and all four of us, Mom, Marty, me, and Alex, were in Marty's Gremlin with a new driver behind the wheel: Mom.

"Ay, Marty." My mother's voice was clear now and she sounded scared.

"Don't worry, Lupe, don't worry," Marty said. From my view in the back seat of the Gremlin, I watched him pat Mom's hand. "I'll take care of it."

We were stopped on the side of the road, only two houses down from our new home, a split-level with a garage, our address just over the border of Massachusetts in a development with its name displayed on a formal brick entrance to our road. It was an impenetrable darkness outside, no streetlamps.

The lights from the police car behind us cast a repeating red, blue, red, blue onto the black vinyl bucket seats my brother and I faced from the back seat. The four of us sat in silence in the tiny two-door vehicle where all I heard was my heart thumping. Already in my short life, I'd learned that the police were not necessarily our friends. The last time we'd been approached by the police, as we'd pulled over to the side of the road, a cop made Marty clean my carsick puke off the already filthy New York City sidewalk, just because he could.

The sergeant came to my mother's window and asked for her license and registration.

"Good evening, Officer. This is my wife here and I'm teaching her to drive," Marty said as he leaned over to make sure the flashlight made his pale face visible. "We've just moved here from New York City and this is our new home, right down there." He gestured. I followed his direction and could now see that we were within sight of our house. Marty handed the cop his documents. We waited again, me still not breathing and still not comprehending what we'd done wrong besides maybe my mother shouldn't have been driving.

The officer came back, leaned into the car, and after he handed everything back to Marty, spoke only to him, not my mother, "You see, your neighbors here called in a report of Puerto Ricans casing the neighborhood."

Puerto Ricans? But we're Dominican. And why is he saying it like that, like it's bad to be Puerto Rican?

"You just be careful out here, all right? Maybe stick to parking lots for your driving lessons."

"Yes sir. Thank you," Marty said. "Have a good night, Officer."

We rode the couple hundred feet home in silence as my mind hummed from an awakening. I rolled around in my head over and over that our neighbors called the police on my mother, on us, because . . . we were different from the people here, the white people. An all-white neighborhood. A nearly all-white state. Of course, I could see with my own eyes that we were different. Our skin, our hair, our features, were nowhere else to be found around us. My brother and I came from the kaleidoscope of a city, where our ambiguous brownness blended in as we'd hop from neighborhood to neighborhood—even in Chinatown we were barely given a second glance though we didn't look very Asian. The subway was the great showcase for all colors and cultures, from white to Black and everyone in between, all trying to get to where we needed to go, do what we needed to do. But white folks were the clear minority in my young world up until that point. My mother had one cousin who was blond with blue eyes but even he was mixed, his beige skin signaling his fraction of African origins. There was one young white professor from Columbia University in our building, his giant dog a lucky sighting. Sure, my mother, her cousins, and friends would ooh and ahh after our blue-eyed, golden-haired cousin and practically genuflect to our resident white professor, signaling their seniority, but what I never saw was them—the white folks—looking down at us. This was the missing piece of this country that I discovered that night in New Hampshire. That these white people, all around us in our new hometown and state, thought less of us for our color. So much less that we were assumed to be criminals on our own street where we lived.

That night became a flashbulb memory preserved in me like a bug in amber, haunting me for decades. And I needn't have questioned my very young assessment because our new home state would continue to teach me exactly what it thought of us.

As we claimed a shopping cart and walked into the local grocery store, my mother—who I thought was beautiful and arguably striking—wore in her hair large "rolos" (rollers), as fat and round as Coke cans, covered by a beautiful silk scarf tied at the back of her neck. This hairstyle was the usual and accepted way for a brown woman uptown with kinky hair to set straight her newly washed 'do. The usual day to see this set on my mother in the city streets and stores was early Saturday because she and her ladies had to look super cute for going out that night after a long workweek. And the scarves. I loved the scarves. My mother had a drawer of them that I would sneak into and drape around myself to pretend I was just as glamorous as her and all her friends.

The grocery aisles in our new town were enormous compared with what we were used to; the store itself appeared to be a full city block of unlimited supplies. We shared a mutual bubbly excitement, my mother, my brother, and I, as we first walked in the doors. Then, as we wound through the aisles, the metallic sounds of our shopping cart sounded louder as every person we passed went silent and stared at us, at my mother in particular. They stared, sneered, and stifled laughs. I saw their ugly faces first, before I saw my mother's stoic but pained expression, as she kept shopping for what our family needed until we reached the last aisle, my brother and me silently following. Mom then steered us to the checkout line. After ten aisles of stares and whispers, her face was burning with shame and maybe even anger. Her back was straight, chin up, jaw set as she unloaded the groceries from our cart. Registering this look that I'd never seen on my proud mother's face, I caught another woman just over her shoulder, staring at Mami and whispering to another shop-per. The women looked at me and I sent burning daggers their way with my little eyes even though I was so sad and afraid. I never saw my mother in rolos in public again. The scarves would soon go too. These bigoted slights, big and small, continued to stack up week by week. Once we started in our new schools, my brother was told he was not allowed on his school's football team. I overheard my mother tell Marty, "They said no n***ers were allowed to play on the team."

We weren't in the town of Hudson long. Marty had bought a plot of land in another town about a half hour north to build my mother a dream house. The area was so undeveloped it didn't have a street address but instead an "RFD," for "rural free delivery," a post office designation cre-ated for families living on farms with unpaved roads. But the house wasn't finished in time to coincide with selling the Hudson house, so we packed up and landed in a rental condo in Nashua, ten or fifteen minutes between the two places. We moved twice in what felt like less than a year and the shock of it all, plus missing my family, our whole family, in Manhattan, started to create problems. Each time we packed up and moved I heard no explanation, was given no guidance. This was 1970s parenting. There was no family meeting to sit the kids down and prepare them psychologically for all these changes to come or to get them to weigh in on what they'd like to do and how they were feeling. Just as there wasn't any discussion about the trauma of moving us away from all the family and friends we'd ever known in New York City and the peo-ple who looked like us. You go where your parents go and they'll hear nothing of your unhappiness or fears or anxieties or, for god's sake, your opinion. I would have loved to know when I would ever see my cousins or my abuela again. *And what is this food Mami's making? I don't like it. It comes in cans and plastic.*

"You will sit here until you eat it." My mother pointed at my plate. Unpacked boxes were all around us. It must have been the first day or so in the Nashua condo, aka our way station between houses, because my dinner was on a paper plate and it was a sad-looking hot dog. Not a long, floppy, gray New York City dirty dog with sauerkraut, which I loved, but a desiccated-bun, short, rigid dog with the ever-present ketchup bottle on the side. I had been used to elaborate dinners cooked by my abuela, piles of rice and beans and sancocho and adobo and this amazing soupy chicken she made with leftovers, an incandescent yellow green from spices, plus every kind of plantain: maduros, tostones, mofongo, boiled and mashed, and on weekends, fried pancakes sometimes—yes, pancakes fried in butter for dinner. Divine. So, what the hell was this? I wanted *our* food. Not this gringo shit. *Coño.* I know now, a mother myself, that my mother must have been so stressed, my brother too, and we were all acting out. All three of us, foreigners in our own country, suddenly, no kinfolk within two hundred or more miles. Isolated. Each of us suffering in our own way. So began my descent into controlling things I could control. Like food.

My bony bum sat and sat and sat at that table with that damn hot dog, my stomach growling for hours. Mom even went up to bed and turned off all the lights except the small one over the kitchen stove. Everyone was in their beds but me. I was a six-year-old sitting alone on the ground floor of a condo I didn't know, in a place I didn't know, my head on the kitchen table, eventually falling asleep with my trusty companion, conviction. At some point Marty came down the stairs and carried me up to bed. Saved. Seen. I liked this new guy. Even though it was his doing that we were there.

Our new house was in the tiny town of Amherst off a main road called Route 101, which was two paved lanes that cut through farmland. This was a new development to attract commuting, family-minded professionals with incomes from burgeoning careers just over the border in Massachusetts, like Marty. (Today, it's an eight-lane mega thoroughfare lined with fast food, car dealerships, and commercial buildings.) This was where Marty was going to build his dream home for the whole family, an American dream home for my mother. Customized, influenced by his Michigan upbringing, bigger, and as it was a new development and fairly rural, frugal. About a fifty-minute commute from his Massachusetts office. Marty worked on designing and constructing the house from the foundation up with a guy named Rusty, a sweet, burly man with a ginger mop of hair, a fluffy mustache, and tattoos. On weekends we'd drive over from the condo to check out the construction progress, walking through the wooden skeleton of the two stories as Rusty and Marty pointed out where the kitchen would be (open kitchen, of course, just like his apartment in the city), and bathrooms and bedrooms. For a city kid, it seemed enormous. Not rich so much as just big for us. Four bedrooms and two and a half baths. Alex would get a huge bedroom at the front of the house, and I'd get the smaller but sunny bedroom in the back. Mom and Marty's bedroom and en suite bathroom were also at the front, and at the top of the stairs in the middle of everything was our kids' full bath, while in the last corner was the remaining fourth bedroom, for our new baby sister and all the babies to come.

"This one, Mami." I pointed at a pastel lime-sherbet-colored fluffy rug sample. We were in a showroom choosing what would go in the new house. With few choices presented to me up until this point, the ability for me to be able to pick out the colors of my bedroom and rug had me feeling like I had a tiara on my head again. I wanted a light-green-and-yellow-decorated room with a canopy bed. Princess-like, but non-gendered colors that showed what I thought was my sophistication and originality at six.

The rug that I ended up with smacked that tiara flat off my head. I stood in the doorway of my fully decorated new room, fuming. There was the white twin canopy bed with the light-yellow-and-white-laced blanket I'd asked for, pillow sham, matching canopy, and curtains. The walls were painted my favorite light, sweet green. But the rug. Well, what would Oscar the Grouch's rug look like? It was a high-piled dreadlike shag of two shades of green, one like wet dollar bills, the other desiccated lawn. Together, they formed a surface only a dirty Muppet could love. I had been betrayed. This would never have happened to me back home. Papi would have bought it for me or Abuela would have made sure I got what I asked for. I had been spoiled. Or had I just been used to having my voice be heard?

Come to find out Marty had vetoed my lovely, ethereal carpet ask. Seems it wasn't "practical." A pastel color would stain too easily. As if my mother would ever let me eat or drink in my bedroom. Well, then. Looks like my white savior had his faults, his tendency toward practicality a lifelong passion. There are worse things a parent can be than nonindulgent, I guess. Plus a couple of times a year I had my father, Papi, peeling off twenties and hundreds for me to balance out this austerity.

There was one small mercy in our New England move. My mother learned to drive fairly quickly and the four-hour drives back home to the city during school breaks and summers may have kept my brother, my mother, and me sane. And each time, as we drove south, the Hutchinson River Parkway eventually unveiling a full panoramic view of the city, my stomach would jump. Jump just like when you see someone you're madly in love with after a long separation.

When we visited home, we would stay in our old apartment on Claremont with Abuela, Abuelo, and my mother's brother, Lou, who'd all moved in, ensuring that I would always stay tethered to that version of home. Tethered with a loving weave of continued Dominican meals, music coming from neighbors' windows, thighs sticky with sweat on a plastic-covered couch, opening every lipstick and perfume jar on my abuela's dresser, and reveling in her unconditional, giving love. And yes, seeing my father, Papi, with his gifts of Chinese food, costume jewelry, and stiff twenty-dollar bills so new they could give paper cuts. The bills that made it into my hands were contributions to my glamorous Barbie collection that I'd curate and purchase from the wide aisles of suburban mega stores once we got back to the woods. My collection was an all-woman (and unfortunately all-white, because that's all that was sold for years) Studio 54–Solid Gold escape fantasy I was building back in my New Hampshire bedroom.

My uncle Lou had moved into my old bedroom abutting the kitchen. Lou was my mother's younger brother, the youngest of the three siblings. Poor Lou. A former child prodigy, a handsome, sweet only son, Lou had been diagnosed with severe paranoid schizophrenia by the age of sixteen. I would find out later in my studies that though schizophrenia runs in families, it usually takes an environmental stressor to trigger it, such as trauma, abuse, or drug use. Rounding out my knowledge of Lou came the revelation from my aunt decades later that Abuelo, my grandfather, had beaten and tortured his son so much, my uncle did not stand a chance. Abuelo had beaten everyone. He beat my beloved grandmother, Mama, he beat his daughters, just as surely as he'd been beaten by not only his own father but the government of his homeland, the Dominican Republic. Abuelo had been part of the rebellion against the dictator at the time, Rafael Trujillo. In the dead of night my grandfather had been pulled from his bed at home, tortured, but he survived. While he was in the hospital recovering, his sisters put a plan in place to get him out as they surely knew that next time there would be no hospital, only a funeral. They dressed up Abuelo as a woman and smuggled him out of the hospital, put him in hiding, and somehow got him on a plane to New York. My grandmother—his mistress—followed him soon after with their children—my mother; her younger sister, Maria; and her brother, Lou. Abuelo would send for his wife and their children afterward, setting them up farther north.

My abuelo's "beatings" of me were seemingly playful "pow-pows" to the bum with his rolled-up newspaper. He was always reading the newspaper or watching the news. Sometimes he'd pretend to chase me around the apartment down the long hallway with the rolled-up paper or just reach over from his recliner while he was watching TV to tap my butt as I passed and say, "Pow-pow! Pow-pow!" and we'd laugh and giggle. Knowing what I know now of how much tragedy he caused my mother, grandmother, and uncle, when I think back, I fantasize taking that newspaper and forcing it down his throat.

"Hi, Carmencita! Oh, my Carmencita! How are you? How's New Hampshire?" my uncle Lou asked me in the rapid, dulcet cadence he has to this day as I sat at the tiny table in our kitchen during one early visit back to Claremont—now my grandparents' kitchen.

"It's good. Good," I answered, putting down my sweet café con leche and Goya crackers that I loved to soak in the coffee like Anglo-American kids soak Oreos in milk. I'd sit there with Abuela, watching her do laundry, squeezing water out of clothes, then hanging them on the line that went out the kitchen window into the alleyway, five floors up, just as the whole building did even in the freezing cold. Or I'd watch her prep and cook dinner, both of us fairly silent, just enjoying each other's presence. Sometimes while I waited for her to make me something delicious, I'd squeeze the plastic fruits in the pretty bowl, especially the grapes, that had a permanent spot on the table.

"Oh, that's good. That's good." My uncle paused. He was in his usual white tank undershirt and black belted pants, his heavy glasses hanging on his brown face and his neck kinked to the side as he looked past me or at the ground as he spoke. A side effect of his psychiatric medication was tardive dyskinesia, involuntary tics of his face and neck. Lou would consistently swing his head down toward his shoulder as if wiping a drop of sauce off his chin onto his shirt. After being on medication most of his life, his neck is permanently hunched over, his head never to sit straight again.

I waited patiently until he finished speaking, as he liked to stop by only briefly and manage whatever conversation he could with me. My grandmother, in her bata, a housecoat, looked over and smiled at us. My mother was probably roaming around the neighborhood seeing friends and cousins.

"Okay, Carmencita. . . . Okay. Jesus loves you! Jesus loves you, Carmencita! Did you know that Jesus loves you? And that if you accept Jesus Christ as your Lord and Savior that there is a place for you in heaven?" Lou asked.

"Yes. I know. Thank you."

"Das good, Carmencita. Okay, you eat, you eat. Jesus loves you!" Lou waved at me and slowly backed into my old bedroom just off the kitchen, where he spent nearly all of his days, leaving only to go to church. Now, four decades later, Lou still says those words to me every time we speak. "Jesus loves you!" I haven't been religious in decades so instead what I have chosen to hear over all these years is: "I love you, Carmencita. I love you." And I usually take love wherever I can get it. Unfortunately.

Marty never came with us on these trips back home. He left New York City behind and has been back maybe three times to visit me over a span of thirty years. Once he drove from his home in Rhode Island just for the day when my daughter was born. Once he did the same when I married her father. And the same to help me move after my divorce. And though we saw Papi the several times a year that we'd drive back home to the city, during our childhood Papi came only once to visit Alex and me in our new house in Amherst, New Hampshire. Maybe a year or two after we moved in, Papi drove the couple hundred miles just to stand outside in the driveway and say hello to us, his two kids. He wouldn't come into the house. Or he wasn't allowed in because it was Marty's house, I don't know. I remember Papi's macho ship of a sedan, looking out of place in a town full of sedate family vehicles. His gelled pompadour now sat a bit lower on his head and he wore a light blue or white button-down shirt. For the first time, I saw him as sincerely out of place. Only a few years in New Hampshire, out of the city, and my visual comprehension was shifting. It was like I had white lenses over my eyes—the white gaze. He looked darker. More harsh. Less "cool." Embarrassing. Feelings I'd never had about him in New York City. I remember that I was old enough—maybe ten—to catch myself with this negativity and that it didn't feel good to recognize what I was doing. And it made me question what was happening to me, and to us as a family, living in a place that felt like an alternate reality where assimilation seemed like the only way to survive. Lose yourself so as not to lose your mind. Erase the differences.

Mom did lose herself in one good way I witnessed in those early New Hampshire years: in Marty's arms. I would catch them often, sneaking kisses and long embraces in the kitchen, which made me feel some kind of way because I'd squeeze my little grade school body between them, push them apart, and squeal: "No kissing! No kissing!" These embraces lessened and then disappeared a few years after our move.

The gap between the "new us" and our own family back in Manhattan kept getting larger. And it became all too clear to my mother that unlike the freedom and support she had in the city, in Amherst she was isolated and alone. Mom had once had a job to go to, coworkers to see, cousins and friends, and the freedom to drop us kids off with her mother or her sister and walk out the door into the world. For my mother, living in the city had meant physical and mental freedom, literally. Hungry? Walk to a bodega anytime and get what you need. Hands full of laundry and a baby? Ask your neighbor doing laundry next to you to hold your baby for a moment, trusting her fully. Get in a fight with your parents? Walk over to your cousins' across the street for some flan and chisme. Get in a fight with your husband? Grab the kids and go down the hall to your neighbor's so you can breathe. Both my mother and I have done this. City living can be lonely but you're never truly alone. And even if you're broke, like I have been, you can walk and walk and fill your eyes with sights and your ears with music, all times of the night and day.

New Hampshire living, with its three-mile drive to the nearest shop and no job beyond caring for us kids, no brown, Black, or even Asian faces, must have felt like a vise on her, cranking down slowly. And there were other limitations she grew to resent. Once a week, Marty would write up, rip out, and give Mom a check for the week's household expenses, mostly groceries. (I will always remember the distinct sound of that rip.) I caught the moment of the exchange once at the kitchen table. It happened in silence, but my mother's look spoke a personal tome on gender and race intersectionality in 1980. Her face fell as she took the check from him between her thumb and first two fingers, as if it had a bit of a stink. Her eyes held on to the dollar amount written on the check, as she brought it down and set it on the table, all happening in slow motion in my eyes. She had a scowl that spoke of resentment. I remember too a slight breeze of shame wafting by me. From earning her own money, living her freedoms, dressed to the nines, red lips and beauty-shop hair, to sitting at a kitchen table, makeup-less, hair pulled into a utilitarian bun, toddlers at her feet, two hundred miles from all she'd known. A lesson in power and money. A parable. Her white knight extracted a price. She signed herself over to a supposed white savior, which meant leaving behind all she held dear. A Faustian immigrant bargain where what she saw before her was what she had to gain, blind at first to what she would be forced to give up in the process.

Mami began to channel her disappointment and resentment onto us kids, making sure not to do so in front of Marty at first. Unfortunately, she'd learned from a skilled abuser, her father, a recipient of the legacy of physical and mental punishment that tends to get passed down from generation to generation. I went from not remembering much of my mother's voice or touch to remembering all too clearly the smack of the flat of her hand against my tiny leg, bare on a summer day. She left a red handprint that I stared at, incredulously betrayed. I remember the empty-gut feeling of her betrayal. *I thought she loved me.* Before New Hampshire, I don't remember Lupe ever hitting me or even holding me. But now she would pull and pinch my ear so hard it burned for hours. Yank my hair. Threaten to make me lick the inside of the toilet if I didn't clean it well enough or that she'd shove the rye bread down my throat if I didn't eat it. (Rye and anything anise or licorice make me retch. So once, under her threats, I tried to eat it and instantly threw up.) I became terrified of her, though I loved and needed her so, as we do our mothers. Over time, my terror would transform into anger and righteousness as I built myself into her foil and a protector of my little sisters. But for those first New Hampshire years, until I was in my midteens, we lived under an increasingly anxious hum of my mother's moods, bile-tipped tongue, and quick hands. But not in front of Marty until years later. Even though I was so young, I remember noting how her demeanor would change when he got home, from sour to sweet. It made me continue to question the concept of trust.

New Hampshire became our home mostly because there was a new little sister. Mom had gotten pregnant, the catalyst for our move out of the city and for the quickie wedding. My sister was six years younger than me, tiny and fragile, the umbilical cord wrapped around her neck preventing her from getting the nutrients she needed to grow as she should have (or so Mom said the doctor told her). She was petite, big-eyed, with a large head and the thinnest of appendages. Years later, I joked (cruelly, I now acknowledge) to my mom that she looked like ET when she was born. But sweetly, to her face, I called her after one of our favorite books I'd read to the kids, "Thumbelina." Meanwhile, she grew into gorgeousness with her big doe eyes and a wild mane of curls, though she never grew taller than a bit over four foot eleven.

Of course, it may be a stretch to say it was maternity's fault that Mami turned sour. After all, she'd been much happier with Alex and me, but we were in the city then. It seemed to be the additional maternity combined with our remote foreign location that clashed with Mami's dreams and desires. The yoke of isolated new motherhood after her two oldest were already school-age and parenting in a place with no family support. It would make many a sane woman go crazy, let alone a smart, charismatic, driven woman like my mother. Marty would leave the house by seven every weekday morning for his nearly one-hour commute to his Massachusetts office in the burgeoning tech corridor of Route 128, briefcase in hand, then not get home again until 6:00 P.M., ready to be served his dinner. Lupe was alone all day, for eleven hours, in a big house with a new baby and two frustrated, perpetually irked, wilding-out kids. Her life went from glamorous fabrics and nights dancing to a home filled with wanting, needing, asking, screaming, crying. She called everyone on the phone back in the city nearly daily at first, while Marty was at work, honoring her own umbilical cord as she whispered in Spanish, laughed, and clucked her tongue.

Alex and I coped with our dismay in other ways. My brother had been my protector. But increasingly I became his annoying, cloying little sister. I'd find him in his big bedroom, head in a comic book or magazine, record spinning. He'd shoo me away. But he could be generous sometimes and let me borrow—swearing on my life to its protection and return—his first-edition X-Men or Spider-Man comics. But Alex and I began to have uproarious fights—our relationship soured into love-hate for a few years—but he still was everything I compared myself with. He led and I followed. He escaped our bland, rejecting new environs with superheroes and science fiction and piles of books. So did I.

We still bonded around Saturday morning television for a while, the same routine as back at Marty's apartment in the city. We'd get up early and sit too close to the screen for hours before Mom and Marty got out of bed to make us breakfast. I was a teen before I figured out that in those hours of cartoons, it was baby-making time. We ended up with so many babies from those sleep-in Saturday mornings. Four little sisters in total, each arriving somewhere between eighteen and twenty months apart. "Irish twins," as some used to say. I remember one day, after already having three baby sisters, bumping into my mom's belly in the kitchen, feeling how hard and round it was under her untucked blouse, then saying to her, only half-joking, "Mom! Another one?" I became a little "mami" to them myself. A role I didn't want or ask for but that was foisted upon me by my eldest-daughter birthright, even if we didn't share the same last name or father. A role that cost me a true sisterly relationship with them. Robbed me of it to this day. On the other hand, Alex and I shared the bond of being Wongs, a couple of city kids sharing the same big hole of hurt from missing our family back home. A family of three—me, Alex, and Mom—before this new family grew.

"Wonder Twin powers, activate!" I held my fist out to fist-bump my brother as we mimicked one of our favorite cartoons. "Shape of . . . a waterfall!"

"Form of . . . a gorilla!" he said.

The cartoon characters were an alien brother and sister, purple-skinned, who would bump rings, say the slogans, and then the boy could become any animal and the girl any shape or form of water. Aliens we were and aliens we remained.

FOR FIRST GRADE, WHEN WE moved to Hudson, my mother continued the Latin family tradition of Catholic school for all. My brother went to the all-boys school one town away, Bishop Guertin, and I went to the all-girls Presentation of Mary Academy. I don't remember much beyond being completely overwhelmed and unmoored. No one was brown like me, or Black or Asian, or had an "ethnic" name. I had trouble telling the girls (all white) apart. The uniforms were scratchy and ugly, a maroon, gray, yellow, and white plaid that would haunt me for decades. It was the first time I came into direct contact with nuns wearing habits, as all our teachers at the time did. The castle-like behemoth brick building was filled with them, navy or black skirt suits with veils allowing only a front pouf of hair or bangs to be seen. I must have spent that whole year simply processing. Processing and figuring it all out, managing everything coming at me, all the change. I do remember being feisty, though. My mother got an earful from the teachers early on. And then, when we moved again, it was time for a public school that was a bit more like home in only two ways: no uniforms and boys.

"No, my name is Morning Dove," I insisted. "My mother made me change it when we got here!" I was seven years old and newly enrolled in second grade at the local public school. This ridiculous lie was my way of answering the new question "What are you?" Something hard for me to answer, because in New Hampshire I had already gotten the message that being anything but a white American was not good—*not good*—in these parts, a place where I was a drop of brown sap in a mountain of snow, or something else brown and not so sweet.

So, when my class had a Thanksgiving project to draw and color a mural representing the first Thanksgiving dinner, white people and brown people sitting at the same table together, I assumed there was not only equality in the depiction but some kind of elevation of these brown people who looked like me and my family. I jumped on it. If these white kids were drawing and coloring Native Americans and the teacher was teaching us about them in honorable tones, well, I was just going to have to reinvent myself, wasn't I?

"Your name is not that," a boy sniped back at me.

"Yes, it is! You don't know," I cut him back.

I even designed a hieroglyphic name for myself, melding the influence of the Egyptian wing of the Met with this new Thanksgiving myth. It was my first exposure to the holiday as far as I can remember. We certainly didn't celebrate it back in NYC—the mass marketing and consumerism of the holiday had yet to influence our plantains-and-dumplings uptown immigrant bubble. The name I designed was an outline of a bird with half a sun above it. (Gotta give myself props for the mash-up.) Surely I made up this tale as a way to insert myself into the story of Thanksgiving that was obviously so important to these white American people. I saw myself only as the "Indian," the brown one, that we drew and colored with crayons in our five-foot-long class mural. It was obvious that I wasn't a white Pilgrim, characters that the whole rest of the class could see themselves in.

This identity I created was a delusion that I spoke of so much, my teacher had to tell my mom at the parent-teacher conference. I don't remember what my mother said to me afterward but I never mentioned Morning Dove or drew my glyph name again. But I also got no answers as to how to manage these feelings of being thought of as an oddity, a lesser human being, that this new place was pushing on me. And it pushed and it pushed.

Between my offensive appropriation and my embarrassing habit of tackling boys during recess to kiss them—and I do mean tackling, to the ground—Lupe had had enough of my shenanigans. It was back to all-girls Catholic school for me for third grade. And time to see racism trickle down from grown-ups. Back to the nuns and their habits, to scratchy uniforms and scolding for doing so much as staring out the window (which I did often). Back to the mostly French Canadian–named students and the military-tight lines of us walking down the halls, in forced silence, even to the bathroom. To Catholic masses in the all-white-and-gold marble chapel one Friday a month and every religious saintly holiday. To nuns who never let uneaten food from home be thrown away at lunch. (I ended up finding a lone trash can outside the building where I'd dump my mother's at-times-revolting sandwiches like sardines on white bread. The horror.)

"Yes, she's doing very well in all her subjects." Sister Rachel smiled. I beamed at my mother. The year before, in third grade, a parent-teacher conference meant a teardown. My grades were top-notch, but I was constantly in trouble for talking too much and not focusing. Attention deficit was to blame, and I was bored. Mom caught on and instead of punishing me, stood up for me. She told the teacher that I needed to be challenged so I was let loose into books and workbooks from the next grade up, as advanced as I could take. That helped quiet me down, a bit.

"That's so great to hear," my mother said as she put her hand on my shoulder after she was told I was a straight-A student yet again.

"She must get it from her Chinese side," said Sister Rachel.

My ears perked up.

Mom just smiled and said, "Sure."

I stood in shocked silence.

Yes, I was a Wong, but Papi wasn't the one there to make sure my homework was done. He wasn't going to parent-teacher conferences. I don't even know if he knew where I was going to school. But Lupe was there. Always pushing, always expecting. The tiger mom of lore but Caribbean born, not the Asian parent. And Sister Rachel thought it was okay to give Chinese genetics credit instead of the mother standing before her? So, Chinese people were "smart." But brown and Black people were not, and in my teacher's eyes maybe could not ever be.

On the car ride home, I was nervous to ask but I had to: "Mami. Sister Rachel said I'm smart because I'm Chinese."

"Mm-hmm." Mami looked straight ahead at the road. She said nothing, but her face communicated a script I couldn't fully decipher. What I was able to glean from her expression and lack of words was that my mother wasn't telling me something in particular. She hinted at it with a sly smile. But it wasn't the Mona Lisa I was looking at. She was more like a Cheshire cat. In her mouth she held something secret. Her face amused by something she was holding back. It was a rare countenance for her to have. As rare as the truth of what she was concealing.

CHAPTER 3

... Because I Sold My Soul
for the American Dream

CATHOLICISM LENDS ITSELF WELL TO OBSESSIVE-compulsive disorder. Say the full rosary before bed and then another three Hail Marys just to make sure. Cross yourself three times every night before you go to sleep and kiss your right thumb after the last. If you accidentally cross yourself more than three times, you then must continue in multiples of three, and do it for six, because four means death in Chinese. But was it six times? Or did I accidentally do seven? Six is the devil's number so I have to go to nine. Okay, rosary again, and then cross three times. And so on. A kid has to manage her anxiety somehow. Catholic school gave me an outlet, or more like a crutch.

When I was eight years old, I made an altar in the small alcove behind my bedroom door with four medium-size moving boxes in two-on-top-of-two formation. I covered them with a lovely scarf from either Abuela or Mom, and when I knelt, the altar was just neck height. On it I centered a large Jesus portrait framed in ornate cheap white plastic that my mother had given me and around which I placed various religious items I'd received during my increasingly intense Catholic education. I tied scapulars (devotional fabric squares of saints hung on ribbon) onto my bed frame, ensuring a sure path to heaven if I died in my sleep. Smooth rocks that I'd found (a habit my mother instilled in me with her inherited Santeria mix of devotion, a religion built from a combo of the faith of the African peoples in the Caribbean and the colonizing European Catholics), along with pictures of the Virgin Mary, including Our Lady of Guadalupe, after whom my mother was named, rounded out the mini chapel of my third- and fourth-grade dreams.

Every night before bed I knelt and prayed as that ugly green shag carpet burned into my knees. I offered up the pain to Jesus. I prayed for stigmata. I prayed for miracles. I prayed for some kind of drama and excitement to happen in my life. I prayed to become a saint like those I read about in the school library. They were illustrated with glamour and romance, even the saints who were nuns, all flowing robes, veils, and almond eyes. When my mother told me that she admired my altar, I declared to her that I wanted to become a nun. She told me the same once, many years later, when the five of us children and babies buzzed around her on a summer day. We were squabbling and bickering, interrupting her favorite pastime of sorting her junk mail, when she hissed at us: "I was supposed to be a nun! I should have been a nun!" I picked up a baby, gave my mother the stink eye just beyond her sight, and took all the kids to another room to play. I worried that they'd take her words to mean that they weren't wanted. That they were mistakes. Which was what she was saying, in essence, but a nun? Did she see herself? Knocking boots every Saturday morning for over a decade, perpetually pregnant for years once we moved to New Hampshire. Walking around sometimes at night in a see-through negligee to say her good nights to us kids.

"Mom. Put away your boobs!" I'd admonish.

"Wha? Dees boobs? You fed on dees boobs!" she'd cackle.

A nun, she said.

I scoffed then, but it was something we shared: the desire to lose ourselves in some kind of passion and devotion.

Then, the house began to talk to me. I'd lie there at night, blankets pulled up over my ears and the top of my head so the demons couldn't pull my hair, only my eyes and nose peeking out. My prayers were done, our growing family finally quiet, asleep, the crickets and critters outside a low rural soundtrack. Then, my walls would speak. *Crack. Crunch.* It was a house made of wood that I saw being built with my own eyes, but the sound of the boards settling flowed through my filters of fear and religion as I convinced myself that a spirit was speaking to me. I asked it questions silently, telepathically: "Are you friendly? One thump for yes, two for no." In time, the wall would thump once. I was carefully pleased. If it was an amiable spirit, then I could talk to it and keep it happy. Just like I tried to keep everyone happy.

When the walls would knock before I fell asleep, I'd ask the presence more questions, like was it a boy? One knock for yes, two for no. Or are you a girl? Oddly, it always answered that it was a boy. Which was fitting, because as those early years went by, a shadowy figure of a man, wearing what looked like the fedora Abuelo used to wear, would appear, standing still at the foot of my bed or crouching in the far corner of my room. But one night, he moved from his position. I felt as if my eyes were wide open and I was awake but I was paralyzed as he appeared to lift himself to stand.

I managed a gargled scream that woke the house: "Baaaalllaahhhhh-hgggg!!" In seconds my door swung open and light poured in.

"Ay! Qué paso? What happened, m'ija?" my mother said as she came to my side.

My breathing was heavy as I grabbed her arm. "Mami! There was a man. There was a man here. He was sitting right there. Then he started to get up and come to me."

"It's okay, okay, I'm here," she consoled.

"He's not usually that scary, Mom."

"You've seen him before?" she asked.

"Mm-hmm. He visits me." With that revelation, my mother's face went as pale as it was able.

"Ha!" came from the doorway. "So, there's a guy, who visits you at night? Wooooo!" Marty teased, making ghost noises as he stood at my bedroom door in his boxer shorts.

I glared at him, hurt. My mother turned to him and did the same.

She believed me. Belief in the spiritual realm was our cultural birth-right, not unnatural in the slightest. It was to be respected. That night, in one of only a few moments of tenderness I remember, and maybe from her own fear, my mother slept next to me, lying on my beanbag (which of course was yellow to match my bedding and drapes). She did two things after that night, tipping her hat to the dance of our dual cultural reality. She spoke to my pediatrician, who told her that my night terrors were caused by anxiety (Bingo!), and then she had a priest come to the house to bless it and get rid of bad spirits.

I hushed my little sisters to stay quiet as we hovered just out of sight of the priest and Mami, who were making their way through each room of the house. He whispered prayers as he held a tiny leather book and a burning incense stick. Mom followed him, head bowed, holding her rosary and moving her lips in prayer. This was the same year that an exorcism was performed at my school. It was in math class. I remember, in terror, hallucinating the numbers in white chalk on the blackboard lifting themselves away from the surface as the teacher told us that we had a priest visiting the academy that day, in the chapel right then to perform an exorcism. She asked us, a class of nine-year-olds, to pray for the poor strange girl who was possessed by the devil.

"The devil, you know, walks among you always, even right now. Lower your heads and close your eyes and pray. He's waiting for one of you to have a weakness—he preys on your weakness—so he can jump into you, like that girl upstairs. Be strong. Don't let him in."

I visualized the damn devil himself that day, scarlet red and horned and thin, winding his way through our rows of desks, stopping at each one to check who was weak. Even with that precedent, it was wild that Mom had called a priest to our house who wasn't from our parish, and notably when Marty wasn't home, to get rid of my "ghost." Marty was, as we all were, raised a practicing Catholic (but with selective adherence to dogma, such as being against birth control, hence all the siblings, yet okay with the sin of marrying a divorcée), but his flavor of faith differed greatly from my mother's, which was formed of Caribbean Catholicism and Santeria. The Catholic soup I swam in from first grade until my teens was formed by the nuns in New Hampshire, our local Catholic church of mostly French Canadian—adjacent folks, and my mother's amalgamated interpretation of all these new influences and norms plus her colorful Caribbean inheritance of Afro-Indian religion. Soon enough there were also the daytime TV grifters like Jim and Tammy Faye Bakker. Mami looked for salvation and favor wherever she could get it. She hedged her bets.

But I wasn't sold on the priest having any power to do anything. I felt like my experiences in the night were mine. My friend in the wall. My scary man. However, I didn't discount the doctor's assessment. I was grateful that my inner anguish had an outward symptom that could be observed, acknowledged, and pointed out to my mother with science, a subject I was beginning to transfer my passion and faith into. There was so much more order, predictability, and truth, which was comforting. I needed comforting.

A weekend family ritual that gave my anxiety a run for its money was our trip to the town dump. Unlike the service of our noisy, friendly neighborhood garbagemen back home in the city, with trucks and metal bins that filled our ears at dawn with a cacophony, residents of our New Hampshire town had to bring their garbage to the local landfill themselves. Picture a cliff—a precipice built of packed sand—sand!—with a two-story drop that you had to *back your car onto* to throw your garbage into the abyss. My skin still prickles thinking of this.

To Marty, driving the whole family plus a week's load of our garbage up the dirt hill, then backing up to the edge of the landfill, was a certain kind of fun. He was the son of the earlier immigrant wave who worked in the Ford plants in Detroit alongside the Black exodus from the South, as his father, Grandpa G, did. His mother, our grandma, was a stay-at-home mom to two: Marty and his sister, my dear pixie-poet Aunt C. As second-generation and the first in his family to go to college—like many of the other Italian immigrants in the area who lived segregated from Black Detroit but worked alongside them—Marty carried a groovy "I'm down" vibe, though lined with a residual white male Americanness that would reveal itself decades later to be the greatest mythological trap of this nation. He married an Afro-Latina immigrant, which was rebellious for his world in the seventies, but beyond the gesture, if you erase everything, our language, our food, our music, what's the rebellion about?

"Aww, are you afraid we're gonna fall off or something?" Marty asked me from the driver's seat.

I didn't answer him. Only pouted and prayed. He was laughing (again) at my fear.

That first year in Amherst, Marty had gotten my mother a boat of an AMC station wagon, maroon, with the fake-wood-paneled sides and a backward-facing seating area that currently had the seats down and our black garbage bags on top. Marty backed up to what looked to me like the edge of the world and our impending death via trash suffocation. I prayed not to die as I envisioned us falling backward, the wagon crumpling on impact, turning all of us into trash too.

Marty got out of the wagon, opened the back door, and began throwing the black bags one by one over the edge. Mami sat in front, holding my baby sister, another one in her belly. Then came the thud of the back door that signaled he was done.

"You wanna come out and see?" he asked.

I didn't answer.

"C'mon. Let me show you." He waved for me to get out of the car.

I didn't move a hair—I couldn't move—until my mother said to me, "Go."

From her this was an order and I dared not disobey. I stepped out of the wagon, making sure that no one was standing behind me to push me over the ledge, including Marty, my prankster stepfather. (Trust, always an issue.) Thankfully he stayed on the driver's side.

"See? It's not that bad. I'm not going to drive off the edge. Plenty of room!"

I was the opposite of assured. There could not have been two feet between the back bumper of our vehicle and the edge. The ground beneath us not the concrete I'd prefer but sand. I dared not look over the edge. I kept my distance but by god, did it smell. Worse than the open fish markets on the streets of Chinatown on a ninety-degree summer day. In that moment I decided that I had to make peace with the fact that this was to be a weekly part of my new life. Weekly. I was going to have to manage my anxiety and terror. Somehow. After all, there were other people pulling up, conducting the same weekend ritual, and surviving.

My inner pep talk wasn't very successful, though. Later, rather than ride up to the precipice, I'd ask Marty to drop me off at the entrance of the dump, where the guard was, to wait until the deed was done so I could be picked up afterward, spared the living nightmare. Until the day the whole family forgot to pick me back up. They drove right past me onto the local throughway. When I eventually got in the car after they turned around nearly a mile later, I was seething, my mother was smiling and shaking her head, and Marty was laughing. "Oh, ho, ho! We forgot you, but then Alex was like, 'Where's Carmen?'"

I never asked to get dropped off again.

Though I noted that it was my brother who remembered me.

One time, another sedan backed up right next to us at the dump. Per usual, I had a death grip on the door handle and looked out the window into space, trying to focus on my breathing. Then I saw her. A Black girl who looked about my age, sitting in the car that pulled up backward next to us. I couldn't believe my eyes. It had to have been a few years in New Hampshire and I hadn't seen one other non-white face yet. Ay Dios, could I believe my eyes? Was I not alone? She had puffy pigtails on each side of her head with big white balls on the ends of the elastics, just like we used back home.

The girl caught my eyes and abruptly stuck her tongue out at me menacingly, breaking my spell. I pulled back from the window, stunned. My face got hot and I looked at the floor. I wanted to cry. For a moment, she had been hope for me. An oasis in the desert. A potential best friend. Maybe even extended family. Where did she go to school? Would I ever see her again? But instead, I got an ugly rejection.

Only as an adult did I realize why she stuck her tongue out at me. She surely, like me, had been stared at, questioned, ostracized, teased, even bullied in this town, this state, for being simply who she was. And there

I was, a damn fool, staring at her just like the white people did. It didn't matter my intention. I did to her what the white folks did to me, to us. So, who's to blame her for treating me just like them with all their rudeness?

I wish to this day I could go back to that point in time to apologize and tell her no, my staring was a face frozen in surprised joy. I needed to make sure that she wasn't a wishful mirage or specter, as my brain was known to conjure. I thought she was a potential sister in this lonely place. But everyone deserves not to be a projection, no matter what skin they're in.

"MAMI?" I HAD ON my sweetest most grown-up voice as I sat on the kitchen counter, eight-year-old legs dangling and swinging as I watched my mother cook something from her ubiquitous American women's magazines. I liked to watch out of curiosity and help when I could out of boredom and sometimes to try to bond with Mom, but the Anglo food was barely palatable. After growing up on Dominican and Chinese cuisine, this new American-food-only-in-this-house menu of meatloaf, overbaked cod, and macaroni salad had me nearly seeing my ribs. At least Mom took our rice cooker with us, so we had white rice available every night, a concession to her beloved first and only son, the very-Wong Alex.

"Mami, I, um, I, well, so Julie went to Disney World," I stuttered.

"Mm-hmm." Mom kept at the confection she was attempting; her plastic apron did not fully protect her skirt from the flour.

"Well, I was wondering . . . can we go to Disney World one day?"

Mom paused. Had I pissed her off with such a grand request? We were solidly middle-class but not a family with enough money to take now two babies, curly-topped me, a big brother, and two parents on a flight to Florida to see Mickey Mouse. A girl could dream.

Lupe turned and patted my knee with her floury hand. "You know, maybe one day."

I took in a big breath. "Really?!"

"Sometimes if you ask the universe for something, it gives it to you."

My mother was instructing me to manifest. I had no idea how it was going to happen, but you'd better believe I prayed and wished and prayed again for it to happen. Her smiley encouragement and surprisingly inspirational quote gave me a weird kind of determined hope. And I was relieved that she didn't get angry and scold me for being so selfish as to ask for a vacation.

Maybe a week or two later, as I sat on my bed with my head in a book, Mom came into my bedroom and plopped down a shopping bag filled with clothes. "Well. Your Papi has been living in Florida so I called him up and asked him to take you and Alex to Disney World." You could have scraped me off the floor, as this was surely a grade school miracle. "I bought you some new clothes because you'll need to dress nice for the plane."

I was that little girl with the fur coat and go-go boots again. I dug into the bags. There was a new light-green-and-white-striped sleeveless shift dress with a matching short-sleeved bolero, an outfit that blew my mind. An adorable terry cloth top-and-shorts combo that I can still feel between my fingers, more shorts and tops, and even socks and sandals. It was really happening. My first plane flight, and alone with my big brother, no adults. This was the kind of excitement I needed back in my life. But excitement is the fraternal twin of fear. Florida gave me both.

Papi called our house in New Hampshire fairly often. Always during the day when Marty wasn't home. Mami would yell for me to get on the phone after she'd spoken to him and he'd yell-ask (he's a yeller on the phone, always and forever): "What you do in school? How your grades? A's? You make A's? What you eating? You eat good there? When I see you, we go Chinatown—get your favorite! Steamed fish, big steamed fish . . ." Every Chinese American kid knows these questions. Grades and food. Languages of love. And though we saw Papi twice or more a year when we'd go back home to our family in the city, we didn't see him there that year and I didn't dare ask why (never ask Lupe why). I'd find out later when he sent Alex and me postcards from his travels to Malaysia, where one of his brothers had settled, and Singapore, where the other had settled. But Florida? I'd had no idea he was there. Serendipity as to the timing of my Disney World request.

"Ay, Carmencita, keep Papi awake, okay! Keep Papi awake! Das your job!" My father was pleading, half-joking, as he made a grade-schooler responsible for avoiding a deadly car accident as we drove in the middle of the night on a Florida highway. He kept nodding off but wouldn't stop to rest. Alex was asleep in the back seat and thankfully, I was too anxious to be anywhere near sleepy. The whole ride, probably from Orlando to Miami, I watched Papi out of the corner of my eye as his head would fall, then jerk upright, dangerously close to swerving off the road a few times or into oncoming traffic. "Pinch me! Pinch me, ayy-yaaaa!" He grabbed my hand to put it on his arm. Even though I was scared to put my hands on any grown-up, let alone a parent, I pinched and punched Papi's arm with my little hands as needed for the rest of the ride. And somehow, we made it to our destination without injury.

We did Disney World, where I prayed like I'd never before prayed in my short little life. I was sure that Alex and I were going to die on Space Mountain as we shot through the "warp speed" tunnel. I rode that ride for my brother, who insisted on it. Whatever he could do, I could do, I assured myself. If he liked it, I had to like it too. Serves me right to have been making every promise to God with my head whipping left and right as we shot through a plaster faux outer space, Alex sitting in front of me chillin' as I screamed the screams of the damned. But wouldn't you know, as soon as we got off that first ride and walked back out into the sun, my terror transformed to utter euphoria and I begged to go on again, and again, and . . . Alex and I rode that ride eight times in a row that day.

Next, it was SeaWorld, Reptile World (I love snakes and always have), and even Monkey World. But then there was the day that Papi had had his fill of draining his wallet on his two kids in these "worlds." It was time for Papi to scratch his inescapable itch in his favorite world, gambling. Alex and I spent hours alone in the hot, humid sun of Miami, no water or snacks, sitting in the car outside of a greyhound racetrack–gambling den while our father did his thing inside.

"When is he gonna come baaack?" I whined to my brother. Papi had told us it was going to be twenty minutes or half an hour ("I give you twenty dollars when I get back!"), but we were running into a couple of hours now, sitting on the sticky, steaming vinyl of his sedan. I remember the wet sensation of curls sticking to my forehead and the back of my neck, drenched with my sweat.

"I'm gonna go sit over there," Alex said as he got out of the car. He was a young teenager but had the look of a man about to crack. My brother was pissed that our irresponsible father had left us two kids alone in a gambling-spot parking lot for hours on a steaming Florida day, no water. At least our windows were open.

"But wait! You can't leave me here!" I begged after my brother. I was alone in the car, watching men going in and out of their cars to the track and vice versa. Alex didn't answer me. He strode off to sit on the front steps of the powder blue building. At least I could see him from where I was. I rested my head on the window edge, exhausted and wilted. I knew Alex wasn't abandoning me. He was angry and in big-brother, man-of-the-house mode. When Papi finally returned, there were no apologies. No talk of why or how he'd been gone so long. He was quiet and so were we. I don't think he won anything. But not all was lost in the long term. I learned a lesson about who our father was that I didn't know up until that point as I'd never lived with him. That maybe he shared the same feeling toward me that Marty and my mom shared when they forgot to pick me up from the dump, or when Mom would pick me up an hour or more late after school, in the winter when I'd have to wait outside in the cold. Not a priority.

When we came back from our adventures in Florida with Papi, I gave a debrief on the wonders of Disney World to my mother, including the pretty blond friend I had made, the daughter of the motel owners ("They had a pool and the rooms had these little boxes where you could put quarters in and the whole bed would shake!"), and then that we'd been left outside alone in a parking lot while Papi gambled, and how I kept him awake as we drove in the middle of the night. At that, Mami's face turned dark, and we never had a trip alone with Papi again.

Our father was a gambling addict and living in Miami because that's where his "business" was. He had gotten me my first plane ride, motel stay, Disney World, and new clothes. It was difficult to be too angry with him when I was young because, like any good manipulator, he compensated with gifts and adventure. Marty couldn't necessarily compete in that arena. We were far from our once-eye-opening trips to the Met in the city and money was getting tighter as more babies joined the family. Instead, in New Hampshire we had weekend jaunts to the local potato chip factory, the maple syrup maker, apple picking (which I detest to this day), zucchini festivals, and flea markets. But Marty could give something critically important that Papi never could: the American "white picket fence" dream, banana-seat bike riding, suburban life of a nuclear family with a dad who carried a briefcase to work every day and brought home the bacon, along with a stay-at-home mom wearing an apron who rang a bell (literally) for all her wandering kids to come back in the house for dinner. It was *Good Housekeeping* and Little Golden Books and "Dick and Jane" come to life. At least, in the beginning.

"Wait, wait! Everybody under the table! Shhhhhh! Now, be quiet and don't make a peep until he walks over the step into the room, okay?" I was coaxing my baby sisters to hide under our dining room table, a six-foot wooden behemoth with long bench seating on either side. When Marty would come home from work every day, a gaggle of excited toddlers and squealing preschool girls climbed him like a jungle gym: "Daddy's home! Daddy's home!" One hanging on to each leg, swinging as he walked like he was a *Gulliver's Travels* giant. Except this time I convinced them to hide under the table in silence so that he'd open the door and wonder where his usual mélange of greeters could be found.

Mom stood on the other side of the wraparound kitchen counter in view of the garage door where he'd enter, making dinner as she did every weekday for six-thirty, giving Marty the chance to change into casual clothes before we all sat down. She watched as I shuffled all the girls under the kitchen table. As I heard Marty's keys in the door, I scrunched down with them too, finger over my lips in a "Shhhhh."

"Hello?" we heard him say into the echoing, empty space of our family room.

Mom stayed quiet, in on our little game, pretending she knew nothing as she clanged pots onto the stove, getting ready to cook.

"Is anybody home?" Marty asked.

"Shhhhhh," I whispered at my sisters, their beautiful little curly-topped heads looking like they were going to explode with excitement and anticipation.

"Well . . . I guess no one's home but me and you, Lupe." His keys hit the foyer table. "Guess I'm gonna have to eat all the dinner! And dessert too!"

One of the girls let out a peep of "Ack!"

"Shuuuup!" I warned.

Marty's footsteps got closer until he finally stepped up onto our raised dining area. I whispered to the girls, "Now!"

"Surprise!" was yelled in five different voices, from my tween alto to a baby "Suh-pwise!" as they jumped all over him in a swarm. I stood back, watching them all hug and hold him, so happy. My mother's face joyful too at the scene before her. Marty's face a bright grin. I never saw him as happy as when his baby girls were climbing all over him. But it wasn't my scene. I was only the director. This wasn't my nuclear family. He wasn't my father. What my sisters had with Marty was something I'd never be privy to. It was inclusive by nature and definition, a golden halo of belonging. I stood there, just outside of it, a choreographer admiring her dance.

There was something comforting about the ability to run alongside the clock every day, to lean into the predictability of white American suburban life. Wildflowers and lawns, caterpillar invasions and tadpoles, learning how to throw a football in the front yard, and now enough neighbors that we had an actual postman drive up to the mailbox in the afternoons. Marty's textbook briefcase, suit, and trench coat, the white-collar workingman's uniform. Mom making dinner every weekday night at the same time, her ever-present apron and the scent of dish soap.

It was in actuality monotonous and dull compared with the life I had lived previously in a colorful, urban world, but it was communicated to me through the white American culture around me as the ideal. The

American ideal. And my stepfather created that world for us. At that age, I didn't question the values behind it. Didn't see how something presented so prettily in every form of media could be a prison. Or how it could take Alex, my mother, and me, and scrub our souls of our culture like a giant eraser, the remnants of the rubbings, our brownness, to be blown off the page.

"Ju see? See how he talks? That's how ju should talk," my mother said to me. We were watching the evening news, as we did every night during or just after dinner. Mom would flip between Peter Jennings ("Ay, so handsome," she'd say) or Dan Rather, who was new to evenings then.

"But Mom, my cousins say that I talk 'white,'" I said. It was unsolicited feedback that was a deep cut coming from my own family. If we weren't accepted by the white people where we lived, and now I was growing not to be accepted by my family back home, what kind of lonely limbo was left?

"Listen. White people do not have a monopoly on speaking English correctly, okay?" Lupe loved to use the biggest English words and concepts she possibly could. She culled them from TV news and our subscriptions to the newsmagazines she and I would devour as soon as they crossed our front door. And to her, the bigger the English word, the more formal, the better. We had a dictionary permanently in the drawer under the telephone on the kitchen counter.

"Nooo! No 'pee-pee' in this house! Use the correct terminology!" She pronounced it: "termahnolohee." "It is 'ju-rinate'!" She'd yell this as I was helping her potty train one of my little sisters. I'd eye roll out of her sight and once I got the toddler to the toilet I'd whisper, "Pee-pee! Pee-pee!" and we'd giggle.

Mom's adherence to Americana at its most Anglo included a devotion to American daytime soap operas, naming my first little sister after a favorite character on *All My Children*. This was a time of four channels on the television, ABC, CBS, NBC, and PBS, no Spanish-language telenovelas. My sisters and I were allowed a few contemporary sitcoms like our favorites, *The Jeffersons, Happy Days, Laverne & Shirley,* and *Barney Miller.* But *The Love Boat, Charlie's Angels,* and *The Six Million Dollar Man* were tempered by loads of PBS, the evening news every night, and *Jeopardy!* This meant a healthy dose of British dramas like *Brideshead Revisited,* world-travel affairs like the Australian *A Town Like Alice,* and British (sometimes offensive) humor like *Fawlty Towers,* BBC productions that handed me a decently fake British accent when I wanted one. Fluffier flavors like *Scooby-Doo,* Walter Mercado, and *Kung Fu* were reserved for our quarterly visits back home to the city, along with witnessing the birth of my future addiction, MTV.

I appreciated Mom working hard to try to give me the tools to succeed in the very white male professional world of this country. That included not only vocabulary but wiping clean any non-Anglo accent and almost completely erasing my first language, Spanish. My school was French Canadian and the only language offered was French. So French it was. My early exposure to Chinese dialects, Spanish, and then English helped with my language studies. One nun couldn't understand how I did so well on pronunciation exams in French. I'll never forget how it perturbed her. It made me nervous but satisfied to see her so unsettled at my success at her language. I learned the sweet sugar high of crushing the low expectations of others.

However, Marty didn't appreciate Mom's attempts at speaking English well.

"Lupe! There is not an 'e' before every word starting with an 's'! It is not 'es-spoon'- -it is 'ssssspoon.' "

I wish I could tell you that I was conscious at the time of the snobbishness and tension in his tone and connotation. However, I must have known subconsciously because what I did was react reflexively, to protect and defend her, turning it all into a joke not at my mother's expense but in her favor.

"Yeah, Ma, can you pass me the 'es-spoon' and the 'es-patula' and the 'es-salt,' por favor?" I'd pantomime her, humor becoming my way of settling the increasingly taut air in the house.

"I'm gonna take dis es-spatula and es-smack it on jor head!" She waved her spatula in the air at me, laughing and smiling. I know now that under her chuckle there had to be some kind of pain. Because thinking of it in the present, looking back at that interchange, that's what I feel. Marty's teasing was not funny. It was an attack on her identity. Her heritage and origins. It was "I'm better than you."

Lupe never made Dominican food unless it was in the middle of the day and Marty wasn't home. Disappointingly, she did not inherit Abuela's cooking genes, and she tended to cook the food only for herself as if it would be a sin or betrayal to sneak us Dominican food in our very "gringo" house. "Ma, it stinks in here of yucky!" I'd say about her boiling yuca, my teasing tone a Marty-infection I'm not proud of. Typical first-generation-American kid back then, rejecting the foreignness of a parent but making sure only I could do that. Only defending her when Marty did it or anyone else said a word against her.

Mami also listened to music in Spanish and sang along only during the day, when Marty wasn't home, us kids dancing up a storm in our open kitchen, many a summer day when salsa would come on. She got rid of her rolos, stopped wearing her scarves and her once-ubiquitous red lipstick. She even bought a pair of denim overalls from the thrift shop, big enough to go over her growing belly (my third sister) and easy to clean after digging up the front yard, planting her beloved but doomed flowers. What a far, far cry from custom-made skirt suits and beautiful heels. If it wasn't for my mother's brown skin, kinky hair, and accent, the person she was before Marty would have been unrecognizable.

THESE WERE THE YEARS that I decided I'd start calling Marty "Dad." Alex never joined me. (Like with the ketchup.) Calling Marty "Dad" allowed me to bridge some of the distance between being an outsider to a family I lived with and grew up with and my increasing desire to be an official part of it. I never saw it as choosing sides so much as wanting to find a place where I could belong. I would always be Lupe's daughter and she, my mother. I'd always be Dominican and Chinese with a Papi but I wanted to be less of a "bastard" child, as the church told Alex and me we were. It felt like a last step into that American dream. A "legitimate" two-parent family.

"Can he adopt me?" I asked Mom about Marty, Dad.

"No, m'ija."

"But why? I want to have the same name as the girls and you!"

I'd forgotten that at one point I wanted that, badly. On one side, there was pressure from classmates and teachers and the world, who treated my Chinese name and parentage as a circus sideshow, and on the other, at home, there was the pressure to want to belong and be a part of their family. I am glad it never happened, but I understand why I wanted it.

"Okay, pass me the Phillips-head," Marty—Dad—told me, as I hovered nearby in the garage on a warm weekend day. We were surrounded by so many tools and wood and nails, it looked like two aisles in a hardware store.

"Uh, which one is that?" I asked.

"Head like a star."

Easy. I passed it to him. I learned enough about construction and odd jobs in that garage with Dad that I was later able to mount drapes with an electric drill, paint walls and trim, sand and stain furniture, even pick the locks of the house with Mom's bobby pins when she forgot her house keys. (That last one was all me, though, inspired by *MacGyver* and starving for after-school snacks.)

Summers meant helping Dad light the fire in the charcoal grill on weekend nights, his nights to cook. It meant playing badminton with him in the yard, this grown man showing me no mercy, treating me no differently because I was a small girl. And late summer, early fall, it was time for the drop-off of our wood for the winter. Our house used a wood-burning stove in the basement for heat. The load of wood that arrived took up half our lawn and looked like eight full trees without their branches stacked up on top of each other.

Dad would dress in a red flannel shirt, jeans, heavy construction gloves, and Timberlands, stand at the top of the pile with his chainsaw screaming its gritty gasoline scream, and cut up the trees into manageable logs while we all stayed inside, watching through the window, steering clear of debris.

"Oh, woof! Almost done," Dad said as he stomped into the family room entryway, working to get some of the tree gunk off his boots onto the mudroom rug. "Lupe—can I get a water?" Mom would pour him a big cup and he'd gulp it down, standing in place, covered in wood powder and sweat. The smell of newly cut wood mixed with the saltiness of his sweat filled the room.

I would join both Marty and Alex for step two, wearing a rolled-up flannel shirt from Dad—which fit tiny me more like a woodsy muumuu—and his work gloves, also enormous on me, but they kept the sap, spiders, and splinters away. Alex managed the logs, walking them over to Dad to chop with his axe. My job was to pick up the quartered logs and stack them like puzzle pieces. What a sight I must have been. Not bad for a couple of brown city kids.

I had been looking for acceptance from Marty since I first put ketchup on my eggs, but I was also genuinely curious about his culture and habits, which were as different as if I'd been set down in Fiji, even though we were both born in the same country. Our worlds were especially different when it came to money.

Papi exposed me to cash and its ability to buy Barbies. Marty exposed me to money in a way that would be the foundation of a twenty-year career covering money and giving financial advice in national magazines and on television. Even if I hadn't made it my beat, what he did was show me the world of money as it was for white-collar men in America and their families. It was to be saved, managed, and invested, not only spent. This introduction to this world was an enormous gift and a key to my success in many ways.

"Hello, there! We're here to open a bank account for this one here. My daughter." I stood next to Dad, a bit nervous, as he addressed the customer service representative at our local bank. We usually didn't go inside the building. I'd go to the bank with Mom when she was running errands, but she'd usually do drive-through banking with its vacuum system. Technology! We'd pull up. The teller would send us a container through a tube for Mom to put her check in then send back—*whoosh*. The teller would return the canister—*whoosh*—filled with the cash from the check.

But I was twelve years old now and Marty said that it was time for me to go inside with him and open a savings account.

"Oh, that's great! C'mon over and we'll get started." The man dressed in a suit on a Saturday waved us over to his desk. There was a lot of paper and signing things, some questions regarding my name of course, as it didn't match my dad's, and then he stamped a little passbook with my first deposit entry (funnily enough, cash from Papi) and slid it over to me. I had a bank account.

"Thank you," I managed.

As we walked to Dad's car, I remember holding that little book open, staring at its lines where I'd write in more deposits and later get to add them all together. Something told me that this was some kind of initiation. I was a brown girl in the 1980s. This seemed like something white dads did with their boys, if they did it at all with their children back then.

But know that the greatest gift Marty gave me was not Anglo culture. It was that he didn't treat me differently from Alex, a boy. Dad competed with me at board games just as hard as he did with my brother, the two of them sometimes ganging up on me until I left in a huff. "I quit!"

"Quitter!" they'd each yell after me.

Dad let me roll under his AMC Gremlin with him when the hatchback needed repairs, pointing out the catalytic converter, teaching me how to change the oil and tires. I helped him load the half cow he'd buy to feed us for the winter, cut up and packaged, into our basement freezer, explaining what "chuck" meant or "sirloin" and why it made financial sense to buy it this way. On the way to dropping me off at school every morning, he had me run into the store to fetch *The Wall Street Journal,* with his fifty cents jangling in my pocket. And when Marty would be lost behind the pages of the *Journal,* scouring the market returns of the day, he'd enthusiastically answer me when I'd ask: "What's a stock?"

There was one question, though, that I knew he wasn't answering the way I hoped he would. One question, one topic that maybe me and Mom and Alex could teach him, but I'd ask anyway.

"Dad, the kids keep asking me, 'What are you?' What do I say?"

"You're American," he'd answer.

He may have given me the pat, useless, erasing answer when it came to race and ethnicity, but he never treated me as lesser for my gender. Mom, yes. But not me.

It would be decades before I discovered why.

CHAPTER 4

... Because We Lost Our Way

IN NEW HAMPSHIRE ALL I SAW AND ENCOUNTERED AROUND me was whiteness. In my school, my neighborhood; our crayon box's "flesh" crayon, a pale peach; the cover models of *Cosmopolitan* in line at the grocery store; my Barbie dolls; the movies I loved, like *Raiders of the Lost Ark;* the shows we watched at home as a family, like *Little House on the Prairie*—a distinct shift from *Sanford and Son* and other racially inclusive shows of the 1970s—the detested *Hee Haw* and Lawrence Welk programs Marty loved to turn on during weekend afternoons when there was no football. I couldn't find us on paper or on screens. (Besides Lynda Carter's Wonder Woman, who my mother told us was Latina, but still, a white Latina.) The message was that American whiteness was best or at least better by default and there was no escaping the bullhorn.

Media may have affected me more because I soaked myself in any and all forms of content from the moment *Newsweek* hit the kitchen table to the text on every toothpaste tube and cereal box in the house. I was ravenous for words and information. A born temperament of inherent curiosity turned up to ten was only part of it. I liked to swim in the warm, safe soup of words and images that I compulsively ingested. Our local library was my sanctuary as soon as we moved to Amherst. It was the place where I downed books like a frat boy at a kegger: glug, glug.

It was about escape. Sitting on the floor of the library lost in a book, or in my other getaway, the movie theater, I didn't feel anyone's eyes on me, judging, asking questions about why I was in their space. *What are you? Why are you here? Where did you come from?*

I found respite in our trips back home to the city, but even there, unfortunately, by twelve, I started to see how my own color was seeping away. My Spanish was being displaced by French, the only language offered in school. It became harder to understand my beloved abuela as both English and French squeezed space in my brain, burying my Spanish deep, one shovelful of New Hampshire at a time. My English pronunciation was East Coast newscaster, just as my mother wanted, no Dominican-NYC flavor like my extended cousins, who'd taunt me with "You talk white!" My clothes were prim, proper, pastel eighties "good girl." I looked like a forty-year-old accountant, not cool like my cousins. Code-switching became my destiny whether I liked it or not.

In hindsight, my morphing into a cosplaying New England white girl wasn't only about survival. I wanted all the advantages they had in the world because I didn't see why not. The only way I knew to go about it, and the only way I was allowed to move forward, was to look, speak, and act the part, to contort myself into their image, follow their rules, like what they liked. I learned to hate my "unruly" hair and ironed it as straight as possible, feathered and lacquered with Aqua Net and mousse. I wore their clothes and makeup, the ones I saw in the all-white teen magazines and on my friends (money was stretched, though, so no matter how hard I tried, I was teased about my clothes, which broke my heart as I worked so hard to be fashionable with what little I had). Wannabe-preppy pastels, boxy jackets, nothing tight or too short, which would be normal attire back home in the city, but where I was would be seen as fulfilling their stereotype of a loose Latina.

How I wanted to belong with my cousins in the city too. But it wasn't to be, as in contrast to my more demure and uptight northern neighbors, my Dominican cousins' style and language began to grate on me.

"Chin*y, chin*y, Chineeeeese!" one cousin threw at my other Dominican-Chinese cousin, as he pulled up the corners of his eyes. Someone said, "Hey. Don't say that," and then the boys started in on whose ass Bruce Lee could kick. Oddly, I processed racist language from my family back in the city differently. I didn't know some of it was racist at all. "Mulatto." "Pelo malo" (bad hair). I remember Alex and I would let it brush past us and roll our eyes because this was family, not wanting to face the damaging power of these words because they were coming from our own circle and we didn't want to rock the boat, potentially alienating our family even more.

Back in Amherst, there was the weekly Friday sleepover at one girl's house—it was a feat that I got Mom to agree to a sleepover, verboten in Latin culture, but she succumbed to assimilation there too—where a gaggle of us would rent movies, do our makeup, and stay up all night. The girl's father would ask what kind of food he should pick up for us, asking if we wanted pizza or "chin*y" food. I was a Wong, sitting right there. Everyone knew I was Chinese. It was in New Hampshire that I learned from kids and adults that there were slurs for Mexicans, Jewish people, disabled people, gay people, pretty much anyone who wasn't straight, cisgender, nondisabled, and white. I remember particularly not understanding jokes about white people from different places, like Ireland or Poland. What was funny?

So I built a protective wall inside of me. I learned that a white friend—or, in the future, lover or husband—no matter how good and wonderful, could always be a short or long step away from slipping up in front of me. And they had likely said these words with the white people in their lives and even if not, could have these feelings and thoughts, sometimes even about me. The distrust is in the room even if it's just a light haze.

If I was feeling all this, my mother was as well, to the nth degree. She chafed at it as the years went by and started to act out a bit when she could.

I was watching over my little sisters in the middle of a summer day, sitting at the kitchen table, munching something disgusting I'd make with whatever I could find, like microwaved bologna in a puddle of Aunt Jemima "maple" syrup, while I read. The girls were fairly quiet, playing in their spaces when Mom got back home from whatever errand she had been on. She walked into the kitchen and into my view. We all said "Hi, Mami" per normal, and went about our business but I did a double take. In lieu of her usual black textured hair straightened and pulled back into a low bun, she had an Afro. A round, natural two-inch Afro, and it was red! More auburn, really, but I was shocked. My skin prickled. This felt like a line in the sand, a statement.

"Wow. Mom. Your hair!"

She rummaged around the kitchen as if nothing had happened, not saying a word about her striking change until I mentioned it. "I know!" She brightened up like I hadn't seen her do in so long. "You like it?"

I nodded and smiled. "Yeah!"

"It's radical, no?" She kept smiling wide. Damn it, my mother was so happy. And proud.

I nodded and smiled, a bit exhilarated but also scared for her. I asked questions about where she got it done. ("New lady in Nashua.") Then as she went off to chase a crawling baby, I went sullen and my prickles turned into an anxious stomachache. This place did not do "different" well. Comments about my "frizzy" hair once we moved to New Hampshire always stung. Marty used to say it too. "Run a brush through that!" But back in the city, my Dominican family cooed about my "good" hair. "So manageable," my mother and aunt would say. Here, by the time I was twelve, I spent nearly an hour every morning with a blazing-hot curling iron, caked in mousse and hair spray, to try to get the straight, feathered hair that was ubiquitous in that era.

This felt very left field for Mom, as she'd toed the assimilation line ever since taking out her rolos and putting away her colorful scarves. Here she was, being true to herself and to her hair. The color, maybe not natural per se, but the shape and her natural African texture. It was brave. I was in awe of her. And the look on her face, I'll never forget. There is nothing like that kind of pride. Hair is not only hair to a Black Latina

woman. It is loaded. And in the sea of whiteness in which we found ourselves, a catalyst had found my mother, one that said "Own it." She did,
and in her eyes and grin I saw how good it felt for her to do just that.

But it wasn't meant to last.

When Marty got home from work, I was still at the table, reading my
weekly newsmagazines, and Mom was upstairs in their bedroom.

"Hi, Dad."

"Hey, everybody. Where's your mom?" he asked me.

I smiled a bit slyly as I knew he was in for a surprise that I was hopeful
he'd like. "Oh, she's upstairs."

Marty went up with his briefcase while I pretended to read. My focus
was actually on listening for any hint of a reaction from him or some
interaction. It was quiet for a while. Marty came back downstairs first,
which was odd. He'd done his usual after-work change out of his suit and
tie into a T-shirt and jeans. He was silent and his face was stern as he
turned in to the dining room, which he'd taken over as an office for himself. Computer parts, business magazines, and newspapers in piles against
the walls. It was getting close to dinnertime.

Mami showed up in the kitchen just in time to whip up something. I
looked up from my pages eagerly to see her new 'do anew and had
thought up more compliments, hoping to see that happy look on her face
again. It was not to be. And I never saw that radiant auburn Afro again,
ever. Lupe's hair was now completely hidden under a scarf. Her face
hung and she didn't say a word, just went from the refrigerator to the sink
to the stove to the cabinets, robotically, doing her duty as a housewife.
Her nose was red. She'd been crying. I was shocked. There were many
times I didn't like my mother one bit. She could be cruel and violent, but
this I'd never wish for her. I read both my parents' body language and the
story all came together. He hated it. I imagined Lupe excited to show her
husband her new cool coif—after all, weren't their best friends in Manhattan the Joneses? The Black Joneses who both wore Afros? I didn't
want to imagine how it felt to see his horror or scorn or whatever disap-
proving thing he'd felt about something she was so proud of.

This was bigger than hair. Even then I knew that. This was about her identity. Who she was as a human being. To reject that was to reject her as a person.

Lupe and Marty barely spoke through dinner. He looked angry and she, defeated. While Mom and I cleaned up the kitchen after dinner, Marty watching television in the other room, I whispered to her, "Mom. What happened? It's so pretty." I stared at the multicolored scarf, already mourning what was underneath.

Mami didn't look at me or raise her head as she scrubbed a pan in the sink. "He didn't like it," she said softly.

I had nothing to say. It wasn't for me to question their relationship. But the dynamics were clear. I got the message that if your husband doesn't like your hair, you hide it and change it back. And if he's white and you're not, it goes deeper. So, from a box, she dyed it back to black the next day and then spent years growing it back out. She wore a scarf every day until she was able to pull it back into a tiny ponytail.

My tween years saw my mother assert herself as if she were punching breathing holes in the top of the jar that was holding her captive. Sometimes the holes allowed for more air and sometimes, like her Afro, her punch didn't break the surface.

Every Sunday, our whole family of eight, squiggly babies and all, went to mass in a Catholic parish on a hill one town over. Church is where Mom found an outlet and first brought her hustle and ambition. At my school, we had contests to see who could sell the most chocolate bars to raise much-needed funds. My mother took this as an exciting challenge.

At first, I was horrified at her enthusiasm. Mom's system was to pack all five of us girls—Alex was spared as usual—into the minivan and drag me door-to-door around town to sell bars. She would drive up the driveway, then I—fear of her wrath winning out over my fear of talking to strange people and asking them for money—would knock and ask folks to buy some chocolate and support my school. This was also when I saw the inside of other people's homes and realized that Anglo people were just as chaotic as we were back in the city. There were hoarders and screaming, dirty kids as well as pristine, curated spaces, and everything in between. This chocolate-selling tour served as a further demystification of white people for me.

Then, my mother had an epiphany. Driving door-to-door was not efficient. So, just as nonprofits team up for win-win arrangements, Lupe had the idea to sell the candy bars outside our church on Sunday right after each mass. We would win with the foot traffic of our fellow parishioners from three Sunday masses in a row. Praise the lord it was spring, because Mom had me standing out there with her, folding table set up at the foot of the steps where everyone had to pass by us to get to their cars. We stood for hours and lo and behold, Mom and I sold every single box—piles and piles. I think we ended up in second place in fundraising for the whole school that year. Secondary status annoyed Lupe but I was so impressed (and a bit mortified) at my mother's gumption and ingenuity. Her hustle. She convinced the church to let us do this; she convinced Dad to take care of the babies while we were doing it; she schmoozed all the parishioners, smiling and selling. She was glowing. Lupe had a drive to win. Such a discovery for me. It's wild when you're a kid and see an interesting side of a parent you've never seen before. I was the daughter of not one but two enterprising parents, Mom and Papi. This would shape me in substantial ways to come.

It was clear to me now that Mom was naturally ambitious. Fundraising was a way for her to work and be a success in a socially (and Marty) acceptable way. It wasn't as if Dad said out loud that he wanted Mom to be a stay-at-home barefoot-and-pregnant wife. (Well, maybe he said that to her privately, I don't know.) After all, when he'd met her, she was a working mother. But it seemed like the role she was in then—diapers and laundry everywhere—required a bit too much acting for her. So, this bit of success (a sales competition, essentially) seemed to satisfy a piece of her that she'd lost in becoming a full-time mother to six children. Instead, she started channeling her drive and ideas through my brother and me.

The years I was twelve and thirteen I watched my mother grow and molt the skins of her previous life built on Dominican machismo and marianismo (where a woman's role is subservient and all-sacrificing). She chose one day to dismantle the young machismo she'd built herself—my brother's role in the family as Little Emperor.

As he grew into an older teen, Alex was a bit of a phantom in our house. He did no housework beyond initially helping with the chopping and moving of wood, an acceptably macho thing to do. He wasn't responsible for our little sisters, even if he was home and our parents weren't. They were my responsibility. So there were many days where we'd see him only at dinner, and I'd see him again at night if I needed or wanted his counsel and comfort, or to be a nosy little sister. He was allowed to study and play his records and hang out in his large bedroom, with eighties electronics and a full-size bed and bookcase. The division between us was drawn with the pen of gender and birth order. And the division between him and Mom's new family with Marty remained stark. He was a Wong. He had been the man of the house and he was not going to let anyone, let alone a new husband, take a father role. He had a father, and he had a role with our mother as her firstborn and only son.

One summer day, before Alex was sent off during his high school summers to live back in the city at Claremont and work—doing everything from selling ice cream sandwiches by city hall in downtown Manhattan to moving boxes for Papi—we kids were all home and Marty was at work. It may have been summer vacation, but god forbid we sit still and enjoy the break that summer can bring. Mom was grumpy and had decided that it was a cleaning day. Each of us five girls had our to-do lists, even the toddlers, to clean and do work all over the house. Keep in mind, she had never told my brother to clean anything outside of his room, and that boy only kept his room clean because that was his perfectionist nature. But even there, Mom made his bed sometimes, changed his sheets. I'm not sure what in particular had transpired to get her to suddenly change her stance on our family "royal" besides being fed up somehow. Maybe Dad had upset her. Maybe she was sick of being a housewife and had to take it out on the closest form of patriarchy, her son. Of course, I resented the imbalance too.

Mami had been sweeping the kitchen floor for only a minute or two, the rest of us milling around her, wiping surfaces, picking up baby toys, dusting every nook and cranny. Suddenly she stood upright, stopped sweeping, and yelled, "ALEXANDER!" All five of us kids froze. Not a peep in answer came from Alex upstairs. He was probably listening to one of his alternative pop bands like the Sparks or reading one of his Isaac Asimov books that I'd sneak off his bookshelf and gobble up in a night or two before he'd miss them. Mami yelled his name again and banged the floor with the broom handle. We all had looked away by then. Never hold my mother's angry gaze. As with a predator, looking her in the eye was read as defiance and whatever anger she had at someone or something else would come your way instead.

Alex moped downstairs in his socks. We worked to be a no-shoes-in-the-house family, as many immigrant parents did. My lanky brother stood in the doorway of the kitchen, waiting for my mother to give her reason for interrupting whatever he was doing.

She handed him the broom and told him to sweep.

He kept his hands by his sides and shook his head—no.

Mami did it again, this time raising her voice.

Alex didn't move. He said, softly but firmly, "No."

Well. That was it. We were all invested in this outcome. My sisters may have been too young to understand the implications of this showdown, but I knew the stakes were high. If my mother got my brother—who had never swept a floor in his life—to pick up that broom and work alongside his sisters and mother, well. It would be like the Equal Rights Amendment.

He folded his arms and refused.

Crossed arms were like gasoline to Mom. She was set afire. She screamed louder, shriller, and raised the broom to strike Alex. He raised his right arm to block the blow and protect his head.

"How daaaaare you?" Mami hissed. "How dare you raise your hand to me?"

"Mom," I interjected, "he was just protecting himself!"

"No! No—I swear, no man will ever hit me again!" she wailed, still with the broom poised to hit him again. "I swear!"

And then the blows started. Mami went at him with the broom, hitting his shoulders as he scrunched them up to protect his head and neck. She managed to push him into the corner of the kitchen between the pantry and refrigerator. A baby sister was crying. Our mother letting out angry grunts with every swing. And then he was gone. Alex shot out fast from under Mom's broom. We heard the front door slam. The violence was over, and the only sounds were our stunned silence, muffled crying from one baby sister hugging my leg, and Mami's heavy breathing. I watched her a moment to make sure she didn't come our way. I shepherded a toddler to my free leg. I was poised to protect these babies should she keep going. She'd have to go through me first.

We needn't have worried. Alex's swift disappearing act took the wind out of Lupe. She stood the broom in the corner and seemed puzzled and overwhelmed by what had just happened. Without a word, she walked upstairs to her bedroom, leaving me with the four little ones. We each, very quietly, looked out the windows for Alex, hoping he didn't go far and that he was okay. The little emperor's mini royal court.

I assumed that he was in one of our usual hiding spots behind a fallen tree or big bushes. Or that he had walked all the way down the street that curved around our house where his school bus would pick him up, the road visible through the foliage. Maybe a half hour went by. Maybe more. I tried to distract my sisters with a book and some crayons, all in view of the bay window to the backyard. But I was worried.

Lupe came downstairs, her anger replaced with anguish.

"Where did he go?" she asked me.

"I don't know, Mom," I said. My tone was cold. She's the one who drove him out. I didn't blame him in the slightest. She created a situation and reacted with violence. But what was this she said about not letting a man hit her "again"? That was the first time I'd heard her say something like this and I knew it definitely wasn't Marty. Not in his nature nor their dynamic. I didn't want to think back then that it had been Papi. So I assumed and envisioned it being Abuelo, her father, my grandfather who pow-powed me with rolled-up newspapers, maybe playacting his past with my mother.

Mom called Marty at work and complained to him, sniffling now, crying with her version of concern, leaving out that the reason he "ran away" was that she had been hitting him with a broom. What was Marty going to do thirty miles away in his office? The call was brief. Mom kept crying into a tissue. I hardened toward her, feeling righteous, seeing weakness in her lack of self-awareness, cruelty in her lack of empathy for the pain she'd create in others. Her children who just wanted to feel safe.

An hour or so later, we were all jolted by the sound of the front door opening and closing. The staircase to all the bedrooms on the second floor was set right inside the front door. We heard Alex take two steps at a time up to his room, without a word. I readied myself for Mom to go after him, to punish him somehow. She didn't. She now knew that if she pushed too hard, she'd lose her favorite, her only son. He was only a few years away from college. At dinner that night, no one really spoke. Alex didn't even kick me under the table as he liked to do. But later that evening, before bed, when Mom and Dad, Marty, were in their room, I knocked on my brother's door.

"So, where'd you go?" I asked him.

"Oh, I was under the kitchen window. I even fell asleep!" he said as he smiled the smile of a winner.

The kitchen bay window that I had set myself in, peering out into the woods, and the whole time, he was sitting right below my feet on a pile of soft sand that was never landscaped, with just enough room to hide where no one in the house could see. Sitting there in his socks.

Brilliant.

It was an unsuccessful attempt by Lupe to right the ship of gender equality in our home, but I was glad for the attempt if not the execution. Alex still didn't help around the house and he was never home for the summer again. He spent summers in the city, happy to have another place to go, things to do, money to make, and to be surrounded by family. I missed him very much but also couldn't blame him in the slightest for leaving. I couldn't wait to leave myself.

Along with warming up to the American idea of gender equality, my mother bought into the American myth of meritocracy. It was nearly religious for her. She pushed my brother and me hard into what she felt this land had to offer her progeny. My preteen years were filled with phrases and allegories she had in response to every story I brought to her, every setback. She was determined for Alex and me to succeed. If she couldn't have a life outside the house, damn it, we would. Aspiration was its own religion for her, and she was its high priestess.

"You're asking me: Why don't we throw a pizza party like those other parents because you got all A's on your report card?" she'd say. "Because those parents don't have high expectations of their children! I expect A's from you. You don't get a prize for doing what you *should* be doing."

I'd say to her, "Mami, someone said they were surprised I was so articulate."

She'd answer, leaning toward my face, pointing her finger, "The white peoples do not have a monopoly on speaking correct English!"

If I complained about how hard school was, she'd sound like an angry philosopher: "Your grandfather, he was a prisoner, and you know what he said? 'Lupe, they can take away your freedom, your family, everything you have but they cannot take what's in your head—your education!'" My grandfather's imprisonment and torture and Mami's rough upbringing made her life lessons all the more colorful.

"She *made* you do it? Does she have a gun to your head? Hmm? Does she? No one makes you do anything unless there's a gun to your head!" In case I didn't get the message, she'd bend her fingers into a mock gun, the first two fingers forming the barrel she'd place at the side of my head, her fingertips pressing into my temple as she spoke. Message received.

And even though I was studious, my big mouth, my brash style of communicating, yet growing physical insecurity (based on beauty standards all around me that I never could attain) meant the smart girls didn't want to be around me, nor I them. I found them very nice but too quiet and reserved. I was a China-Latina city kid with loud, colorful parents, Papi and Lupe, a stepfather, and four little sisters. When I complained to my mother about feeling lonely, rejected, and misunderstood at school, she responded with what felt like a curse, not a compliment: "Kings and queens are lonely." I knew she was saying this for herself more than me.

And if that's what was required of our lives, it was an inheritance and false monarchy I wasn't interested in.

Where did she hear these things? How did she formulate these modern Instagram-motivation-style posts that have stuck with me throughout my life, for better or worse? I've always wondered. Only in hindsight do I realize just how intelligent and insightful she could be despite her formal education ending when she was a young teen.

At the same time, these were the years when a rancid aura of resentment seemed to build up in my mother. Alex and I started calling her "Dragon Lady." I worked hard at school and at home, cleaning and taking care of my sisters, babysitting neighborhood kids too, but I was "lazy." And I was "disrespectful" on nearly a daily basis for standing up for myself and my sisters (when we were clearly being yelled at simply because Lupe was in a bad mood or state of mind, not because we'd actually done anything wrong).

These words, her words, became an inner voice that in later years would not let me sit still for a moment to rest. A voice that had me run fast and hard on the capitalistic wheel of the U.S. of A.

What saved me down the road was watching men, like my dad, Marty, and how they were allowed the time and space to sit, read, and think. How Alex was allowed to take care only of himself and sit, read, and think. I wanted that. And why not? I was just as smart. Women were just as smart and capable. When I would complain about Alex's not doing any housework I would say to Mom, "He's got two arms and two legs too!" Gender divisions did not make any sense to me. They weren't logical or intelligent. I refused to accept them.

Combined with how Marty didn't treat me any differently from a son—working outdoors with him, driving a stick shift, changing oil, talking stocks and money—I would realize later in life that I didn't internalize typical gender norms at all. The supposed differences did not stand up to scrutiny. And though when it came to housework Mom enforced old ideas, she did not apply them to educational and professional success. All her empowerment phrases and expectations led me to believe that I was just as good as a white boy or man. That with hard work, there was no reason why I couldn't have what they have. This entitlement of a white man was never dislodged. Lupe built me with it. It's my hardware, not software.

One summer day, as I walked down the garage steps to the warm outdoors in a pretty fitted skirt, my thoughts came to a head. "Wait. Do I want to *be* a boy?" I froze on the middle stair and looked down at my bare legs and fancy long nails that I obsessively manicured with glued-on gems. I enjoyed beautifying too much, I enjoyed the curves forming on my body and the power women's bodies could elicit. "Nah. I like the stuff that goes with being a girl. I just want and deserve what they've got."

CHAPTER 5

... Because You Were on Your Way

PAPI NEVER CAME BACK TO NEW HAMPSHIRE AFTER THE one visit when I was in grade school, when he stood in the driveway, not coming into the house, Marty's house. But Papi showed up financially. Once we'd moved out of the city, he started sending money to Mom for me and Alex. The pressure for him to do so ramped up once my brother got only a partial scholarship to Georgetown University. But the dollar amounts needed were too big for just Papi to handle. So, on a summer Saturday, we said goodbye to the last of my mother's collectibles from Chinatown and Claremont. Mom held a garage sale to raise money for my brother's college education.

I was, yet again, both embarrassed and simultaneously slightly awed at her ability to be resourceful. As with the candy bar fundraisers, Lupe threw herself into it. She made signs to post all over the neighborhood and spread the word that she was selling great things. She was doing just that, and I was sad. Embroidered wall hangings of luscious Chinese land-scapes featuring exotic birds—my favorite, the peacock—considered tacky commercial art by some, but we thought they were gorgeous and so did those who paid decent money for them. Mom had a few smaller pieces like this and one large one that was mounted in my room, filled with glistening colors, handiwork that I would stare at for hours, losing myself in the detailed feathers made by thread, tugging at me, reminding me of my origins. My art sensibilities would grow well past this, but my admiration and connection to them went beyond their aesthetics and taste. They were tapestries connecting us to our past and a father from another land. Mom took them all to sell—except my smaller peacock piece that I begged to keep—and pocketed what I could see in her eyes was a satisfying sum for Alex's education. I didn't dare protest too much against this unloading of our city-brought belongings. In a battle between helping my brother and pleasing me, my mother would choose Alex every time. And I didn't mind so much because my brother was paving the way. Wherever he went, I could go too. So I was a fan of helping him go as far as he could.

I remember watching Marty during all of this. He'd position himself off to the side, arms folded or in his pockets, talking with a neighbor while Mom managed the money and the bargaining. I wondered if he wasn't doing well financially, and if it brought him shame or concern to see my mother selling her lovely things from home to pay for Alex's tuition. So I asked Mom directly, approaching her on eggshells, "Why do you have to sell so much? Don't we have enough money?"

"Marty doesn't contribute to you and Alex. Peter is your father, so he pays for your schools and expenses." This was a big surprise to me. Here I was thinking I was part of the family that lived under this roof, Marty's family, with my sisters, but no, an incorrect assumption on my part. I wasn't his kid. I was Papi's.

"Is Papi not sending enough?" I asked. I was starting to get nervous not only for my brother but for myself and my future.

"He's in Venezuela right now so he can't send too much," Mom said and then went about counting the day's take. She felt no reason to give me any further explanation.

Papi was in Venezuela? What was a Chinese New Yorker doing in South America? This explained why Papi hadn't called too often lately. And I guess it explained the garage sale.

But again, I mulled, how did Marty fit into this? It made me worry and question my place in the family. I'd been living with Marty since I was four and I called him "Dad" now, and I had never lived with Papi. I saw him less and less as our trips back home went from four times a year to maybe two a year in my teens. If Marty, Dad, didn't take care of me financially, and if Papi disappeared or stopped sending money, what would happen to me? How would I get out? I had to leave that house as soon as high school graduation and I was determined to do so, but that would require money. Mom still had babies at home to raise and they needed to be supported. Where would the funds to launch me come from?

This maybe explained the exploitative arrangement that my mother roped me into one summer when I was almost twelve years old, working as the full-time nanny of the two (bratty) kids next door, a boy and a girl, five and six, from 7:00 A.M. to 5:00 P.M. Monday through Friday for—get this—$75. For the whole week. That's $1.50 an hour. The check handed to me at the end of the day on Friday went to my mom. A painful, maddening experience for me so young. No middle-schooler should be farmed out to work a fifty-hour week. But, at that age, I had no choice but to comply.

However, once I was old enough for the money to go into my hands, I never turned down an after-school babysitting gig, even if it meant not seeing friends or showing up in terrible pain from wisdom teeth extraction earlier that day, or getting home late and staying up until two A.M. to cram for a test the next morning. Soon, Papi's financial spigot, which was getting smaller and smaller, flowed only to Alex's tuition, so there was no more money for my clothes or needs at all. My babysitting money bought me everything I wore, paid for my hair, skin, and nail products, clothes, shoes, movies, everything that wasn't meals at home and the roof over my head.

Marty was frugal and he also socked away money into investments no matter how little we had, stretching our family finances. When Mom would want to spend on something (though I can't remember what, maybe installing the deck), or when us kids got giddy over an ad for something on the TV, the response would be: "Costs too much," and "Not worth it." Marty had a steady white-collar job and we seemed to be living a middle-class life, so where'd the increasing frugality come from? The answer coincided with our increasing number of place settings at the table. I remember noting, even that young, that the pattern was, with every birth of another sister, our budget would dwindle, or should I say the same budget had to be stretched. With four little sisters and all five of us going to parochial school, this was a time of me darning my three pairs of worn-down school uniform socks so much they didn't have a line at the toe anymore. A time of Mom and Dad sitting at the kitchen table every Sunday after church, surrounded by newspapers and flyers, spending hours—even on the most gorgeous day—clipping out and sorting every coupon they could find. One of our local supermarkets had Double Coupon Day and we managed to leave the store with enough groceries for a family of eight for a week for around fifty dollars total, instead of over two hundred dollars. This put me in my usual state of dissonance—an admiration for taking advantage of a system, but disdain for the lost hours of life on a Sunday.

At fifteen I took a job as a bagger at the local grocery store. Previously, Marty had asked if I wanted to work as a paid intern at his office that summer, working full-time hours, driving to and from work with him. It was more money per hour but waking up at six during the summer for a fifty-minute one-way commute, then sitting under fluorescent lights collating papers for white men in suits, no thank you, dear god, no. A few Saturdays during the year, Dad would take us kids to his office when he had to work on a weekend. I'd keep my sisters entertained, mostly with the dry-erase board in the conference room. Those weekend days under life-draining lights, the walls and furniture bereft of ornamentation or vibrancy of any kind, locked into me an allergy to office work. This choice to turn down a more lucrative summer gig brought about a self-awareness that as much as I needed that coin, money wasn't everything to me—I valued engrossing, engaging situations and spaces and interacting with people more than a few extra bucks an hour. Marty may have been slightly insulted, as I'm sure he pulled strings to get me the offer, but I was not about to enter his white-collar churn. After all, Lupe told me I could do anything I wanted to if I worked hard enough. And I chose to believe her.

So I bagged groceries instead. Seems like a backward bargain, but it was a major shift in my life. That enormous grocery store opened my world to friends outside of my tiny school. They were still white people of course, but there was a mix of backgrounds, styles, ages, and most important, gender. Going to an all-girls school since third grade, I'd had limited social interaction with men and boys beyond my brother and Marty. What heightened the intrigue of that summer was that at fifteen, my braces came off, I got contact lenses to replace my thick glasses, and I went natural with my hair. No more blowouts. My new coif was a pile of cascading black curls. It was a shocking transformation for me, what kids now call a major glow-up. Janet Jackson, Jennifer Beals, and Lisa Bonet had cracked pop culture style with their glorious natural hair that I finally could embrace too with their new mainstream "permission." I went from looking like a forty-year-old accountant with a bad blowout to an MTV girl. Of course, no self-respecting Dominican mother would let her daughter date at fifteen years old. But I still reveled in my new-found powers of being "cute" and "exotic" to coworkers. I was suspicious of it, but I enjoyed the attention. (I would never fully shed the idea of myself in that nerdy-accountant phase, however, no matter how old I was.)

Mom continued her efforts at moneymaking, but not all were fruitful. The living room in our house became a storage place for Mom's attempts at building cash flow. It was spacious, the size of a large studio apartment, intended to be a formal sitting room with a red brick fireplace, but ended up a playroom and dance studio for us kids. Shoved into the back of the room were boxes and boxes of Mary Kay cosmetics. Lupe was so excited to get started with Mary Kay, a multilevel marketing cosmetic brand with an ostentatious founder, Mary Kay Ash, a lady with white-platinum cotton-candy-swirled hair who always dressed in pink. I thought she was tacky and not in a good Dolly Parton way but in the sly-preacher way that Mom tended to fall prey to. I very much wanted

Mom to reach her dream to one day make enough money for her own big pink Cadillac (the company reward for reaching a certain level). But MLM, multilevel marketing (I call it an exploitative pyramid scheme), requires a large, influential social network and the ability to buy piles of product up front. Even as a kid I knew it was a losing bet.

I'm not sure if Marty gave Mom the money for the start-up kit of makeup or if she got it from our funds from Papi, but within months, it was all still there, boxes dusty, most of it unopened. Mom had the flair for makeup and hosted one session with neighborhood and church ladies, maybe three of them, but she didn't have the social pull or insider status that she wished she had. It was one thing to sit outside the church exit offering up goodies to a flow of hungry parishioners who couldn't escape your position at the exit, but another to—pre-social media—reach people directly in their homes. That required a pull and time that she did not have.

ONE OF MOM'S BIGGEST GOALS, though, had happened: Her firstborn and only son was in a great university. Happy to be on his own and at the same college as his high school best friend, Alex was spared the loneliness of not knowing a soul in Washington, D.C. Our relationship improved greatly too as we both grew up and out of the pain of our ambiguous loss, the angry, competitive grief of our youth. Alex was sad to leave me and the little girls behind but also thrilled to move on. The tension between our parents kept rising and rising, and those of us left at home suffered for it. I felt bad for my little sisters too, all of us orbiting these two adults, wondering about their moods, tiptoeing around their sensibilities. It was a lot, and we each would have to handle it in our own way.

As I grew older, I was placed firmly into the role of Second Mami, due to both Latin tradition and Mom's worsening state of mind that led her to sometimes not leave her bed for a few days, break out in hives, and sit at the kitchen table opening growing piles of junk mail, sticking Publishers Clearing House stickers in the right spots so she could win the lottery. Dad barely spoke in these times. One evening, after Mom had put herself back to bed after picking us kids up from school, he came home from work and insisted that I make dinner for everyone since she wasn't going to get out of bed. I was barely thirteen years old. I was incredulous and protested as he sat down at his place at the dinner table, opened his newspaper, and waited to be served. I had never made a meal before. I was a kid. He was a grown-up. Why couldn't he cook? Wasn't it enough that I was doing my schoolwork and taking care of four children? I went upstairs to my mother, lying in bed, and told her that Dad insisted that I cook dinner, but I didn't know how to cook anything but boxed mac and cheese. I was scared and caught between the two adults. Mom eventually ended up coming downstairs and made us all something to eat, in her bathrobe and in silence.

I registered Mom's sadness. Though I wanted to empathize with her, our conflicts worsened because when Lupe was sad, she could also turn angry in an instant. The mom who sat by my bedside all night when I had night terrors was now the one standing over me as I sat on my bed, screaming that I was lazy and ungrateful and so many other things that it all turned into a jumble of sharp words I couldn't hear but could only file away into boxes in my mind, close the lids, push to the back, and seal shut. In the past, after these yelling sessions, I'd wait until my mother was either in her bedroom or back downstairs then knock on my brother's door, knowing he'd heard everything. Alex would let me in to hang for a moment and talk about a movie he'd seen or a new book he was reading or what band he was listening to on his record player. An assuring ritual. But from the time I was thirteen, Alex was gone.

I filed away the boxes of fear and pain in my mind, but the tremors they made within their confines escaped in the form of constant anxiety and self-harm. I picked and picked at the adolescent bumpy skin on my upper arms, the ritual allowing me to leave my body for a moment. It got to the point that I had to wear long sleeves even in the heat of summer. Unfortunately, my Caribbean skin was not forgiving even when it healed. Hyperpigmentation left dark brown spots all over my lighter brown skin. I even had to find a long-sleeved dress for the prom—both proms, junior and senior. When I got my driving permit at fifteen and Marty gave me his old car, another hatchback like the Gremlin, the independence and feeling of accomplishment and freedom offered me some much-needed reprieve. I could leave the house and limit my exposure to everyone. I could breathe a little.

As I matured and proved myself a sensible listener, Mom and Dad began to complain about each other to me. Mom would rant and Dad would whine. I wanted to be in both of their good graces, so I'd listen and, at times, agree with both. But Mom's overbearing, strict, controlling nature clashed with my newfound teen freedoms, so Marty and I ended up talking much more. He was the first to teach me how to drive (before I enrolled in classes) on my hand-me-down stick shift, and if he was in the garage fixing something or under the car, I'd sit nearby and learn. I wasn't comfortable, though, with hearing him talk badly about Mom, no matter how much I disliked her (which was a mutual feeling. She'd hiss at me: "I love you. But I don't like you."), and tried to dissuade him from doing so, or make an excuse and duck out. Whining grated on me, especially from adults. Unless of course I needed something from him, like permission to use his new car, which was cuter than my old one. Managing difficult personalities became a skill I wish I hadn't had to learn firsthand as a child. But I did.

Because Alex wasn't around much, and our youngest sister was born when he was seventeen, my brother was like a visiting uncle to our sisters and a returning prodigal son to Mom. We all got giddy when Alex was coming home. On one break from school, Alex came home with his girlfriend, Belinda. I was shocked. Not in the way other people were shocked, because Belinda was Black, Guyanese American, but because my nerdy, once-pimply brother had brought home an actual girlfriend, and a beautiful one! My mother hated when he dated (and would when I did too) and was terrified of him getting someone pregnant. But mostly, I think Lupe was just possessive and controlling because if she knew her two Wongs, truly, she would have known not to worry in the slightest about either of us landing in a pregnancy predicament before we were out of

college and married. We both wanted to escape from New Hampshire to
our own independence much too much.

I was impressed and a bit envious too of Alex's girlfriend. First, because she had a quiet, confident radiance I wished for myself, and second,
because they were living as students in Washington, D.C., a city filled
with people that looked like her and us. I wanted choices in friends and
lovers like that. Unfortunately, Mom's family, our Dominican family,
did not agree with my assessment of this smart, sweet, beautiful person
Alex had brought home.

We were stop number two on Alex's spring break girlfriend-
introduction tour. The couple had visited our Manhattan family before
coming to us up north in Amherst. After dinner the night of their
arrival—Belinda sleeping separately from Alex in my bedroom, of
course—I heard my mother's voice downstairs speaking in Spanish in a
tense, loud whisper. Strange that she'd get a family call this late. I went
about getting my sisters ready for bed and then crept to the top of the
stairs, out of my sisters' room, where I was sharing the littlest's lower
bunk, to hear if Mom was off the phone. She was, so I tiptoed down to
see if it was safe to talk to her. She seemed quiet but approachable.

"Mom. What was all that? What happened?"

"Oh, you know. Mama and Abuelo are very upset that Alex's girlfriend is Black," she said as she waved her right hand in the air, swatting
away the nonsense.

"What?" I was shocked. Abuelo was clearly a man of African descent,
Black himself, and Mom had dark-skinned cousins like Belinda (granted,
with blue eyes and green eyes) who used to come visit us at the apartment. "Even Mama?" I asked. To hear of Abuela's, Mama's, racism was
deeply disappointing to me. I looked up to her so much for acceptance
and love.

"Yes. But I told them this is America. She is a student with him at
university. A smart woman. And her skin color doesn't matter. Hard
work does. An education." She blew her nose, and I realized that my
mother had really gone to bat for Alex and for his girlfriend. She'd stood

up to the racism of her Dominican family, a family who all came up together escaping a genocide deeply fueled by hatred of the neighboring
Black Haitians. She'd come a long way from the day when she'd put me
in a beauty pageant at eight years old (I won Miss Congeniality. Ha.) and
a Black woman, the mother of a fellow contestant, approached her with
an invitation to join Jack and Jill. I had taken Lupe's turning down a his-
toric high-society membership organization of Black mothers and their
children, offered by maybe the second Black person I'd seen since our
move out of the city, as a rejection of her—our—Blackness. Maybe at
the time it was, maybe it wasn't, but on that night my brother was home
with this love, she'd dared to piss off her parents and stand up for them
both. Considering the brutality she'd lived under from her father, it was
a brave thing for her to do. And it further separated her from her family.

So did the lack of a quinceañera for me. The topic wasn't even raised
by my mother. It just wasn't what "American" girls did, and after all, we
were American. (I certainly, at the time, saw this as Marty's idea; in my
mind he had taken on the mantle of the assimilation police.) The typical
coming-out party for fifteen-year-old Latinas wasn't even on my radar
until my mother got a letter with photos from a cousin's quince. I was
shocked at the dress she was in, mounds and mounds of blue ruffles to the
floor, and a crown—a crown!

"Ay, look at your cousin. Look at how beautiful!" Mom said.

"Why is she so dressed up?" I asked. I thought it couldn't have been a
prom because it wasn't the season, and she was pictured alone.

"For her quinceañera. The party when you turn fifteen," Mom answered. As if I should just know all these Latin traditions. *By what, telepa-
thy?* Who the hell was going to teach me?

"Can I have a party too?" Even though my *Vogue*-magazine / Anglo-
media–trained eye found the flounces of the dress distasteful.

"Oh no. Your money is for education," Mom said as she put the photos back in the envelope.

"Party or college. Wedding or college," Marty chimed in from the
other room. "Those are your choices. We're paying for only one of
those."

I understood that this was a blended-family rule, though Dad wasn't paying for anything related to me. Of course I'd choose college, but not having a party that my cousins and other brown girls had made me feel sad, even if I was intimidated by the dress. A specifically Dominican party just for me? Like the white girls' sweet sixteen? Another line item in our long list of lost culture, though I didn't hesitate to always choose college. Mom didn't resist this one. She was all in when it came to success for her kids in America.

WITHOUT ALEX AT HOME, I did my best to manage everyone's needs, expectations, and personalities, working hard to keep the peace between my sisters and my parents, to stop Mom from hitting the kids, to not go crazy from all the pressure knowing that my little sisters were growing to begrudge me more and more. Putting me—a child—in charge of young children, adultifying me, robbed me of the ability to have a sibling relationship with my sisters. Though I tried. I rallied them together when I could to do something as sisters, like Twister or double Dutch or throwing a wild dance party in front of the big mirror in my bedroom. I even took a thick rope from the garage and tied it up on a big branch of the giant tree in front of the house to make a swing for them. Until I sat on it and busted it, leaving me with a bruised tailbone.

In the spirit of joyous cooperation between sisters, I had the idea for us girls to surprise our mom by baking a cake for her birthday while she was out running errands. We worked together harmoniously, for once, and frosted a pretty white box-mix cake. We were proud of it. Everyone contributed in some way. I directed one sister to crack the eggs, another to scoop the ingredients, another to use the mixer, etc. Then Mom got home in a foul mood. Her brow was furrowed, the two wrinkles between her eyebrows growing more and more prominent each year. She started yelling about god knows what as we all gathered around her, her five girls, in the kitchen to show off the cake we baked for her. But there was no stopping Mom's tirade.

"Mom! Stop! It's your birthday, and the girls and I made you a cake!"

I scolded, the youngest sister holding on to my leg. Each of them frozen in their spots.

"I don't care about your goddamn cake, coño!" Lupe shrieked. She picked up the cake on its plate, lifted it, and smashed it onto the floor. It exploded. Frosting, cake, broken glass scattered all around our shoeless feet.

I was livid. And hurt.

Lupe then picked up her bag from the counter, brushed past me to go upstairs to her room, and said, "Now clean it up."

Every birthday, whether it was mine, or hers, or one of my little sisters', became a pile of tinder. Not one went by without Mom turning it sour somehow. Same with confirmations, graduations, any event where someone else was being celebrated. Even Christmas. Our home was turning bitter, fast and hard. In the moment I didn't understand the reasons behind her acrid mood and berating countenance, especially on days that were supposed to be happy—it was a day that was supposed to be about us kids, someone other than her. It felt like betrayal. Why would a mom ruin a kid's birthday? How could she? Yes, I knew she was frustrated and angry about almost everything all the time. I knew she was tired of this place. But I also knew it wasn't fair and we were kids. Just kids.

And as we weren't allowed to be sad or complain or be tired or scared or angry or wistful, any emotions we girls felt were seen as weaknesses. Emotions made you a target. This meant that even though we five girls should have been close, should have banded together in sisterly love and support, we couldn't escape turning on each other. Mirroring our mother's distaste for each other. Yet still, as children, very much wanting to love and be loved.

School was no haven for me either. There were the typical nasty tween and teen girls, but added to that were the low expectations of me from teachers and administration that intensified over time. At a school social, I had my littlest baby sister propped on my hip as I carried her around the gymnasium. A nun approached me and said, "Oh, she's so sweet. When did you have her?" I was fourteen. Enough time in New Hampshire hearing "All sp*cs do is have babies" made it clear this was a normal question for me and only me. I fumed inside at her and all the nuns who were put off by me because I questioned them and got great grades. My academic performance grated at teachers. And I knew why. They wanted me to stay in my place, where I belonged as a brown person—low, in their expectations. I was supposed to be dumb, loose, and compliant. I was none of those things and I threatened their belief in their superiority. Once I realized that this was the dynamic at play, I was happy to continue to make them unhappy. One of my drives became spite.

They made it easy. I would be cited for the smallest things to bring me down in the class ranking. I had my hair in my face too often: a penalty on "decorum." I had a disrespectful look on my face: penalty and banned from the National Honor Society for my attitude. I forgot a comma in a sentence on a history test: penalty, so I couldn't get the perfect grade I had earned. I asked my friends if they got points off for commas. They did not.

My new acquaintances from the grocery store expanded my parameters of bigotry, introducing me to the slurs that would fly out of their mouths as easy as "Nice weather, huh?" I spoke up against them and heard in return, "Well, you seem white to me." When I told them I absolutely and clearly wasn't, they shrugged. No apologies. What a place this was. My home, my school, my work. I refused to get trapped by their stereotype of "Hispanic" women: young, barefoot, and pregnant. I would not be my mother, seemingly and increasingly detesting her life, an intelligent (if disordered) woman, trapped by babies. Oh no, not me. No kids until my education was set and my career in place and I was married, just like these white folks do. But I would certainly have sex as soon as possible. I had to rebel somehow.

By high school I'd become as anti-Catholic as I'd been Catholic in grade school. A full turnaround from when I had built my little shrine in my bedroom, praying for stigmata like the saints. The shrine was still there, in the corner of my room, but it was dusty, and I kept it out of superstition and laziness, not devotion. The biggest influence on my distaste for dogma was unsurprisingly its patriarchy. Nuns who couldn't be priests, the riches of advancement out of their reach, as they were merely wives to Jesus. Receptacles and servants. There was the church's nonresponse to the AIDS crisis. The blame of our original sin placed on Eve—my mother would say, "And that's why childbirth is so painful"— the drumbeat of virginity, virginity, virginity to young women but not to men. Vilification of birth control. And my eyes opening to the position my mother was in, her constant chafing against her state. It was all unfair.

Remember, I wanted what men had. I wanted all the possibilities and respect that the male gender had. All the forgiveness and leeway and time and assumptions of competency. All of it. Anything that didn't bend toward equality, I detested and spoke up about. Even things that seemed silly, like Elizabeth Taylor marrying for the umpteenth time. The schoolyard girls called her names and said she was going to hell, and I said, "Why can't she get married as many times as she wants? Men do it." Or when the nun in religious studies class said that all those who did not get baptized were going to hell. I raised my hand and asked, "My father is from China and they are mostly Buddhist. Does that mean that a billion people are going to hell?" I don't remember how she answered, beyond the glare in her eyes.

I had to wait until I was sixteen to truly rebel. This was when I was allowed to date, so of course my first date was on my sixteenth birthday. It was with a cashier from the grocery store, a tall, thin white guy who was as close to the Europop posters on my walls as I could get in those parts. He said I reminded him of a Native American character on the show *Bonanza*. I had no idea who she was, but it was a new one from being called "Flashdance!" or "Cosby girl!" nearly daily by customers and back room stock guys. I was so nervous and inept that night of my first date that my hands shook nonstop for an hour. We went to Pizza Hut and he gave me a set of colored pencils as a birthday gift. The seal was broken. I was going to date like crazy. And I did. After all, I was driving my dad's old car, paying for gas and insurance myself. I was responsible and drove my sisters to and from school every morning, blasting Depeche Mode and Tracy Chapman, asking my sisters to help keep me awake, just like Papi did with me in Florida. I was sleep-deprived too, but it was from my studies and working thirty hours a week, not gambling.

I decided several months after my first kiss on my sixteenth birthday that it was time to lose that thing the nuns and my mother valued so much, but only in women: virginity. I didn't have an official boyfriend so I literally approached the best-looking guy in town (he didn't have a lot upstairs, but that didn't matter), black haired, blue-eyed, and pale, like a buff male Snow White, and asked him if he'd do the deed. He agreed. My mutually rebellious friends set up an after-school rendezvous at one of their homes when parents were at work. Done and done. Another checkbox on my to-do list of life. I didn't feel anything that sex can make you feel, like loved, treasured, or pleasured. But that wasn't the point. I was getting rid of a burden. I used multiple forms of birth control and had plotted out a plan if I needed an abortion. The funds I needed for the full cost, the ride to and from, and the lie to hide it. I may have been a mutinous daughter, but you'd better believe I became an operations manager when it came to protecting my ability to go to college and have a career. And the stakes were about to get much higher.

In high school, the yuppie late eighties had arrived, and suddenly, for a year, Marty was flush with funds. Dad was very tight with money at home, socking away a substantial percentage of his take-home pay and investing in the market, but suddenly every Sunday night he'd take the whole family, five girls and two grown-ups, out to a nice white-tablecloth restaurant for an early dinner. It was wild to me and totally new to all of us. I hadn't had a white tablecloth since Chinatown and Papi. And the reason why I got Marty's old hatchback was because he'd bought himself a brand-new two-seater red sports car. Lupe was livid. She called him selfish and said he was having a midlife crisis now that he was approaching fifty. He said he earned it, and bought her a new car every two years or so, so why complain. It was a boom-boom time for the American economy as a whole, and we felt it directly as a family.

Until one school day, as we kids were setting up at the kitchen table for homework time, the phone rang. I picked up. It was Marty. He never called home during the workday.

"Dad?"

"Yeah, can you put your mother on the phone?" he asked.

"She's not home yet." She was probably running errands. I envisioned him in his suit and tie. His tone was tight and shaky.

"Okay. Can you tell her that I'll be home early?"

"Yeah, sure. But why?" I asked.

"The market crashed. I lost my job," he said so matter-of-factly it was nearly robotic.

My blood got cold. Lost his job? The one person who was supporting a house of six, seven if you counted me. It was October of 1987, the day of the stock market crash known as Black Monday.

Overburdened (again, I was still a kid) with this shocking news, I told my little sisters that Daddy was coming home early because he lost his job. In retrospect, of course, I shouldn't have made that my job.

Dad made it home before Mom did. I was at the kitchen table reading, my sisters, having done their homework, sitting in front of PBS watching *3-2-1 Contact*. I had no idea what to say to him besides "Hi." He returned my greeting, my sisters each softly saying "Hi, Daddy," not budging from their seats. Marty walked past us and went directly upstairs. When Mom came home, she asked why Marty's car was in the driveway. I had the sense to walk up close to her, help her with the grocery bags, and say softly, "He lost his job. He's upstairs."

Mom's face dropped and paled. I took the remainder of the bags to the kitchen, letting Lupe head up to see her husband, who surely wasn't well.

The next day I devoured the newspaper and the newsweekly magazines that showed up later to learn what happened. What I read didn't bode well for Marty getting a new job soon, but he had been so successful, especially the past year, that I felt confident that he wouldn't be out of work too long. I would be very wrong.

All of a sudden, Dad was home all the time. At first, he'd get up at his usual time and go to his computer room, what he called the office he set up in what had been our formal dining room at the front of the house.

He had gone from banking to technology when we moved to New Hampshire, a very young field at that time, building up in what was known for a short period as the East Coast Silicon Valley: Route 128 in Massachusetts. Marty built his own computer out of discarded parts from the office. The room also had piles of financial papers and magazines, *Barron's, Money, Fortune*. The sound of the turning of magazine or newspaper pages from his workroom became our soundtrack when we got home from school. At first, Mom seemed to be supportive, at least in front of us, going about her business taking care of the house. And then we got another phone call that changed my life substantially.

I was reading on my bed after dinner and heard a soft knock on my door. "Come in," I said, and my mother, with a strange look on her face, walked in, tissue in hand.

"I need to talk to you," she said as I got up to make room so she could sit on the bed, still covered in the frilly sunshine-yellow quilt that matched the canopy and my drapes from when we first moved in. "Go close the door." She came in through the door and was closer to it, but I did what I was told.

"It's about your brother. And Peter," she said. Alex had graduated from college and was living in a small spare room back in our old apartment on Claremont while he looked for a job in banking, helping Papi with his business deliveries in the evenings after his office job. As far as I knew, Papi had a wholesale costume jewelry business.

"See, I get the pieces and then I pay Chinese ladies to put it together— ladies in Queens—and then I bring to department store to sell" is how he explained it to me. What was cool for me was that when we went back to the city, I didn't get only my hundred-dollar bill but a big cardboard box full of costume jewelry, stuff he was selling to a big department store, for example. What my sisters or I didn't want to keep, I would bring to school for my friends.

"Your father was arrested last night," Mom said.

"What?!"

"And your brother was with him."

"Alex? Alex got arrested? What the hell did he do?" I couldn't imagine my newly college-graduated brother going to the dark side of the law. He knew better, though that's not completely true. I'd yell at him for watching the pirated movie cassettes that Papi would get for him. But arrested? For pirating movies?

"You know your brother has been helping out Peter with his business, going on the deliveries at night," she said. I nodded. "Well, your father"—why did she keep saying "your father"?—"he was transporting drugs."

"Drugs? What kind of drugs?" I asked.

"I don't know. But your brother was with him," she said. I was terrified for him. Lupe was dragging this out.

"So, Alex is in jail?" I asked, caring obviously much more about him than Papi.

"No. He explained to the police that he just graduated from college and this was his father, and he was helping him with work, but he didn't know anything about what was in the boxes. And Peter told them that Alex knew nothing—that he didn't have anything to do with it." She paused. "So they let him go."

"Oh my god, he must have been terrified."

"Yes. The police saw that too. He was very scared and crying. They could tell he was telling the truth."

"You found out about this today?" I asked.

"Yes. Your brother called me," she said. I couldn't wait to talk to him but also I knew he'd be very hurt and embarrassed and probably needed space before we spoke.

"So, your father is in jail for now. And it looks like it's going to be for a long time," Mom said. My eyes got wide. That must have been a lot of drugs.

"Is this going to be on Alex's record? He's trying to get a job!"

"No. They didn't press charges," Mom said. I was relieved. "The trouble is that . . . that means that we are not going to have Peter to help pay for your college." I was gearing up, looking at schools, and was definitely depending on Papi contributing to my education as he had for Alex's.

"Okay. I'll . . . we'll figure it out." I would need scholarships, grants, and loans, and would have to save up enough money to buy regular clothes, which I didn't have much of, being in a school uniform five days a week, plus everything for my dorm. I was sleeping on worn-out bedding I'd had for ten years. I'd figure it out. I had no choice.

What was tearing through my mind in that moment was the image of my brother being interrogated by police. Scared, alone. His graduation from Georgetown was a huge family accomplishment. First on both sides of the family to go to college and graduate. We had even picked up Abuela and Abuelo from New York on the drive down to Washington, D.C., for his graduation ceremonies. Papi drove down too. Ten people sitting in the sun in rows of folding chairs cheering on our first family college graduate. So proud. Then months later, in handcuffs? I couldn't believe it.

My thoughts next turned to the person whose fault this all was— Papi. And it started to fall together in my mind. The bosses sitting on the dais in the restaurants. The slick-rick way he carried his money, always so much cash. Living in Venezuela. The story my mom told of him beating her with the butt of a gun the night she decided to leave him. And there was our experience at the greyhound racetrack in Miami. So I had thought he just had a gambling problem.

I told myself it was just marijuana. That wasn't so bad, I thought. It didn't kill people like hard drugs did. Right?

My mother never confirmed the details of that arrest, the drugs he was transporting, how long, exactly, he'd be incarcerated, etc. These insights into that night came to light only recently, over thirty years later.

In 2019, on a typical visit to Papi's one-room apartment in Catholic Charities housing in Brooklyn, he decided at eighty-eight years old with stage 4 cancer that he was going to unload his belongings as much as possible.

"Here. Here. Take this. And this paper." He was handing me fragile-looking papers, very old. I opened them up and saw his employment document from the Norwegian ship he stepped off of many years ago. Divorce papers from Mom.

"Take this . . . Oh! No. Don't take that one," he said as he pulled one folded paper off the growing pile in my hand.

"Why? What is it?" I asked.

He sighed and handed it back to me. "Okay, okay, fine. Take that too."

I opened it. It was his arrest record from that night with Alex. There in dark bureaucratic typeface was the word "Heroin." Papi was trafficking heroin that night. Hence the long prison sentence, then a few years in a halfway house.

A few months before that visit to Papi, I had gotten more details, this time from my brother. I was walking home from Chinatown, chatting with Alex on my phone, when I realized that I was under the passageway of the Manhattan "House of D" (Detention), where only a few days before an internationally known sexual predator and trafficker to the wealthy had been discovered hanged in his cell, dead.

"Aldo! [his nickname since college] Guess where I am?" I knew he'd get a kick out of it. We were news junkies and talked nearly every day about what was going on in the headlines. "Manhattan House of D, man! Epstein, yo. Right there. Wow," I said as I walked under the windows, looking up, imagining the melee that had happened there days earlier.

"Oh yeah, I know that place. I've been inside it," he said.

"What?!" I nearly dropped the phone.

"Yeah, that's where I had to visit Peter before they sent him off that time . . . after college."

"Oh my god. You never told me that!"

Alex set the colorful scene: "I remember we all had to sit like in half a circle and wait for them all to come out. And they came in, all in orange jumpsuits, and sat across from us. And we couldn't bring anything in and they searched us and everything."

"Oh, Alex. That time. I can't believe what you went through."

"Yeah, yeah. It was wild," he said.

To say the least.

That night years before, when my mother sat on the edge of my bed and told me Papi had gotten my brother arrested, was a catalyst. I started to question everything told to me by my parents, all of them. I could see Alex and Peter fit together, as different as they were in their execution of the American dream. But something was off with me and Papi. At first it wasn't so much about the fact that I didn't look Chinese. My cousins of the same mix didn't look Dominican at all, so I brushed that off. There was something else. It was as if I was growing out of him. Like a phase. Definitely away from him, especially now. Maybe I didn't want to have anything to do with a criminal, drug-running-gangster father. I had college-educated Marty as "Dad." But I was complicit in accepting Papi's ill-gotten money and gifts. Or was I? I was only a kid. And I loved my parents, all three of them.

That night I didn't sleep much. Inside of me a whisper started. I couldn't hear distinct words, but I knew it was about me and Papi. I didn't want to hear it, but it wasn't going away.

It was doubt.

CHAPTER 6

. . . Because We Were Vested

THERE WERE THREE REASONS I WANTED TO GO TO COL-
lege. One, to get up and out of that house and that town. Two, to start
my ascendancy to independence and success. And three, to mix and min-
gle with a wider group of people.

I have no excuse for not going to a school that better suited me and
matched my aptitude except that Lupe wouldn't allow me to go back to
NYC, where I desperately wanted to be. ("Too many drugs," she said,
thinking that the city was Sodom and Gomorrah—as if private suburban
schools were any better.) I wonder too, in retrospect, if she wasn't envious in some way that I could escape to a place that she wasn't able to go
back to. And pressure at home to help with the kids, clean, and have
perfect grades combined with working double shifts on weekends and
after school left me desperate for time to do schoolwork and study. I was
too worn out for multiple applications and essays. Then there were the
application fees. So expensive, and all on me to pay. No help from my
parents financially or any guidance beyond where I was *not* allowed to
go. The whole college application process was on me. I had thought I'd
get some sound advice from the school guidance counselor but all I got

from her were her low expectations for the "Hispanic" in the school, telling me that I'd "need more safety schools," even though I had one of the highest GPAs in the class. She didn't tell one of my friends (white, of course) that. She told her that she should apply to the Ivies, and she had grades lower than mine.

I caved with exhaustion. The school I ended up with replicated my New Hampshire life, dialing it up a notch with even more class issues and conservatism to live with. Maybe I capitulated to earn points with Marty by going to a Jesuit university like he and Alex did. I even pulled the nonsense of accepting an early-decision offer just to get the whole process over with. I gave myself no options. Just took the first life raft that I could grab on to. But one thing made sense: The school was an hour and a half north of Manhattan by train. Maybe I'd finally be able to enjoy some of what the city had to offer a once-homegirl. But first, I was moving to Connecticut.

Our family minivan, packed like a clown car with people and boxes, turned the corner through a gate onto the campus. Greenery everywhere, rolling hills and trees. It was a well-manicured, wealthy-looking place. My stomach fought with itself between anxiety and excitement. Psychologically, I had one leg out of the vehicle already, eager to start my new solo life. But not yet. We were waiting in a long line of cars, parents and family dropping off their first-year kids. Mom was driving, my sisters in a row in the back, except one who was sitting in the middle with Abuela, Mama, whom we'd picked up from Claremont. As much of a pain as it was to drive all the way down to Manhattan only to turn back around and drive north to Connecticut, I was honored that she was there for me. I was the first girl in the family to graduate from high school and go to college. Dad didn't come. He said he had work to do.

As we crawled forward, red-and-white school flags flapping in the breeze, I saw people dressed in red and white coming closer. They were cheerleaders. All white, mostly blond, bouncing, flouncing, whooping cheerleaders. I was a brown, artsy, emo-alt-pop, fashion-magazine-loving teenager who adored both Janet Jackson and New Order. I was wildly allergic to cheerleaders. *What had I done?* As a couple came to our windows waving pom-poms ("Yaaaay! Welcome!"), golden ponytails flying, I saw Abuela's face. She had the same expression of nervous apprehension that I did.

Soon we were walking down the hall of my dorm, headed to my room. And there it was. Pus-beige-painted brick walls, oxidized metal bed frames, flat overused mattress, and all. I heard Abuela whisper something to my mother. "Ma, what did Mama say?" I asked.

"She said it looks like a jail," Mom said. She wasn't far off.

A few weeks into college I'd decorated my walls with ripped-out pages from the fashion magazines I'd brought with me. It was after dinner and I had made a quick friend, during orientation, who lived a few doors down. We were getting ready to go out for the evening around campus. On cue, she showed up at my door, which was open, as was everyone's, and behind her, two fellow first-years she'd met, both in sweatshirts and baseball hats, the local uniform I was discovering. We said our hellos, and one of them stared at my wall. It was models, Madonna, and probably unlike most of the campus, I posted and adored ads and fashion spreads with models of color. In the late eighties there were few, especially dark-skinned. I had one of them on my wall. It was a Ralph Lauren ad. A preppy aesthetic I didn't care for, but the model was stunning, and I was so proud her dark skin and natural hair had made the page.

"Wow. That's a lot of pictures."

"Yeah. I love fashion stuff," I answered.

"Why do you have a n—r on your wall?" the short one asked. So, this was how it was going to be.

"Excuse me? My mother is Black," I said. "I'm Black."

"Huh. You seem white to me," he said as he shrugged his shoulders, satisfied with himself, as if he were giving me an honorarium, a compliment. My new friend hurried the two guys out the door with an excuse. What had I done, indeed.

What I did do was lose my mind that first year. I went absolutely nuts. There was no thirty-hour-a-week job on top of a full course load. No little sisters to help take care of, no house to clean. No parents to referee or tiptoe around. What the hell was I going to do with myself? I got drunk nearly every night and indulged in straight-hookup culture. (I had one girl crush but I kept that possibility—and identity—in the only acceptable place for me, my head.) Essentially, I was a mess. Coming home that first break, once my grades had been mailed and my parents intercepted the envelope, Mom said, "We don't pay for you to get C's." (Though there was no we, only her, waiting tables to help pay my tuition, but she always presented a united front with Marty.) It was the first time in my life I'd gotten grades like that. And she was right. Lupe was leaving my little sisters home with a disengaged and increasingly depressed dad so she could serve strangers previously frozen meals and hope they left her a few dollars alongside their discarded pile of chicken bones. I had to snap out of it.

Consider what—or who—my mother thought she'd married. A successful, college-educated white man who built her the big house, missing only a white picket fence. And at her other hand, an ex-husband sending her money to help care for her first two children. Then, over months, both situations and these men's fortunes flipped. My take now is that the resentment she had toward Marty in particular for not finding another job within a few years wasn't only about disappointment in the "white knight" she thought she'd married. It was a rotting irritation at herself. She made the decision to give up her life—our lives—in the city to follow this man to a place where she knew no one and would endure humiliating racism and isolation. She made the decision to become that wife—having babies and making meals. Putting her needs aside because she assumed Marty would give her an always stable and even improving life—she counted on it. She bet on it. That all her sacrifice, the loss of her family and people, was going to pay off. And then he couldn't make it pay off for her. But it had been her bet. Instead of supporting him, acting as a team, she chose disdain. And he chose (mental) distance. Honestly, I can't say that I'd have felt differently. The disappointment for both must have been crushing.

I spent the following three years of college excelling like mad to get my cumulative GPA back up. I also took on a work-study job in addition to my bulked-up course load. Lupe was relieved with my industriousness and better grades but was not happy with my switch from a premed major to a double major in psychology and art history. My initial premed concentration was to be a path to becoming an MD in psychiatry. With Uncle Lou and his mental health struggles, plus my mother's depression, and possibly other personality disorders around me, psychiatry made sense and scratched that itch I had to make healing the mind a profession. However, one art history class and my mind busted open. It confirmed the feeling I'd had when staring at and absorbing Picasso's *Guernica* in our old *Encyclopædia Britannica* when I was maybe in second grade, seven years old—my perception and understanding of what limits and parameters were in the world were altered for the better forever. No limits.

Art to me is psychology. It is the mind, the internal state, expressed. The two majors together felt like a beautiful marriage. To my immigrant mother, though, it was supposed to be doctor, lawyer, or banker for her kids. Only Alex stayed on her path, majoring in business and then getting an MBA. My studies were a disappointment. Marty's input was that no matter what I majored in, the Jesuits offered a "solid liberal arts education," which he was a fan and product of. His attitude with me those years, and every year since, has been "You don't need any help." Which he may have meant either as a compliment or just being laissez-faire, but I took it as misunderstanding and neglect. I wanted help. I desperately wanted someone to help me, somehow. Even the strongest and most capable need help sometimes.

I went back home to New Hampshire during every school break that was more than a long weekend. I took on loans and Mom was helping financially, but everything from food to clothes to books to any other expense had to come from me. Spring breaks, summers, Thanksgiving, Christmas, all were spent working back at the restaurant where my mother also worked. On New Year's Eve, my mother and I would walk through the door into the house after long shifts just as the ball was dropping in Times Square at midnight. Marty would be watching it on television in the dark, the girls asleep on the couch, and he'd whisper to us, "Happy New Year!" I started out the first hour of a couple of new years in a row bone-tired, smelling of cheap steak, fryer grease, and surface cleaner. Mom brushed by her husband with nary a glance, leaving only a trail of bitterness behind her. I hadn't seen them touch each other in longer than I'd bothered to remember.

Something happened to me while working one summer at the restaurant that taught me a lesson about who I was to some, no matter how smart or successful I would become. Our franchise was owned by a man in the wealthy town next door, Bedford. He was a tall ashy blond, former-football-player-looking man who'd show up once every other week or so to see how the restaurant was going. He was jovial and Mom enjoyed flattering him. She was just as charming as Papi was chatting with his bosses on their dais. Then the owner's son started coming along with him on visits. He was in college like me, home for the summer, cut from his dad's cloth, definitely a kind of "Chad" I had dropped the twenty pounds I'd gained my first year—all the running around on my feet for ten-hour shifts did the work. I looked good. Chad, I'll call him, noticed, and after a third visit, he asked me out. Again, it was my birthday either that day or close, so he planned dinner at a nice (read: nonfranchise) restaurant in Bedford, but first he'd pick me up and bring me to his house to meet his parents. I thought that was a bit much, felt maybe like a new acquisition, but went along with it, as everyone talked about their mansion, so I wanted to see how they lived. I even bought a brand-new dress for the evening that I'll always remember. It was a snug, stretchy white V-neck, pulled into a twist in the middle to accentuate my shape. But of course, to be classy, it covered my shoulders and wasn't too short. It was the most I'd spent on an item of clothing since the prom.

Chad picked me up in his shiny red car. We drove to his house, which was, yes, huge, especially for their family of three. His mother, a pretty blonde, smiled nicely and gave me the once-over. Then we went to dinner, where he gave me a gift box like you buy at the perfume or makeup counter at a department store. I was genuinely flattered after my early college experience of drunk guys sloppily groping me after a few words at a keg party. Chad must have spent seventy or eighty dollars that night, a fortune in my eyes then. When we got into the car after dinner so he could drive me home, he went in for a kiss. Fine. That was fine. Then, as he continued driving, it was as if he'd changed personalities. Gone was the polite and sweet young man who opened my door, pulled out my chair for me, brought me a gift on our first date. His left hand was on the wheel and his right hand was squeezing my thigh nearest him, moving its way toward my crotch. I tried to laugh it away—What happened to the polite guy of a few minutes ago? I was no prude, especially after my first year of college, but I had really been fooled by all the flashiness and fanciness into thinking that he genuinely had wanted to get to know me, respect me, even.

Abruptly, Chad pulled over onto the side of the road into a small gravel clearing. I didn't know Bedford well, so I didn't recognize where we were. There were no cars on the road and nothing but trees around. I asked him what he was doing, my heart beating loudly in my ears as I started to sweat. I remember the gift that was sitting on my lap getting pushed to the floor. I remember feeling smothered and asking him to please stop. He did. For a moment. Only to say "After all I've done for you tonight? You owe me." And he went back to trying to get under my panties and bra, while his wet tongue was doing god knows what on my face and neck. He was heavy and strong. My arms were pinned back. As he breached me with his fingers, in a burst of fury I pulled together all my strength, pushed against his chest, and yelled with a guttural growl, "Get off me NOW!" My tone startled him. An anger that I'd let loose only a few times in my life, a fiery fury that reminded me of my mother when she raged so hard that she looked like she could rip the world apart with her hands. As he pulled back, I looked him in the eye, and at a lower volume but the same tone said, "Take. Me. Home." He started the car in silence and drove. I was sweating and shaking. All I could think of was how much I put into looking so nice and being so charming to his parents and how happy I had been that someone was taking me on a proper date. I felt like a sucker.

So, this is what I got, thinking I was actually on par with these people. I did everything right, I thought, and it didn't matter. I was something to be used. I wasn't a fellow human but a function. Stupid, stupid me, I thought. So stupid. How dare I think that a rich white boy would ever want anything serious and respectable with a brown girl like me? I couldn't just be an interesting and yes, attractive, person that someone wanted to get to know, worthy of a relationship, not just an outlet for lust—unless, as when I plotted to lose my virginity at sixteen, I wanted to be and communicated such.

When I got home, Lupe was up and waiting to hear all about the date. I was disheveled, my hair sticking to the back of my neck with perspiration. I walked straight to the garbage can in the kitchen and threw his gift away. Mom stared. "Wha? Why did you do that?" To my Latin mother who never wasted an ounce of anything, my gesture was shocking.

Lupe wanted to hear every detail. Before that night, I'd never told her anything about any date I'd had, but she knew this kid and knew his father, who was our employer. And I think I got pleasure too in bursting her bubble about that rich father-and-son combo. (I never cared for how she'd be nothing but sweetness and charm to others, leaving the nastiness for her family at home.) I left out the worst part of the assault but made it clear that he'd behaved like a lech. My mother had originally shared my fantasy and joy at this fancy date. She got quiet, didn't say anything I needed to hear like "I'm so sorry that happened to you." She just told me to go upstairs and clean up. I regretted telling her just then.

The next day when we were at the restaurant, at the end of our shifts, Mom came up to me in between busing tables and said, "So, I called his father."

"You did what?" I had no idea that she'd do something so bold.

"I called and I told him everything that happened, and I told him that it was so disrespectful to treat my daughter that way. And that if I ever saw that boy again, I'd give him a piece of my mind."

I was a jumble of impressed, horrified, and embarrassed but also afraid for our jobs. As the week went by and we weren't fired, I exhaled and realized that my mother had stood up for me with our boss. She confronted the father of my attacker—because that's what he was—held him accountable, and risked something. And she came out on top. Her reaction shocked me. For a moment, a day, or at least until the next time she snarled at me, I felt like, wow, she cares. Maybe? But then I remembered that one summer before Marty lost his job and Mom went to work, she had a business idea for a line of kitchen goods, like aprons and potholders. She'd gotten some seed money (I assumed from Dad but maybe it was Peter), had a graphic designer come up with a logo of fruits, veggies, and nuts—"Fru-gee-nuts"—and she rented a booth at the Javits Center in Manhattan at the cooking expo. She demanded that Alex and I go with her to staff her booth, though both of us protested. (Alex and I didn't see a future for her idea, and for me, what teenager wants to do a job like that in the summer?) Two men in their forties, brown-skinned and, I thought, Middle Eastern, came by our booth. I noted that they were pretending to look at the wares but were disconcertingly staring at me. Mom approached them, all smiles, and talked to them for a bit. I scowled once I saw her bashful and flirty. I didn't like this. Once they left I asked her what that was all about. She said, "They said they'd buy everything in the booth, in exchange for you."

"For me?"

Mom waved me and my questions and protests away. I hated the smile that was still on her face. Why didn't she smack these guys? They asked if they could "have" me in exchange for her fucking aprons, and she didn't punch them? She didn't even yell or wipe that smile off her face?

I had trouble reconciling this reaction of hers with her reaction to my assault by Chad. But now I know what the difference was. My mother saw me as an extension of her, a product, something she made and owned. You can look, admire, but don't touch.

Her standing up for me at the restaurant, however, was a workplace lesson that would serve me down the road. And a life lesson on what I represented to many men. It was one, however, I'd keep having to learn.

Back at the house, Marty wasn't having much luck with finding work. Three years into living off of his investments and savings had the house stretched. He sat the whole family down at the dinner table one Sunday when we all happened to be home, even the little ones, and told us in very serious, somber tones that "We're taking out a second mortgage." I wasn't exactly sure at that point how that worked, and certainly my little sisters didn't know, but what was clear was that it was not good.

Bad things happen to all sorts of people. The stock market and economic crash of Black Monday surprised everyone and put thousands and thousands out of work. It wasn't the layoff that increasingly incensed my mother, it was that Marty was not finding work, and though he was home and had two working arms and legs, was not helping around the house while Mom and I were pumping ours at the restaurant. I'll never forget when Marty attempted laundry and shrunk to doll size one of Mom's favorite sweaters. She yelled and yelled at him, saying that he'd done a bad job on purpose so he wouldn't be asked to do it again. I thought that was oddly insightful of human behavior, his purposeful, willful ignorance. So, no, he never had to do laundry again.

Looking back, I feel guilty for often siding with Marty in his arguments with Mom. She was so rough on all of us, particularly that summer, filling the house with a palpable layer of eggshells at our feet. It was hard to breathe in her presence sometimes for fear that she'd catch your face in an expression she didn't like. I'm sure the workload on her at home got much worse without me there to help. And the financial pressure must have become intense. We went from a family that gave a donation check to church every week to receiving food pantry goods and a donated Thanksgiving meal.

I felt for my four younger sisters, now alone at home with a fractious mom and dad, no big sister or Alex around to buffer or thwart their moods. I certainly wasn't always their savior. Yes, if I had a few extra bucks, I'd treat them all to McDonald's drive-through ice cream after school, and if I had a day off in the summer, I'd drive all four girls to the beach for the day or treat them to a day at Canobie Lake Park, the local amusement park with rides and games. I wanted to bring joy into their lives so much. But unfortunately, I was also a kid myself, put in charge of raising babies. It was a recipe for failure for both me and our relationship as siblings. I did my best to make cleaning the house fun with friendly, competitive games and to just try and try to keep everyone—especially

Mom—happy. But I was too young to manage it all. Exhaustion, too much responsibility, threats of stark punishment, were always looming over me. My anxiety and resentment were at times too much so I screamed, yelled, and hissed at these little girls in ways I shouldn't have had I been a mature caretaker. Instead, I lost out on being a kid myself. And they lost out on the best of me.

It was often just too much for me as a kid. It tinged my relationship with my siblings with an ever-present sour taste, casting me as a hair-triggered substitute parent rather than a sister, all authority, punishment, bribes, and gifts. To this day and most likely forever, this pains me. I mourn not having a true sibling relationship with them more like I had with my brother. I've accepted that I will always love them much more than they love me. Because they were under my care but also under my feet. And all this ate away at my relationship with my mother greatly. Pushing me into adulthood so soon meant I became the adult in the room, overseeing her too in many ways.

There had been no affection between my mother and me for years, no hugs, no physical contact. Even the laughs we used to have were long gone. Lupe became a raw nerve, a roiling river of resentment, unloading on me daily her complaints about Marty and, once in a while, other family members, Papi or even Alex. It was hard for a teenage daughter to sympathize with a mother like that. I felt unseen and unheard myself, uncared-for, functioning only as a repository for a parent's rotten feelings. Yes, I agreed that Marty could do more around the house and look for a job. But hearing it like a banging, thumping drum, when what I needed was the acceptance, love, support, and reciprocity of a parent, soured me. In my last year of high school, Marty and I had started to talk a lot more beyond our usual movie or news or stock market conversations. I began to confide in him about my relationship with a boyfriend at the time and we achieved a buddy-buddy status. He'd listen and ask some questions. Mostly, he'd just listen and nod. But then, over the following college years, it turned into him also complaining about Mom too often. Asking me to talk to her, to *do* something. To change her, pleas to "get her off my case."

Good news for the family finances came in the form of a surprise phone call. It was a former colleague from Dad's last job who asked him to join him at an up-and-coming software firm back in the tech area in Massachusetts. It was a bit of a step down for Dad, but it was still in his field and a salaried position with benefits. Everyone in the house was relieved. And you would have thought that maybe this would have bettered the dynamics between Mom and Dad, but it was becoming clear that their marriage was becoming unsalvageable.

"Mom, where are you going?" I asked, as Lupe frantically grabbed her jacket, purse, and car keys. It was evening, dark, and after dinner.

"That son of a bitch is at her house and I'm going to go there and get him!"

"Whose house? What are you talking about?"

"He says he's doing work and working but I know he's not! He's having an affair with her and I'm going to give her a piece of my mind," Mom hissed, holding her keys in her hand, pointing at me with one of them.

"Mom. You don't know that! Doesn't he work with her? Maybe they are working." I couldn't imagine Marty having an affair. He had made himself out to us as the victim of Mom's rages, and as we were victims too, maybe we identified with him too much. Marty having an affair would have made him a villain in my eyes. I couldn't do it. Now I know that whatever he did or didn't do didn't make him a villain at all. It made him human. Both these people, both our parents, were human, however they chose to express it.

"Mom! Mom, what are you going to do?" I yelled after her as she sped—squealed her wheels—in reverse out of the driveway.

My sisters, who were home with me, all looked at me with concern. "It's okay," I said. "It's okay. Nothing's going to happen." Then we all turned back to whatever we had been doing, watching TV, reading the paper, cleaning the kitchen. But we did these things in a tense silence, waiting for a car to pull back into the driveway.

Maybe an hour later, both Mom and Dad walked in the door. Marty looked beaten down and Mom was steaming, as burgundy as her jacket.

Dad went straight upstairs to their bedroom. As Mom hung up her things in the hallway closet, I went up to her and asked furtively, "What happened?" I see now that I was shaped into a young accomplice in this unhealthy relationship with my mother. I wanted her to get away from me but at the same time, I acted like a sympathetic listener when it suited my curiosity or needs.

She spoke loudly so we could all hear and told us that she'd gotten there, saw Dad's car parked at the house, and knocked on the door, and *she* answered. Mom demanded that "my husband" come outside, and then she berated the woman. I can't recall more details than that, just a blur of scenes flying by in my head. Imagining Lupe yelling and screaming at this woman. Or, as Mom was saying more calmly, giving her a piece of her mind. And I remember looking around at my sisters and their worried, sad faces. We all were thinking the same thing. That Mom was a crazy mess of a woman, filled with jealousy and vitriol. She blew it out of proportion, surely, I hoped. Regardless of who was guilty of what, or not, it was painful for us all. And the pain colored our days as the accusations of infidelity began to run both ways.

The summer before sophomore year, to add to the chaotic family dynamic, we were surprised by a beloved visitor who was going to stay for a few months, my grandmother, Abuela. She'd been diagnosed with advanced breast cancer, and as Lupe tended to do, with no heads-up or notice, she drove to Manhattan one morning and came back that same evening with Abuela and her bags so she could receive her chemo treatments and care with Mom. My grandmother, whom I adored, looked smaller and thinner than usual. She was usually a pleasantly filled-out woman. And shockingly, her hair was gray. I somehow believed that all these years her hair had been naturally black. I later found out she'd dye her roots every two weeks so the gray had zero chance of revealing itself. Thankfully I was home when they arrived. We set Abuela up in our once-expansive living room, filling up more and more with Mom's boxes of mail and unsuccessful business launches. Marty brought down one of the girls' bunk beds to set up a mini bedroom (though no door) for her.

The reason for Abuela's arrival made me sad and anxious but I was also deeply happy to have her there with us. Mom and Marty mostly fell into their best behavior, and I had my favorite person just down the staircase. But I couldn't talk to her anymore. New Hampshire and our in-house ban of Spanish had erased my first language. I had noticed it drip away, year after year. And once Mom started working at the restaurant my junior year of high school, our visits to New York City and opportunities to practice my first language were gone.

I was ashamed and surprised at myself. I didn't know just how much I'd lost. And now my abuela was with us, shriveling from chemotherapy, and I couldn't speak with her? Comfort her? I was angry and frustrated at what I'd been taken from and what this place had demanded of me, taken from me. It wasn't just New Hampshire. The whole country outside of neighborhoods like ours in uptown Manhattan had a belief that assimilation was best. That erasing anything not white American was how you became American. In retrospect, some of my shame came from being complicit. From feeling that I had personally betrayed my abuela, betrayed our roots and culture and family by participating in this assimilation. And though Mom could have prevented this by standing up to Marty, she would have had to stand up to the whole world outside of our New Hampshire house too. At the time I didn't feel I could blame Marty too much. He told me of how his father, Grandpa G, had made it to Detroit from Italy as a child, and when he went to kindergarten not speaking a word of English, the teacher would beat him with a paddle every time he spoke Italian. Mom and Dad had both gone along with what you had to do to make it in America. Assimilate. I was angry at New Hampshire, white America, more than anything or anyone else.

Despite the language barrier, I tried to connect with Abuela. I knew we both loved fashion magazines. She always had a small pile of the most recent Spanish-language women's magazines, like *Vanidades,* on her dresser, always featuring a pale white woman's face. So, one day before I traipsed off to work, I brought down a stack of my fashion magazines to give to her. She had to have been bored in that room, too weak to do much of anything, though Lupe had brought in a small television for her. I hoped that the piles of pretty print would help.

As I handed them to her, all I could say to her was something like "Mama, [these are] for you" in English. She smiled and thanked me. I stood there for an awkward moment, looking for Spanish words in my head I could use, but I couldn't find any. English it was to be. "Going to work now. Okay, bye" as I hugged her. "Love you!"

My heart hurt as I walked out the door, my car keys jingling. My mind a jumble of dark thoughts and emotions. Not only distress at the lost connection to Abuela but the loss of the life I could have had as a little girl had we not moved. And now Abuela was dying, and it was too late. She was only in her early sixties. Why did we have to give up our family, our culture, language, history? Why did we have to leave the city? Why did Mom agree to this life? I wish she hadn't. But at the same time, I was determined to make sure that the painful price I paid—and she paid—got me admission to an even bigger American dream than my mom had, no matter what.

Mom took Abuela to doctor appointments for treatments on days off from the restaurant. Then, before I left for my second year of college, the rounds of treatment done, Mom drove Abuela back home to Claremont. By December, she had passed away. Alex called me in my dorm to tell me. I was crushed. The person who saw me and loved me without condition was gone. And I couldn't even speak with her, communicate, in the end.

It wasn't all work and sorrow that summer and those that followed. Alex and Belinda had a beautiful, boisterous wedding in Washington, D.C., where we all got to meet our new Guyanese family. I was the lightest-skinned and youngest in the wedding party, only nineteen years old. But that didn't stop Belinda's bridesmaid crew from taking me in like their own little sister and taking me out to the bachelorette party at an all-Black male strip club in D.C. Sheltered and "square" as I was, I was shocked at the rawness of it, but liberated. These women were so free yet tightly bound with each other, models of friendships that I'd aspire to. A group of big sisters and aunties who were to remain in my life until this day, more than thirty years later.

Back at college in my senior year, the Bill Clinton vs. George Bush,

Sr., election became a schism between me and my roommates on campus, the friends I'd had since my first year. I was hated in my own house for speaking my mind and pointing out their racism. (When your roommate says "I don't date Black guys. I don't find them attractive. I would date Will Smith, though. But that's not racist!" you try not to lose your mind.) My roommate had the bed near the window and chose to put up a BUSH poster for George H. W.'s election campaign, not for something more fun, like celebrating women's anatomy. I tried to argue that as it was *our* room, not her room, that was *our* window, not hers, and I certainly did not support that man or that sign. No dice. The poster stayed and I had to see it every day, not only in my room but from outside the house every time I walked to the door. Tensions were so high, my body dwindled to a scary-small size. I was all nerves. I couldn't eat. I had a heavy course load and had to take on a work-study job to bolster my income and cover costs. Our town house was far from both the campus and my work-study job, so every day meant walking miles upon miles in all kinds of weather. I tried to keep my eye on the prize, graduation. Again, dreaming of freedom, just as I had back in New Hampshire. Dreaming of the people I could share things with

There were a few good things to come of my college years. I remain friends with some professors who encouraged me to succeed and took the time to see me as a whole, intelligent person. One professor, a Yale PhD in psychology, blew my mind wide open by teaching me analysis rather than the rote learning I'd only had so far. And then there was senior year, when I made friends with the theater kids and the Black and brown kids' tables in the cafeteria, a group a year or more below me, making up a bit for my class's incredible lack of diversity. It was too late to get too close to any of them, but they all may just have saved me by including me, embracing me, giving me acceptance and a bit of a social life.

Once, late that year, Marty drove the three hours down to Connecticut to bring me back home for a holiday break so I could work at the restaurant. By the time he made the seven-hour round trip and pulled into the driveway, it was late at night, everyone in the house was asleep, and I was eager to get into my own bed. As we approached the front door, Marty said, "Oh, your sister took your room." The oldest of my four sisters.

"What? What do you mean she took my room?"

"She took your room. She's sleeping there," he said nonchalantly. Sleeping in my adored yellow frilly, canopied twin bed.

"But . . . where am I going to sleep?" I was incredulous. It was the middle of the night and I had nowhere to sleep in my own home? Or, I guess, now my former home, was the message being sent to me.

"I dunno. Couch?" Marty shrugged.

Hard to convey the gut punch it was to come home late at night, exhausted from midterms, to find your bedroom is not your bedroom anymore, your bed not your bed anymore, and no one thought to give you a heads-up. Even if it wasn't going to be a choice, could someone have let me know so I didn't discover this at midnight after a long drive? It felt like I'd been kicked out of the family and they were in a rush to see me go. Yes, I left the house to go to college, but both Alex and I had had no choice but to do so, as Lupe made clear. I did think that at least I could have my room until graduation, as they had done for Alex. I was so hurt that no one thought to tell me about it.

As I sat on the uncomfortable overworn family couch in the dark, I wasn't as mad at my little sister as much as my parents. My sister would have needed permission or even an order to move into my room. She couldn't have done it on her own even if she'd wanted to. This was just Mom doing her thing, Marty doing the spineless move of going along with it to keep the peace for him, and then me not allowed to have feelings about it. It was clear that night that the place I had wanted to leave so badly had already let me go.

Graduation day. I had managed to stick the landing of that double major, a BA in both psychology and art history, only one class short of a minor in Asian religions. The whole family was there except for Papi, of course, who remained behind bars, his sentence for drug running still in force. And without Abuela around to nudge support for their grand-daughter, as he'd supported their grandson at his graduation, Abuelo, my grandfather, wasn't going to make the effort. He didn't support women getting an education anyway. It was a beautiful, sunny day and mostly a blur until it was time to leave and I had to say goodbye to my sisters and parents and my life with them as I knew it. I packed up my belongings into Belinda's little red sedan and was off to share my brother and his wife's newlywed apartment in a not-yet-gentrified Park Slope, Brooklyn. Ever generous, Alex and Belinda had asked me to move in with them so I could find work in NYC and save up for my own place. I had given Alex an earful about coming home at midnight a few months earlier to no bed or bedroom, only a couch-surf in what had been my home, so they both were particularly sympathetic. I was moving into their tiny "baby" room with just enough space for a futon couch, which had to stay a couch in order for the door to open. But that was all I needed, and I was grateful to my core.

As Alex, Belinda, and I drove off to start my post-grad life, I wasn't able to relax and take in what I'd accomplished those four college years until we crossed into New York City. The rows of buildings welcomed me home with a psychic embrace. It was done. I was back, baby. I crossed dimensions. I hadn't realized just how pained I had been at that school, especially that last year. The grip of stress in my mind let go just a bit. I thought, now it's on me. My freedom is on me. I can do what I want. But I had to get a job first. I was broke.

CHAPTER 7

... Because We Needed to Be Free

ONE DAY IN MY EARLY TWENTIES, I WOKE UP, WENT TO work, and by evening was asked by colleagues to kick Tupac Shakur and Mickey Rourke out of the men's restroom in the lobby. I was not even two years out of college. After a brief starter-job pit stop in Boston, working at an art gallery on Newbury Street, the pedal hit the metal in my professional life once I got back to New York City.

After those few months of I'd-rather-not-remember Boston living, I was back in Manhattan with a new job as the second assistant to the chairman of Christie's auction house. Christopher Burge was a legend in the building and the business, having started working at the auction house in 1970. I was making $27,000 a year, and in 1994 that was enough to save up money living with my brother and his wife to get my own studio apartment in three months. *It was happening.* But first, Alex and Belinda were excited for me to come back to the city and stay with them. I wasn't swayed in the slightest by the fifty-minute commute on the subway from their place in Park Slope, Brooklyn, to East Fifty-ninth and Park Avenue in Manhattan. The new job required a serious upgrade on the wardrobe, so I took out the one already indebted piece of plastic I had in my wallet and brought it to my newest discovery, the sale at Zara. With a flat iron for my hair, a clothing iron for my new duds, a spritz of starch, shoe polish skills, and a fake fancy watch bought off the street corner, I was looking the part of an Upper East Side professional (as long as you didn't look too closely at the shoddy seams of my fast fashions). I had my newscaster's voice—trained well from our family's practice of nightly news with dinner, Lupe's insistence on articulation, and my knowledge of New York City society from reading every magazine and society page I could find. I would need all of this, an arsenal of work and intent. It had to work. I had to turn the five figures of debt I'd gotten into paying for my education into a solid investment. Quickly, though, I got in trouble.

My job was to be backup to the executive assistants to both the chairman and the president, a number two to the two. The president was rarely there, but Christopher was always around. I found Christopher, the top auctioneer of the firm, jovial and welcoming and we had good rapport. I was fairly well-liked except for one thing: Someone had reported to human resources that I was wearing pants in the office. Pantsuits, to be exact. Matching, well-pressed, professional gray and navy pantsuits. This was against company policy. Women, in 1994, per worldwide company policy, were allowed to wear only skirts or dresses, no pants. I hadn't read the company handbook that clearly or I'd glazed over it, not thinking it could possibly be enforced, as it was not 1954. But I was wrong.

"How can it be more professional to wear a skirt if your skirt is not professional? Have you seen Jane? Look at her, then look at me, and tell me which one you'd like clients to see and who looks more professional," I argued to the head of HR.

Jane was the chairman's assistant. She too lived in Park Slope but dressed as if she were going to the food co-op, not to the office where millionaires, billionaires, and snooty Europeans came through the door every day. She wore skirts, all right—long, wrinkled paisley skirts. I had to find an argument for wearing pants to get rid of this insanely ancient and sexist policy, and yes, I threw a colleague under the bus. I felt very bad about it because I liked her, and she was nice to me. But unfortunately, the comparison was true. Plus, I needed to wear pants for two reasons: First, it's just goddamn right for women to be allowed to wear pants and second, the apartment I ended up getting for myself (a walk-up studio overrun with mice) was walking distance from work. It was on First Avenue and work was on Park Avenue, a walk of several long city blocks. I felt very exposed and was harassed when I wore a skirt to work.

Looking back, I have to say, Jesus, I was a piece of work. Fighting a sexist office policy at my second job out of college, barely twenty-three years old. I was nuts. But I won. The policy was changed within a week. Two decades later, in the late 2010s, a good friend and fellow nonprofit board member landed as the new head of human resources for Christie's. She was their first Black executive and I made sure to tell her about changing the no-pants policy. She thought it was a hoot. I saw her months after she started and she told me, "I heard the story about the pants!" Twenty years later, that felt good to hear.

And now I admit that my ambition, my being very good at my job, and my using Jane as an example of unprofessionalism got her fired and me hired for her job as number one assistant to the chairman, Christopher. She had been there for twelve or more years. Her last two weeks when we had to sit in the same office space were very uncomfortable. Rightly so. I found out that she was the one who reported me to Human Resources for wearing pants instead of talking to me directly, sitting two yards away from her every day for eight or more hours, smiling at me. It wasn't a good situation overall.

But I did throw myself into that job like the dream it had started out as for me. I threw myself into every job I've ever had like gangbusters. I had made the most in tips at the restaurant. Before that, I was the fastest, most accurate cashier at the grocery store. I was competitive with myself, and I took to heart Lupe telling me that I'd have to be ten times better than white people to get anywhere in life. So I made myself that extra. Always professional, learned quickly, read every single auction catalog that went past me, and art publications (nearly a stack a day), became an expert on this new thing called email, software installation, and its use. I thank Marty for that, Dad, and his mini home office strewn with com-

The fateful photo, kept in a box for more than
forty years. Me as a newborn, held by my mother,
with my future stepfather, Marty, and a friend.

Mom (Lupe—known as "Cita" then), only nineteen,
and Peter/Papi Wong, thirty-four, at their
engagement party in Chinatown, Manhattan.

My mother's
wedding day
to Papi, with
her father,
my abuelo,
in Chinatown.

My abuelo (grandfather), Eugenio, as a young tailor in the Dominican Republic.

My lovely abuela (grandmother), Ana Rita, whom we called "Mama," in an official Dominican Republic government photo.

My mother, Guadalupe Altagracia, as an adolescent in the Dominican Republic.

Me and Papi at our apartment on Claremont Avenue in Manhattan.

Mom on a weekend trip to Mount Airy Lodge.

In Vermont with my brother, Alex, playing in the leaves with Marty on one of our weekends out of the city with Mom.

Me, my brother, our mother (pregnant with the first of my four younger sisters), and Marty at our first house in New Hampshire.

Our body language says it all. Mom's attention is on Marty, who is taking the photo, while I cling to her, hoping for crumbs. I am scared and lonely in this new place we call home.

My first (and only) beauty pageant—a rite of passage for a Latina daughter—where I won Miss Congeniality. The other girl was one of the few brown people I'd seen since we moved out of the city. I loved her instantly but never saw her again.

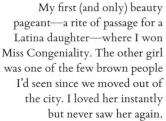

The "dream" home in process that Marty had built for our growing family in a new town, Amherst, New Hampshire.

Me at Disney World in Orlando, Florida, on a vacation with Alex and Papi. It was my first time away from home. Note the hometown T-shirt.

A photo I "directed" of my four little sisters on the steps of our school, which was also the home of a few dozen Catholic nuns. I was in high school then and would drive us five kids to and from school every weekday in a little hatchback.

Me and Papi at Alex's graduation from Georgetown University in Washington, D.C. My brother was the first in the family, on either side, to go to college and get a degree. I liked to remind him years later that I was the first girl in the family to do so.

First year of college, ready for the spring dance. Note the fashion tearsheets and posters on my wall. The one with a Black model was derided more than once.

A sunny day in Santiago, Chile, 1995, when I was working for Christie's auction house, first on Park Avenue, then in South America. Photo taken by my soon-to-be first husband. My work colleagues called me "gorda" (fat girl) and "negra" (Black girl).

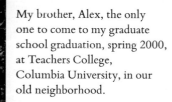

My brother, Alex, the only one to come to my graduate school graduation, spring 2000, at Teachers College, Columbia University, in our old neighborhood.

On the set, hosting my CNBC show with friend and guest Lisa Takeuchi Cullen.

My brother, his three daughters (also Wongs), Papi, me (after a day of doing TV), and my daughter, the littlest one, B, all out for dinner in Chinatown, NYC.

My brother and I return to Florida decades later, this time to Miami, in 2019, with our daughters, on a visit to see Alex's godmother, my mother's best friend of her youth.

My biological father, finally found. Florencio ("Frank") with my big sister, Veronica.

puter parts and yes, the nuns in high school who insisted on teaching us coding, like BASIC.

There were limits, however, to how far I could climb, because as I discovered at Christie's, your work is not the only thing higher-ups judge you on. I couldn't work myself out of the color of my skin and lack of a wealthy, influential family. Regardless, it was to be the most interesting place I've ever worked and a rocket leap from daydreaming on my yellow-canopy bed in New Hampshire to meeting the people from my magazines whose faces I had memorized and memorialized. A world that had lived in my fantasies in my green-and-yellow childhood bedroom was now one I was a part of myself.

On to the night of Tupac: It was 1995, and the evening auction event was a fundraiser hosted by the supermodel Christy Turlington. She had been my favorite fashion model for years, even more so once I found out she was a fellow Latina. It was a gala-type dinner in the usual auction space, during the season of the twice-a-year Latin American art sales. A mix of art from Bruce Weber original photos to well-known Latin American artists, all to raise funds for Christy's mother's charity for girls and women in her home country of El Salvador. Of course I volunteered to work that night, checking in guests as they arrived. The guest list was surreal and that night devolved into a drunken mess—guests glamorous but without decorum, my boss losing his temper at the podium. Managing their exodus at the end of the night turned into an exercise in herding VIPs while protecting the artwork on the walls with our bodies.

Finally, the dining area almost fully cleared, I made my way down the hall to the front lobby, which had a few lingering guests chatting, laughing, still holding their wineglasses. A young, tall assistant, as preppy-rich as they made them, was in heated discussion with the women behind the front desk. I approached with curiosity.

"Everything okay?" I asked, feeling the wee bit of authority that being the right hand of the chairman gave me.

"No, it's not okay," the young man said, turning toward me. He then asked me to get Tupac Shakur and Mickey Rourke out of the men's bathroom where they'd been hanging out for a while.

"Why don't you go in there and ask them to leave?" I asked.

"Oh, I can't do that."

"Why?" I asked. He waved his hand dismissively at me as if that was a silly idea. "What about one of the security guys?"

"They're out there." He gestured outside the front door, a scrum of flashing cameras, security busy herding paparazzi. "Oh, wait—*you* can go in there," he said to me.

"Me! How can I go in the men's room to kick out freakin' Tupac?" I was incredulous.

"Well, because, you know. He wouldn't get mad at you" as he waved his hand at my face. *Because of my color.*

Ah. So this guy wouldn't address Tupac and Mickey because he was scared of a Black man. And I was the only person of color at a professional level. There was not one Black or brown person working there unless they came after hours to clean, move artwork, or guard the doors. I got it.

Challenge taken.

"Fine. Just cover for me if I get in trouble for being in the men's room." I walked over to the men's door down the gray hall, took a deep breath, and was just about to knock to enter when the door swung open. Mickey Rourke first walked out swiftly, and then came the magnificence that was Tupac Shakur. He looked at me, sheepish, like a kid caught in the act of eating cookies before dinner. His eyes were lined with the thickest long black eyelashes I'd ever seen on a man. His skin smooth like polished bronze. He was barely taller than me. My face must have revealed my surprise and marvel at his beauty because he paused and smiled at me for a moment before he followed his friend Mickey down the hall. I didn't sleep a wink that night. There was no social media, no camera phones, nothing but my own mind to preserve and catalog every moment of that celebrity-filled, Leo/Naomi/Christy/Coppola night into my memory. Who knows when I'd ever have a night like that again?

"We are never doing that again! Never again!" Christopher sputtered to me after a terse "Morning" as he arrived at the office the next day, slapping the morning newspaper on the desk behind me. I gave him a moment to settle in and looked through the pages. There was coverage in the *New York Post,* but it was fairly glowing about the sheer mass of celebrity that showed up. It did mention a bit of pandemonium, if I recall correctly.

I knocked at Christopher's open door once he'd had a chance to settle in. "It was pretty rough, wasn't it?" I said.

"Do you know that they damaged paintings for this week's sale? Damaged! No. Never again," he said.

The walls and floors of Christie's displayed rotating pieces from upcoming sales. Not only was there the large landscape behind me worth six figures, but at least half a dozen more hung in the crowded entrance hall and around the lobby.

As I sat down, I said a little prayer to myself hoping that he didn't hold this against me and all Latinos. I knew he would, probably, at least just a bit. Maybe the whole building did too. And there was only me plus two white Latino staff specialists and one intern in the Latin American department, out of a couple hundred employees stateside and even more at the headquarters in London. I pledged to excel as much as I could to try to overcome the bad taste the sale had left in my boss's mouth.

Not long before that night, I was still living with Alex and Belinda when Lupe showed up at their apartment unexpectedly, bringing the troubles of home back to the city. Alex and I had heard from our sisters that it had gotten so bad at home between Mom and Dad that Marty had started sleeping on the couch every night. I hadn't spoken to my mother in months. The last time we spoke, she'd called my number at work and scolded me after I answered with my usual professional greeting.

"You know, you need to answer the phone more professionally, like this: 'Good afternoon! [in a singsong saccharine tone] How can I help you?'" Like she knew what she was talking about or had any experience, I thought. I was so tired of her criticism. Tired of her puppeteering my life. Never taking the time to ask me what I wanted or how I was feeling. Never assuming that I knew what the hell I was doing and that maybe she didn't. All I got from her was, as she'd say, "constructive criticism." I was exhausted by her voice. Living on my own and away from her had given me the space that I'd needed to finally exist just a bit more in my own skin, to hear my own voice in my head instead of hers.

Lupe had been at the apartment only one night as I strolled the ten-minute walk home from the train after work, enjoying the warm sunset and tree-lined Park Slope streets. Then I spotted Mom standing at the front door of our limestone building, probably locked out, as Alex and Belinda weren't expected home for another half hour or so. My face fell. I did not want to be alone with her. Alex's presence was always a salve between us. She behaved better around him, and he managed her without losing his cool. I approached the stairs with my keys in hand. I noticed that she was wearing snug jeans with high heels and a short-sleeved blouse, her hair done. She looked nothing like she did back in New Hampshire. She was dressed like her old city self, sassy. I wondered where she'd gone looking so unlike her more proper self. And then I saw her belt.

"Mom, is that my belt?"

"Oh, yes," she said, faking sweetness.

I scowled. She had gone into my suitcase, which I was living out of, rummaged through my belongings, and took what she wanted. It should have been just the borrowing of a belt. Maybe some mothers and daughters delightedly share clothes. But all it did was remind me of how she used to search my room every single day when I was in school. In high school I discovered that she would rummage through my drawers daily. She once found and confronted me with a can of high-caffeine Jolt soda that I'd hidden to drink in case of emergency so I could stay awake all night after work to study for finals. It was only caffeine, but to her it was a gateway drug, and I was going to turn into a drug addict. Confronted, I cleared my mind and closed my ears as she screamed at me for fifteen minutes, trying to make me cry but failing at that endeavor since I was twelve.

Then there was the discovery of my brother's borrowed copy of the bestselling, slightly racy NYC novel *Bright Lights, Big City,* with a painting of Tribeca restaurant The Odeon (now my favorite neighborhood hang) on the front, stashed under my bed at fourteen. I knew she wouldn't find it acceptable for me to read. She confronted me with that find the next day. And almost worst of all was when she found spermicide in the back of one of my drawers when I was seventeen. That discovery meant a pickup from work and a solo drive with her to a parking lot where we could talk without anyone in the house hearing. I convinced her it belonged to one of my friends and I was hiding it from her crazy-strict mom. Managing Lupe meant learning how to gaslight back. Her snooping is why I never kept a diary. There was nowhere in that bedroom or dresser or closet, nowhere, that she didn't scour nearly every day. I learned that the only truly private place, the only thing that was mine and only mine, was my own mind. I wrote whole movie scripts and book plots in my head, enjoying a revisit once in a while for decades to my favorites that managed to stay remembered in the files of my imagination.

One day, as a teen, when I came home from waiting tables after a long shift, my apron bulging with one-dollar bills, I sat down at my desk to pull out my haul from the night before and count it all. I tallied the batch of bills in my apron and then added it to the saved bundle in my desk drawer where I kept my money to make deposits at the end of the week. But my count didn't match what I'd had the night before. I counted again what was in my drawer. I was missing fifty dollars, more than a weeknight's regular haul. I saw stars of rage and stormed downstairs.

"Mom! Did you take money out of my drawer?"

Mom didn't look at me as she kept washing a pan in the sink, paused, and said, "Yes."

"You can't just go through my drawer and take my money. I earned that money!"

"Well, I'm your mother and your money *is* my money, so I take what I need." She raised her voice. I couldn't believe what I was hearing.

"No. No. That doesn't make any sense. You make money yourself, why do you need to take mine at all?"

I don't remember exactly how she answered, but it was a jumble of bullshit and guilt and how I didn't put my 10 percent of earnings into the "charity" jug, a large glass jar that sat at the end of the kitchen island where we were all supposed to tithe. I knew that money went right into her pocket and she was flat-out lying to us, using charity as a ploy. It was a grift. So I asked her questions she couldn't answer:

"What charities are you giving it to, huh? Where are the receipts for the donations? Show me the receipts. Because those places give receipts for taxes." Marty's money lessons had taught me too much for her.

The "charity" jar was gone a few days later.

Lupe's lack of boundaries created walls in me. No one would or could know all of what I was thinking or planning, my motives and desires, maybe ever. I've softened the walls of my mind fortress over the decades, but it's hard to dismantle structures that needed to be built at the time. Sometimes I have to remind myself that my mother may have blended the concrete, but I am the architect.

I think back at the look on her face when I hissed at her for wearing my belt. She had started dressing more like a city gal again, tighter clothes, heels with jeans, proud of her body and who she was after her split from Marty. She was again that woman who had cut and dyed her hair into an auburn Afro. And for the many years I thought about this moment in our relationship, I'd sometimes think, did my disdain for her look, for her grasp at being sexy and cool again, make me like Marty? I felt guilty for it. Or maybe I just wanted my mom back. The one with her hair in a prim bun and her clothes proper. Mostly, and primarily, my anger stemmed from her lack of respect that what was mine was not hers. I had worked, had strived so hard to have my own space, as tiny as it was, simply one suitcase with nearly everything I owned. And she wouldn't even allow me that one thing. Wasn't it enough that she lived in my head?

I had saved up enough money after living with Alex and Belinda for three months to afford my own apartment. I found a second-floor walk-up studio above a bodega on the corner of First Avenue and East Sixty-first Street. It was maybe 350 square feet with room for an Ikea haul of a futon, one dresser, and a tiny kitchen table with two chairs. The bathroom shower was made of standing plastic, like a shower in an RV. There was one window that led out onto a fire escape and looked onto the brick wall of the building next door. I dug into my bank account to pay for a window gate so I could sleep at night, avoiding a home invasion. The midnineties was a time in the city when it wasn't always safe for a woman to walk outside after 9:00 P.M. or take the subway after eight. In fact, Christie's had a policy that if you worked past eight, you got a car home. A perk, but also a safety issue.

I was thrilled to have my own place, but I underestimated just how lonely I'd become. I opened the door to the possibility of having people over but I had no friends, and there was no such thing as internet dating. So I spent weekends sleeping in too late, watching marathons of *Absolutely Fabulous* on my cruddy small TV, or walking across the street to watch three-dollar matinées at the Regal movie theater, eating popcorn for lunch, or visiting the Metropolitan Museum of Art, which was pay what you can, a fee I tried to always make at least five dollars. My only apartment guests were the mice who left droppings in the drawer where I kept a pile of fortune cookies from my cheap Chinese food dinners. At night I pulled my bedsheets over my ears so the furry guests didn't snack on them too.

THE OFFICE ADHERED FAIRLY well to the deal I had made with myself the summer that Marty offered me the office job: no gray walls. Christie's walls were the furthest from plain I had ever seen. Right in front of me, just above my head, once hung a privately owned Frida Kahlo painting that hadn't been seen by the public in decades. There was the sale and display of Leonardo da Vinci's Codex, his hand-drawn book of inventions and sketches. It was magnificent. Bill Gates sent his father for a private viewing and they won the auction. In my teens, I was a big fan of *Star Trek: The Next Generation,* a show I and a few of my sisters would watch with Marty. Patrick Stewart (the captain of the crew in that show) came one night to read from the handwritten manuscript of "'Twas the Night Before Christmas" that was up for sale. The other bit of showbiz excitement in the building was the filming of the auction scene in *The First Wives Club,* a film with Bette Midler, a pre-*Sex and the City* Sarah Jessica Parker, Diane Keaton, and Goldie Hawn. Christopher was the auctioneer in the film. Madonna came for a private weekend tour of the Rudolf Nureyev sale. (Unfortunately, I found out about that one the following Monday.) Princess Diana's closet-cleaning sale was in 1997. She, however, did not make an appearance, for which I would have insisted on being present. Behemoths in the art world were a weekly occurrence at sales, bidding and visiting the executive office. Pablo Picasso's biographer. The son of the founder of the fashion house Givenchy, who was just starting to build his now incredibly successful jewelry line. In the three years I worked there, I saw more art and celebrities and important creations than I thought I'd ever see in my life. I was glad I made that promise to myself to always take a risk to make exciting choices, not easy ones.

I had no friends of my own yet in the city, but Alex and Belinda were kind enough to let their little sister tag along to their social events. Belinda had started working for the government right after her graduation, so she grew a solid and diverse crew of work friends who would come over to their apartment, or we'd congregate at another's. One night the gathering was at her boss's place and the whole team was there. My brother and I were the non-Feds, along with a few other spouses or partners. I was shy and mostly shadowed my brother. And then I heard a goofy, wholehearted laugh that sounded like a mini party on its own. I was curious so I followed the sound to a guy sitting in the middle of the couch between two woman coworkers. He was a piece of work. A brown-skinned, broad-shouldered Christopher Reeve type of Clark Kent, with a wide grin and perfect white teeth, pushing his stylish glasses up his nose. His hair was even Superman-ish, thick, black, and wavy, a lock escaping onto his forehead occasionally. He was beefy too. Six feet and built. But goofy. Gorgeous but goofy. An unfortunately irresistible combination.

And then he saw me. His eyes widened and he stopped paying any attention to the conversation around him. He stared and followed my movements around the room. By the end of the night, I was experiencing my first date in the city. His name was Derek. He was a coworker of Belinda's, a fellow chemistry major, who'd had a full scholarship to Manhattan College. An Ecuadoran American from the tippy top of Manhattan, Dyckman Street. There were red flags even on that night, of course. He was slick. Dressed like an investment banker on a government salary but still living at home with his parents and grandmother in a two-bedroom apartment. He teased me for using "ten-dollar words" and being so buttoned-up. A form of manipulation I now know is called negging: negative compliments. He was amused with himself and my feisty barbs back. I was roped in.

There was such a pull of familiarity in him, a fellow Latino striver. Someone like me who was trying to make it in worlds where there were none of us or only one of us. Doing it against the odds. And once he took me home to meet his parents, it was as if I'd been reunited with my abuela and my whole family back on Claremont and Tiemann Place. It was all that I'd missed and longed for so much all those years in New Hampshire. My grandparents had passed, and my cousins moved away, but here was a new family—one so much, I thought, like the one I'd had before. There was no extricating me from the grip of this nostalgia. It was a spell. I felt as if I had a Latina identity again and a Latino family that surrounded me, fed me. But the acceptance of and focus on me, as Abuela had given me growing up, wasn't there. They commented that I was so lucky to have the job I had (in a condescending tone, another neg) and outside of that they focused all their energy completely on their successful son, a little emperor just like my brother had been, who stood nearly a foot taller than both his parents but might as well have been perpetually a golden child in their eyes.

All four of us sat around the television on Saturday nights, on the plastic-covered furniture behind folding tray tables to hold the heaps of food his mother would make us. It was futbol and then *Sábado Gigante,* a wacky live game-and-talk show—a staple in Latino households—that I hadn't seen in years. The women on the show were in tiny clothes and high heels, fawning over the old, rotund, toad-looking man who hosted the show. This disgusted me. But I swallowed my "gringa feminism" along with my arroz then blurred my vision back to leaning into the idea that this apartment and its people could take away the grief of missing my own Dominican family, culture, and identity. Of course, no one can truly replace those who've passed away or give you back something that's always been yours. I was fooling myself. Derek was narcissistic and obnoxious but again, familiar. (His best friend was a cokehead who wore ski goggles on his forehead when we went to clubs. Like a Backstreet Boy.) I was with a kid from the 'hood made good. And then he made better. He received a full scholarship for his MBA at Kellogg, the number two business school in the country at the time, at Northwestern University in Evanston, Illinois.

We somehow stuck it out as a couple with daily phone calls and me charging $99 round trips to the Chicago airport for a weekend every month. Then Derek would come live with me in my little studio apartment during breaks and summer, rent-free. This was where the cracks first started to show too clearly for comfort. One Saturday late afternoon during the summer before his second year, he came home to the apartment after shopping with his older brother, loaded with bags. This non-rent-paying grad student was setting down big bags from the most expensive store in the tristate area if not the country, Barneys.

"Barneys? What the heck are you doing shopping at Barneys?" I asked.

He chuckled. "Gotta keep up with these MBA guys, you know!"

"But with what money?"

"Oh, I just used my credit card," he answered.

I had used my credit card too for my work clothes, but I shopped at Zara sales where five hundred dollars could buy me a whole season of outfits plus shoes.

Derek held up a suit that looked so expensive it hurt my eyes. "Two thousand dollars!" He grinned. "This is gonna look so great at interviews."

The sum knocked me numb. I couldn't imagine in a hundred years spending more than a month's take-home pay on one outfit.

"Oh—I got something for you too," he said. Well, now he was talking. I mean, he was living with me rent-free, I paid for most of our meals out, plus I flew out and back to see him and maintain our relationship, how about throwing some of that flash my way?

He pulled out a bundle wrapped in what looked like a plastic bodega bag and handed it to me. This was not from Barneys. I unwrapped it wanting badly to hold off on judging, not wanting to believe that he'd do me so wrong. It was two plain sweaters, one navy, one gray. The navy one looked like it had been used and worn, and there were what looked like crumbs on the front. They did not have shopping tags.

"What—what is this?" I asked, disbelieving.

"Oh, I just picked them up for you on the way home," he said as he continued to unpack more clothes from his Barneys bags, their stiff, expensive hanging sale tags mocking me.

"Picked them up from where?"

"Oh, this lady was selling them."

"This lady. On the street," I said.

"Yeah. On the street." He dared me to say anything about it.

"So, you go to Barneys, spend thousands of dollars, and then for me, you spend a few bucks on used clothes from the street?"

"I got you something, didn't I? Didn't I?" And there it was. The dismissal of my worth. *How dare I?* How familiar. So I made myself smaller. But at the same time, inside, bigger and tighter. So that when he got a deal to do half the year of graduate school in Santiago, Chile, but tried to tell me I didn't need to go with him, I wasn't going to let him deprive me of the opportunity to live in South America. To me, living and working in another country, improving my Spanish, was a great career move. Too good to pass up. And to not do it alone, even better.

"Oh, no. I'm coming, all right," I said to him. And I talked my way into an office manager job in the Christie's office in Santiago, covering for a maternity leave and installing the company email system in two other countries as well.

Chile in 1995–96 was a culture shock. I had thought I knew what Latino was. I was only half-right, thinking only of the northern half: Mexico, Central America, the Caribbean, and even Brazil and the north of South America. But Chile, Argentina, and Uruguay?

"Mami, why didn't anyone tell me that everyone down here is white?" It was my first call to my mother from our new rental home. I made sure to call the New Hampshire house every two or three weeks or so, Mom picking up the phone usually, but I also checked in on my sisters, missing them very much. Our first rental was a tiny house surrounded by high stone walls—as all houses there were—quaintly decorated in 1980s abuela fashion. The house belonged to the head of the Christie's office in Santiago; she charged a small rent for Derek and me to stay there for a month until we found another place. As was the norm (and many times still is), a housekeeper lived in a tiny room behind the kitchen, no wider than a twin bed and a half. She went home to see her family only on Sundays. She was Indigenous, as I also noted most of the people in the city who made up the service class seemed to be. My same color and small stature, but not my features. There was a tiny bell placed on the dining table for us to ring when we needed something during meals, and there were additional buzzers in the bathroom, next to our bed, and in the main room. This all rang too loudly to me of American slave history. I'd never seen or experienced anything like it. My red-white-and-blue bristled at it, while Derek reveled in it. Of course he did. It was as if he had his mother back at his beck and call. Me, feminist Madame Self-Sufficient, was horrified.

One night I got out of bed to get some water from the refrigerator. Derek hissed at me "Use the button!" I wasn't going to wake a grown woman from deep sleep to fetch me water as if I were a toddler. Ridiculous. As soon as I opened the refrigerator, the housekeeper's door, directly behind the fridge, opened and she begged me in Spanish to let her do it. I insisted on doing it myself.

The next morning the office director took me aside at work and said, "Listen, you're making Graciela very upset."

"I am?" I felt horrible. I did not think about the impact of what I was doing on her. Just about how much more comfortable it made me feel.

"Taking care of you is her job. You're not letting her do her job, okay?"

Noted. That night at dinner this equal-rights gringa rang the little bell in the middle of the dinner table to ask Graciela to clear our plates for the dessert she'd made. She popped out of her waiting spot in the kitchen and cleared our plates, smiling a very pleased smile.

My Spanish was an issue, however. Or I should say, my lack of Spanish was an issue. So I spent the first three full weeks after we landed in Santiago completing forty-hour weeks of private language tutoring paid for by my bosses in New York. My first language had disappeared so much that when we landed (after a cigarette-smoke-filled fourteen-hour flight from Miami), all I could muster were greetings and thank you. Spanish classes were a revelation because I went from a five-word vocabulary to reading the newspaper and being able to speak with clients in three weeks. I asked my mom about this during my calls home to New Hampshire to talk with her, Marty, and my sisters.

"Ma, how did I go from 'Hola' to reading the paper in weeks?"

"Well, Spanish was your first language," she said.

"It was?" I thought back to my cuchi-cuchi-doll days and remembered that the words I heard spoken to me and around me were Spanish. Of course, I didn't have to ask her why that was a surprise to me. There was much of our early lives that Mom held close. As an older aunt said to me many years later, "Your mother held things very tight." And I didn't often press. I'd learned that doing so led nowhere, or to hostility. Lupe divulged only what she wanted to and when. I had to glean what I could when I could, and this tidbit was a revelation.

Office life there, however, was rough. The director was a petty, tiny woman of European descent who at first treated me like one of her servants. She also called me, as did many others, "negra" (Black girl) and "gorda" (fat girl). Sure, I'd gained weight—on the sublime Chilean food, pisco sour cocktails, and delicious wine so plentiful it was sold in the grocery stores with soda, and at the same price—but calling me "fat" at a size eight was a stretch.

One workday she took me along to a client appointment about an hour outside the city. We pulled into what can only be described as a gated compound the size of a city block. There were security guards dressed in black at each corner as we pulled in. Two came to the car to open our doors. We were handed over to another set of staff who guided us into the home, which was much more like a museum of Spanish colonial art than someone's house. Every surface, every wall was adorned with saints and crucifixes, wood and bronze, and gilded paintings.

The client was a stout white man with graying hair, dressed casually in a button-down shirt, open a few buttons, showing a bit of his tan chest. He sat at the head of a colossal carved wooden dining table. None of us sitting was taller than five foot five, which meant we all looked like children in grown-up chairs, the dining set was so large. Then I began to participate in the most formal dining experience I'd ever had. We each had our own server. Though the word that comes to mind is "servant." I say servant because they were women dressed in full British maid costumes, white doilies pinned in their hair, with matching aprons and collars over black dresses cinched at the waist. I barely ate, my eyes gluttonous with all I was taking in. I noted again that my skin and shape matched the servers. I did my best to not shrivel up in insecurity, reminding myself who I worked for and why I was there.

As Linda and I got back into the SUV taking us back to the city, I had to ask, "What does he do? Where did his money come from?"

"He sells guns to the Middle East. You know, like Iraq, Iran. His father started the business after the war, but this one really made the family fortune."

Our lunch host, a gunrunner. One with a German last name. I didn't want to seem like an investigator or gossipy, but I had to learn more, so I asked Linda as much as I could about how his family ended up there before crossing a line. Essentially, as I now know, after World War II thousands of German Nazis escaped to Chile, along with Italians, and to Argentina and Uruguay. I didn't know how to manage what I'd just found out. It made me upset and uncomfortable. But I did my job. Pretend, pretend, pretend. That's what I did to get down there anyway—pretend that my relationship with Derek was somehow a good one despite knowing it sincerely wasn't (hence the overeating and drinking). Pretend that I knew what I was doing. Pretend that I belonged there. Una negra, una gordita. Not thin and European like those around me. Pretend that having a servant who lived in a closet behind the refrigerator who only saw her family during the day on Sundays was normal. Chile was a mindfuck of the highest order for me on class, race, and history. I thought of my mother often as I lived there. How she too had made a huge cultural shift when she first came to the United States, and especially to New Hampshire. The pretending. Combined with the thrill of newness. One addicting, the other diminishing. It was a sticky trap.

But, ay Dios, did I love that country. It was a magical landscape filled with warm, creative people (outside of my work), art, and food. I was introduced to alternative rock en español and bands like Café Tacvba and Aterciopelados, going to packed, gritty concerts and nightclubs. Outside of Christie's, with Derek's classmates, I felt much less an impostor and more like I could enjoy where I was at.

Until I'd met Derek, I knew I was flawed but I wasn't completely self-loathing. Unfortunately, our dynamic was that he'd do his best to keep me feeling insecure and small. It took a decade for me to understand how and why I'd settle for such a situation. This was a repeat of how my mother made me feel: small, a victim. And maybe too how she'd felt at times in her marriage, whether it was when Dad handed her a check for the week or when he didn't like her hair or made fun of her accent. Plus there was pressure from the outside on me and Derek, as people said we were "the Latino power couple" and society in the nineties was pumping out movies where best friends vowed to marry each other if they hadn't found a spouse by the time they were twenty-eight years old. I put my own pressure on the relationship, determined to make it right. Determined to make it work. This would always be my downfall. I fixated on the "fix" instead of moving on to what would work for me too.

We wrapped up six eye-opening months, including two weeks in Buenos Aires, where I finally tasted a real steak, and a week in Montevideo, Uruguay, a city that felt more like Eastern Europe than South America. My colleagues in each city were grateful for my tech support and coaching and hosted Derek and me for meals in their homes. In Montevideo we heard of the director's husband's kidnapping and ransom, the dirt pit he was kept in, and his reunion with his children. This was the cost of having just a bit of money there. Wondering if you'd come home, ever.

Back in the United States, Derek graduated and landed a job at a small investment bank fairly quickly. We moved into a pleasant one-bedroom apartment in an elevator building on the Upper East Side. But within months, Derek had the opportunity to transfer for six months to his new company's offices in Mexico City. This time, we'd be moving for his work and he'd be paying the expenses. Christie's had succeeded in breaking my meritocracy dreams upon our return from Santiago. I had been there three years, still stuck as an assistant in the executive offices (yes, during the price-fixing scandal with Sotheby's, whose CEO's phone calls I'd have to pass along), with no desire to go into the marketing department, where I was encouraged to go. I wanted to be an art specialist. Quiz me on any contemporary art, jewelry, Hong Kong sale, or American furniture; I had become an enthusiastic encyclopedia of knowledge, but no matter. My family didn't know people. I didn't come from money. There was no place else for me to go. So I decided to see if I could finagle the same deal I had gotten in Chile with their Mexico City office, to no real avail this time.

"Well, you know what that means!" Derek said.

"What?"

"You're going to have to marry me!"

In Chile, we wore cheap bands on our fingers and pretended to be married to ensure that we'd be able to get an apartment, as cohabitation was frowned upon in such a Catholic city. And yes, I had hoped one day I'd be married, but I wish I could tell you it felt good to hear him say it. Instead, it felt as if I was swept up in another current, a riptide, unable to see which way was up. All signs pointed to marriage, so I was just going to do it. I proceeded as if I had no choice.

I started planning a small wedding that we could afford in an old house with a barn in New Hampshire over Thanksgiving break. I even found an off-the-shoulder long-sleeved wedding dress that would hide the scars on my arms, which had returned from my anxious picking. But Derek's mother vetoed the whole thing. She didn't want to travel anywhere. The wedding should be in New York City. I was livid. Derek did whatever his mother told him to do. There was no way we could afford an NYC wedding. So we eloped. One day I put on my pale lavender skirt suit from Burlington Coat Factory with a matching Zara velvet scarf and pumps, Derek was in one of his suits from Barneys, and we took a cab downtown to get married in front of a justice of the peace. Our nice, retired neighbors next door were our witnesses. As soon as we all sat down at the nuevo Latino restaurant we chose after the service, I knew it was over and that I had made a big mistake. In all the ways that mattered, our relationship ended that day, in that moment. My gut told me, stating plainly the truth between my ears. There's a photo of Derek and me taken from across the table that day. My eyes say "save me," though I managed a smile. I barely recall the phone call afterward to my mother, her reaction, or anyone else's in my family once I shared the news. No one else registered at this point besides Alex and Belinda. If anything, they were—as they'd always been—supportive. Apprehensive and concerned, but supportive.

Derek didn't even want to sleep with me that night. Or many nights after that. This didn't stop us, though, from relocating to Mexico City. Unlike our previous travels, this time he was the one going off to work in the mornings while, with no studies to head to, I was left home to occupy myself and try to figure out what to do for work.

I adored Mexico City, still do. But all of its beauty and sensations—and yes, danger; it was more dangerous then—could not change that I wasn't working full-time, was alone much too much, and was living off my savings. Derek was spending the majority of evenings each week with his colleagues, not me. I tried to relax with the expats, but from these white people, European and American, I heard again so much of the dog-whistle bigotry I'd heard at Christie's about overpopulation and some people just being genetically inferior or better suited for sports. It sickened and angered me. I was the model minority again. All while my new husband barely engaged with me. It was heartbreaking. I was terribly lonely and anxious. During this international relocation, unlike in Chile, I lost over twenty pounds from a mix of anxiety and a horrible stomach infection that kept getting misdiagnosed. Finally, tired of being sick, unemployed, and ignored, I told Derek that I had to go back to New York City. He promised to move his job and be back too in about six weeks. This time also would allow me a head start to find a new job and settle in. I noted that he agreed to my departure all too easily, almost happily.

It was a rough summer by myself subletting on the Upper West Side, but at least as soon as I hit home soil, all my stomach issues went away. I was relieved to see Alex and Belinda and I was even glad that Lupe came to visit me. After I'd eloped, communication with Mom was rare. Phone calls back home were expensive, and I saved them for a couple of times a month, speaking, as usual, with Alex the most. It wasn't so much a purposeful split or line in the sand with either Mom or Marty or Peter at that point in my life. It was simply we each were living our own lives. Who knows where Papi was at that point—only Alex kept track of him. Dad was working and was never one to reach out, ever. We kids had to do the reaching. Mom also didn't call; instead I'd call her once a month, maybe. In retrospect, it was interesting that as someone who always had an opinion or criticism of my life, Mom ran flat with me during that time. I took it that she was occupied doing her own thing, working too, with my youngest sisters going into high school. We were all planets in different orbits.

Back in the city, hitting the interview trail again, I landed another executive assistant spot where I thought (mistakenly again) that I had a chance to move up. I got us an apartment in Brooklyn Heights, one stop away from Manhattan. Belinda had had my niece, her first baby, and my brother and his family picked up and moved a few counties north to a house in a commuter town, the suburbs.

I was suddenly alone in the city. No Abuela or Abuelo. No Papi or cousins. No Alex or Belinda, or even my husband. And let's face it, was my husband ever going to come back?

CHAPTER 8

... Because I Thought I Could Start Over

"SAY IT. JUST SAY IT," I SAID.

Derek and I were sitting, tense, on the couch in our Brooklyn Heights apartment. We had barely lasted four months there as a couple after his return from Mexico City. He was hemming and hawing in that moment, and though I knew what he was trying to tell me, I wanted him to say it out loud. *Coward*.

Barely above a whisper, head bowed, he finally said, "I want a divorce."

Two thoughts flew through my head. One, *good*. No more of this bullshit. No more being woken up in the dead of night by a duplicitous spouse climbing into bed still wet from his sin shower. No more being lied to on the regular by someone who had vowed to love me. And two, *fuck me, I've failed*. A twentysomething divorcée? I failed. I'm a failure.

A month or so before this couch moment, Derek had just come home after a business trip, and as he changed out of his travel clothes in the bedroom, I stared at his black overnight duffel bag, open on the living room floor. I wondered what that bag knew that I didn't. Then, just behind the bag, I spotted a folded yellow paper. It must have fallen out onto the floor when he dug into it for his toiletry case. If the paper was on the floor, why not pick it up? And if it was something he didn't want me to see, why would he have been so careless? In what felt like slow motion, I reached to pick up the paper, opened and read it, itemized line by line. My vision narrowed as I realized what it was: a resort receipt for an adults-only hedonism spot. Derek hadn't been traveling for work. He was getting nailed with his buddies in the Caribbean while I was drudging away, playing the ever-faithful wife. My reaction to this piece of seemingly purposeful self-sabotage on his part—keeping the receipt loose in his bag and letting it fall out—was appropriately volcanic. In response he packed that same bag right back up and left, not to be seen again until the couch-divorce-ask about a month later.

On that couch in Brooklyn, I had to ask him, "Why are you in such a rush?" We'd been separated for only weeks and married for less than a year. I knew I had made a mistake marrying him, and there was no way it was going to work, but that didn't mean I was ready to be alone again or tossed aside so quickly.

"Well, I'm gonna move in with her," he said. It was the receptionist from our recent trip to his company's headquarters in the South of France, Cannes. Instead of more tears, my practical side kicked in. I straightened my back. I asked Derek if he was moving to France. He said yes.

The complicating factor was that I'd just gotten into graduate school full-time. My dream: an accelerated master's program at Teachers College, Columbia University, in applied psychology. My goal was to jump into a PhD from there. And the plan had been that as I'd supported Derek financially during his graduate school studies—both him living in my apartment initially and then my covering us both in Santiago, Chile—it was his turn to cover me. I was already in student loan debt—this program was going to double it and I was going to have no income. Left yet again financially hanging high and dry by a man in my life. Papi right before college, and now this one.

When I got the offer, Derek had said, "Why do you want to go to graduate school anyway?" My answer was I had found that no matter where I went job-wise, I was stymied and passed over continuously for less experienced, less competent people because higher-ups just couldn't "see" me in more prominent roles. I was brown. They all were not.

After Christie's, I had thought, what the hell, I knew what banking was, what investing was (thanks, Dad), maybe it was time to cash in on that and go where the money was. I lasted four months as the assistant to the head of private client services at Goldman Sachs. He was a nice enough guy, but I was terribly bored with the gray walls and piles of dot matrix printouts. Plus part of the job was reviewing his associates' expense accounts that included strip clubs. Not a place for pants-wearing, feminist me.

Just because I could do Wall Street didn't mean I wanted to do Wall Street. It was time to head toward the things I had always treasured and enjoyed: magazines. My lifelong escape into traveling and experiencing the world in my head, from wars to fashion. I was off to Time & Life, the largest magazine company in the world in the late nineties. I won a job offer when the head of HR asked me a question that I really couldn't answer. I waited a beat and responded truthfully. "I actually don't know. I don't have an answer to that." Bingo. Hired. It helped that she was a Black woman. You bet it helped. Unfortunately, you can't always get everything you want. A newshound, I wanted to be at *Time* magazine, of course, but the opening she had was at *Money*. I said sure. Marty had always had a subscription to *Money* and *Fortune* and *Forbes,* and I talked stock prices and economics with Dad. It was our sports. At least I was going to be in the door at the company.

But again, I made the mistake of thinking that being an assistant was like being an apprentice. In many industries that role was a stepping-stone into rising up the business, even at many magazines—see *Vogue.* But it became the same as at Christie's. The new, young editor in chief at the magazine did not see it that way, and as only one of two people of color on a large editorial staff, I could see (and feel) just how easy it was going to be to keep me in my corner. When I applied to the graduate program, I had the (illusory) security of marriage, so I figured it was a great time to do what my husband had done: Go to graduate school and move ahead that way. We brown folk had to keep working on wins and achievements to get on par with the average white guy or gal who just sat still and rode the wave of advancement.

Remember, Mom wouldn't let me apply to Columbia for undergrad. No going to college in the city. Well, I did it anyway, even better, graduate school. Tell me no and I still do it, if I want it badly enough.

Derek's "Why do you want to go to graduate school anyway?" led to "You're married now! You've got me—and who's going to take care of the babies?"

"Babies? You've got two arms and two legs. You can change diapers too!"

"I am never changing a diaper in my life!" he screamed at me.

That was the nail in our long-overdue coffin. I married a patriarchal, chauvinist macho Latino. Of course. I had married the version of my mother who was traditional, the version that was okay with marrying away her independence and professional ambitions. The one who let Alex off the hook from housework. Also the one who was cruel and taunting. Gaslighting and cold. Narcissistic. And I had placed myself in my family pattern (born out of Mom-and-Dad dynamics) of victim and villain. The feelings Derek elicited in me were too recognizable for me to resist. It took years of therapy, self-help books, and work in my head to see this. I did the work because I truly couldn't believe that I'd let myself marry someone who wouldn't change a diaper. He might as well have been a caveman in a suit, his mentality was so far from what I cared for or even tolerated in anyone.

"Why the hell are you with me, then? You know I'm ambitious! That I support myself and want a career. You expect me to put that all away and pump out babies?" I yelled back. I couldn't escape a vision of my mother in my head. How we kids had messed up what she had wanted for her life—at least that's what was communicated. I did want children at some point. Maybe one. I had so much love set aside in me for a child. But I knew that waiting until I was older meant being a much better parent, financially more secure, with career momentum going, and hopefully, a supportive partner.

Derek walked out of the room. We both made a big mistake taking those vows. We had very different expectations—we had written whole stories about each other in our heads—that were no more real or tangible than projections on a screen. I had built mine on nostalgia for a time when I lived among my Latin family and community, hoping to re-create that feeling of comfort, connection, and acceptance with his family. But his parents also complained about and questioned my going to graduate school. Why would I do that now that I had their amazing son to father babies?

Back on the couch with him, in our divorce talk, I knew that there was no way that I was going to miss out on graduate school. But I needed money to live on. I also knew that I had Derek in a bind. He wanted what he wanted: to get out quickly because he'd knocked up a French receptionist. In France. And I wanted what I wanted: to keep achieving. That's where my focus was in that moment. We were beyond broken. I needed to make sure my life stayed on track because all I had was me.

"Okay. You'll get your divorce. But I took care of you when you were in graduate school. I deserve the same."

"Fine. How much?" he said, resigned.

I quickly calculated a lump sum of what I'd need to survive and stay in school full-time. I gave him a low-five-figure number and he agreed. Within a week I had a check that he'd drawn from credit. I didn't breathe again until the check cleared. I was going to be able to pay my rent and achieve my dream of going to Columbia. My Barneys-suit-wearing ex may have been in debt up to his eyeballs, but I didn't feel bad for him. He was eager to write me off quickly and I was eager to start graduate school.

I can't sugarcoat how crushed I was by the end of this marriage, regardless of getting into my dream school. I was alone, left for another woman, and I felt incredibly dumb and shameful for falling for Derek's hype. But he never truly loved me, and I didn't like him as a person, so what I really was mourning was the idea of having a loving, fully functioning marriage and family. An idea of what lifelong love is that I had culled from reading and watching the outside world, not my parents.

And an idea of who I thought I was as a person. I had failed at something big. Getting married was another rung on the way to "success." Falling down that rickety ladder in my mind hurt me to my soul.

Walking onto that Columbia University Morningside Heights campus five days a week saved me like probably nothing else could have. Saved me from wanting to step in front of a taxi and go to sleep already, not to die, but to have a break from my life via a hospital bed and drugs, people taking care of me. School kept me going. That and anger. It's interesting how much anger can be a motivator. Combined with my natural temperament, it's as gritty as it can come.

I finally broke down and made an appointment with a university psychiatrist in the health center, an older, casually dressed Upper West Side gentleman. He asked me at our intake session, "Do you think about ending your life, killing yourself?"

I raised my tearstained chin, sniffed, and said, "I wouldn't give him the satisfaction."

The psychiatrist chuckled as he wrote a prescription on his notepad. "Oh, you're going to be just fine."

I would not give Derek the satisfaction of not reaching my goal of getting this degree. Nor my mother, who took the divorce very badly and I felt secretly had always actually wanted me to fail—this was not direct knowledge, just a hunch, like a supposed best friend who doesn't cheer you on as she should. Lupe would call and beg and berate me not to get divorced. What my mother was most concerned about was appearances. For me to divorce meant shame and failure for her too, somehow. Even though she'd been divorced from Papi Wong. Even after I told her what Derek had done, how horrible he was to me. It was as if my mother had regressed to the days of Abuelo and Abuela and his two families. She wasn't the mother who raised me to excel in school and be self-sufficient, rather she was the uglier flip side of that. It hurt that she wanted something that made his life easier but my life hell. Again, it didn't matter what I wanted or needed. Thankfully, Alex was a shoulder to cry on. My brother was very worried about me even though he was sleepless from his newborn daughter and a long commute. He was so worried that after one phone conversation we had in the morning, he was knocking on my door by the afternoon. Even if we just went for a walk, he made me feel like someone was there. Someone who cared.

But the end of a marriage at twenty-seven years old, so abrupt and full of betrayal, was still too much for me. I couldn't focus my mind at school, and papers that were due were piling up. This education was all on me—a shitload of money that I'd have to pay back—and my dream. I had to do my best to get it done and done well so I could use it to get to the next thing. Not to mention have something valuable that no one could take away from me. I allowed myself to go on antidepressants for three months. I was going to jump-start my brain back up like a stalled car battery. I could handle the constant crying I was doing, tears dripping onto my textbook as I highlighted passages, reading assignments on the subway. Even the full-on sorrowful wails I'd release when I would make it back to the empty apartment, the emptiness taunting me. But I could not and would not allow myself not to excel at my education.

I WASN'T THE ONLY one who needed a lawyer at that time. After years of ugliness at home, Mom and Dad finally were getting a divorce. There was a feeling of inevitability about it. Some relief too. But as my two youngest sisters were still at home, in high school, I had so much sadness for them. I thought that all I'd feel was relief that my parents, who hadn't liked each other for years, were finally headed their own ways. I think now that what I was feeling was the end of an era. The end of our family as we knew it.

I talked to Dad and he said that Mom had filed the papers. Then I talked to Mom, and she said yes, she did file, because she'd had enough. Enough of years of fighting and her litany of complaints about Dad and vice versa. They both were almost empty nesters, and even though I felt their split was as unavoidable as my own—not a nice word between them in a year or more—it felt like a cliff. When your parents have been to-gether nearly your whole life, even if they hate each other, the reality of them existing as separate people, not even bound in their mutual loathing, is like another dimension. I couldn't imagine what each of them was going to do without the other.

What Marty did was, thankfully, drive down to Brooklyn from New Hampshire along with my brother, Alex, the new dad, driving from his house with Belinda in the 'burbs to help me, the new divorcée, move out of the Brooklyn Heights apartment. I was off to a rent-stabilized, reno-vated one-bedroom fifth-floor walk-up apartment in Washington Heights, back to upper Manhattan where I belonged. The Heights in 1999 was still mostly Dominican, but "nouveau" restaurants and coffee shops owned by the second generation were popping up, and I certainly saw more white faces there than I'd ever seen, even if it was just a trickle at first. I almost felt guilty at the amazing state of the apartment I had found for eight hundred dollars a month. New floors, new appliances, new bathroom, etc. Guilt came, though, from being a recipient of gen-trification even as I shared a heritage with those around me, and those who'd been displaced.

My glutes got rock-solid and exhausted walking groceries up those five flights of stairs, but I had my own comfortable and safe space, even closer to the Columbia campus. The man I had once wanted a life with was gone, but on the day of the move here were two men still in my life helping me start fresh. I was grateful.

Marty's post-divorce situation didn't appear to be as pleasant as mine. I visited him one weekend and what I saw was a far fall from the man with the suit and briefcase of my childhood. You're not supposed to live better than your parents when you're broke in your late twenties. Thank-fully, Dad had income from his new job so he could get a place, period, but the small space he lived in was shoddily built. He had rented one por-tion of the structure with a few small windows, a mattress on the floor, boxes of papers and papers and more papers piled up everywhere. There was not one personal effect or way to know that I was in my stepfather's home. It could have been anyone's. Dad's point of view had obviously changed since his cool uptown apartment in Manhattan, with its iron-railed spiral staircase and funky rattan chairs. I had nothing to offer him besides my presence. No money, no real support, and his new surroundings complicated my feelings too much. How did I manage to get a nice place with little money and make it look good quickly, but he couldn't and didn't? He was thirty years older than me. I guess I had expected more and better of him. This was unfair, of course, as not only was he burdened with paying Mom alimony, but he was getting himself loaded up with student loans for my sisters. And he'd drained his retirement savings to keep the family afloat when he was out of work. My young mind didn't think to recognize that it could simply be the choices of someone who was clinically depressed, something else we maybe shared.

Lupe took a different route after the divorce. She acted as if she'd been let out of a cage. To be fair, that is most likely what it felt like to go from raising six children in an unhappy marriage to suddenly being free of all of it and everyone.

Mom shared with Marty the penchant for hoarding boxes and papers, which required trucks to move from the house and dispose of, but even before she moved, the first thing she did was start traveling. Lupe plopped down some money and joined a group of women retirees for something she'd always wanted to do, tour the Grand Canyon. This seemingly wild expense shocked me, though it shouldn't have. Lupe was a repressed explorer, lover of culture and art and travel, history, all things worldly. But when she had six children at home, how would she have ever done that?

Whatever her limitations were before, Lupe did not see them now. Though I knew she wished to be a citizen of the world, always talking about wanting to visit cities like Paris, I was shocked that she was going anywhere at all, as the only travel she'd done in decades was to Santiago, Dominican Republic, to bury her parents. And when she got back, she decided that New Hampshire was no longer for her. She spent some time hiring contractors to fix up the house, so it was suitable for sale. She replaced our now-rotting light green wood with light blue vinyl siding. She somehow cleared out what seemed like one-hundred-plus boxes that filled up the living room. The house that Marty had built and that we kids had filled up was slowly stripped and done over piece by piece.

Once my depression was medicated, I charged into my studies, treating my role as student as the best job I'd ever had. I plowed through classes, socialized a bit with the younger students around me, who mostly had come directly out of undergrad. Surely, I was still a mess of a person, but I tried—sometimes failing—to limit subjecting people to my needy mental state and focused on my studies. The subject of one of my first papers, what I'd been told was a risk because it was "not a popular topic" in the field, was narcissistic personality disorder. Not only was this prescient in terms of this country's future leadership, but of course I was trying to manage and understand my mother. And maybe even Marty, in a more benign way. However, the biggest gift that paper gave me was the reassurance that even though I'd been told at *Money* magazine that I couldn't become a writer (for no real reason beyond that my racial and ethnic minority status made me "biased" and therefore I couldn't be "objective"), the professor, who'd been teaching there for thirty years, pulled my paper and asked me if she could use it as a model for the class and future classes as to how to write well. Sure, an academic paper is different from a magazine article, but still, whether it was grass or a clay court, at least I knew that I could play.

My graduate school graduation was approaching, class of 2000. I certainly felt as if I'd replaced many parts of myself in a very short time. When I called around to see who maybe would come to my graduation, Marty demurred because of work, my younger sisters were doing their own thing, Alex, of course, would come, though Belinda bowed out with another important obligation, but I wasn't sure about Mom. I hadn't spoken to her in nearly a year.

"She married a guy," Alex told me.

"What? She did what? To who?" I asked. The ink was barely dry on her divorce papers. I was shocked. My newly independent, traveling mother married again?

"You remember that guy that Abuelo owned the cleaners with?"

I thought I remembered a short, tan man who wore a newsboy cap. "I think so."

"She married him."

"Jesus, Alex! Isn't he like . . . super old? Like Abuelo's age?" I couldn't believe it. She hadn't been back in the city for more than a month, or even less. Alex and I didn't know where she went when she first arrived or whom she stayed with. We just knew she was around. I had barely been speaking to her but heard of her whereabouts from my siblings. The move back to the city was a big shock to me at first, but getting married again? Wasn't the whole point that she didn't want to be tied down? That she was enjoying her newly single life? Then I thought about it, thought about who my mother was as a person, and within minutes, I knew this made complete sense. She wanted to come back to the city. She needed a place to live, and she didn't have a full-time job yet. This man had a townhouse in the Heights. Mom did what she'd always done: married to escape one roof for another.

Another catalyst was probably her father, my abuelo, dying. Her life until she left for New Hampshire was lived under his thumb, and surely even after she'd gotten a couple hundred miles away, he was in her head. You can feel relief when an abusive parent dies. Without him, without Marty, and on her own, she was ready to do her. So it certainly wasn't love. This man was ancient and she hadn't seen him in a decade at least.

Alex continued, "So, Mom wants to come to your graduation but she wants to bring him."

I laughed. "Aw, hell no. Hell no! There is no way I'm getting a ticket for some random guy she just upped and married. That's insane! I don't want him there! Then it will be all about her and this new guy!" I'd lived a childhood with her ruining every birthday and graduation. Now that I wasn't under her roof, I wasn't going to let that happen again. I did want her there, though. As much of a risk as it could be. Who doesn't want to look out and see a proud parent at graduation? I knew this was wishful thinking, but I couldn't stop wanting things to change. My mom to change.

I called her to let her know that no, this new husband of five minutes was not invited.

"Yes, I got married," Mom said.

"Okay" was my only answer.

"So, I'd love to come to your graduation, and I'll bring him with me," she said as a statement, not a request.

"No, Mom," I said. I could almost feel her anger rise through the phone. "I don't know this guy. I don't want him at my graduation." There was some back-and-forth about how selfish I was and how dare I not be happy for her, etc. And then she made a decision.

"Well, then. I'm not going either," she hissed.

So that was it. My mother was choosing this guy over me. Fine. Granted, I now know that I was not being a grown-up either. It didn't matter whether I knew this man or not. Or that my mother was always intent on ruining days of celebration. If I had really wanted her there, I should have put up and shut up. She was a grown woman and should have been able to marry whomever the hell she wanted and still see her daughter on those campus grounds, dressed in the cap and gown of Columbia blue. But I wasn't having it and she wasn't having me. We were peas in a pod—stubborn and unforgiving of each other.

On the day of graduation, I looked like the walking dead. I had been up nonstop, many sleepless nights before, finishing final papers. But I was smiling wide and my brother was there, proudly grinning for me too. I was so grateful to him for not letting me do this alone. To be there with no family, especially after a divorce, would have been much too gloomy to manage. But he was there, and I was proud of what I'd come through and accomplished. I had even landed a (low) paid internship as a researcher at Weill Cornell psychiatric hospital in White Plains that I hoped would lead to my doctorate.

By this time, I'd also let someone else return into my life: Papi. His years in prison, then a halfway house, were over just before I married Derek, and now father number one was back. I hadn't heard from Papi in nearly ten years, though he'd been in touch with my mother. (But because I wasn't really talking to her, I'd get all news about him from Alex.) And now we were living in the same city for the first time since I was a baby. It went unsaid between me and Alex that he was going to give our father a wide berth for a while. Alex was a married father now, building the life he worked hard for and protecting the home he bought with his love. The last time Alex had seen Papi, he was in an orange prison jumpsuit, which Alex could have been in too if someone in law enforcement hadn't believed that he was ignorant of Papi's crimes. Though his calls started slowly, maybe once every couple of months, Papi began to settle in. Alex blocking him on his end, it was on me, the daughter, to take Papi's ranting calls and requests to meet up in Chinatown or let him drop off some oranges or the black bean bao I loved so much. Of course, I was going to hold Papi at arm's length too. I didn't give him my address no matter how many times he asked.

"Oh! You uptown? Where, where? By museum, or no?" he'd dig.

"I'm near many things, Papi," I'd dodge.

I don't remember if it was out of boredom, loneliness, guilt, or a combination, but after a year or so of him being out, I agreed to meet up with Papi and go on a delivery with him. Not drugs, of course. Jewelry. Yes, this had been his cover previously as well. But he swore this time that it was only jewelry. That he was "clean, clean" now. What can I say? I wanted to see my father. I had him pick me up a couple of blocks away from my apartment. He was driving a boat of a vehicle, a washed-out old sedan that would have been more at home on the wider streets of Los Angeles. We were headed to a big department store in west Midtown, where he sold his costume jewelry. I have to say I was surprised that he sold to such an established place. Even more so once he told me, as we were driving, how he came to have boxes and boxes to sell.

"These Chinese ladies, ladies from China, no papers, they come here and live in Queens, all together. I buy the pieces, cheap, cheap, and drop them off to them, and they all put them together, and then I come back and pick it all up to sell."

So, he wasn't "clean, clean" after all. Was it legal to use undocumented labor at probably well below minimum wage to assemble jewelry that was then sold at a major department store? Did Papi even know how to have a regular business or job? Did he even know or care in the slightest about what was legal or not? Or was what I was seeing simply another economy that's just as normal as the one we all seem to know? What he was telling me involved so many people, I had to assume what he did now, and back then, was much more prevalent than I'd ever thought. And if it was so prevalent, that made it a substantial part of this country's consumer and financial system. I cursed myself a bit for being so interested in black market economics, but I couldn't resist, because I was a child of immigrants, after all. Immigrants who built their American lives in that economy. My mother was married off to Papi with a financial exchange. I later found out that before she had me or Alex, she was sometimes working off-the-books jobs. Getting paid under the table. It was just the way things were done and most likely needed to be.

We arrived at the loading dock of the store. Papi backed in and I stayed in the car as the three men standing around to receive deliveries stared at me aggressively. There was no cellphone for me to be on to distract myself while Papi unloaded the boxes, exchanged papers and money. The men, Black and Latino, kept up their ogling, so I kept my head up, pretending to be unbothered by their eyes, as I watched people walking by on the sidewalk.

"Those guys asking me who you are, and I say: That's my daughter! My daughter, I say!" Papi said as he got back into the car and patted my hand. I didn't have a response.

"Why my daughter so pretty and your brother so ugly, huh? Why?"

"Papi! Don't say that. That's not nice," I said.

"Aw, but it's true! It's true."

I shook my head at him. I always thought my brother was handsome. Tall and thin, curly haired, with giant eyes. But then Papi made clear why he really thought Alex wasn't good-looking.

"And why he have to go marry Black lady? Why? He went to college—he could marry white lady!"

"Papi. Belinda went to college with him. She's a professional and very pretty." I couldn't believe the racist shit coming out of my father's mouth. He was an old Chinese guy so maybe he'd just never had the opportunity to talk like this to me or in front of me. Or maybe being in prison changed him, hardened him and his beliefs. Either way, I now knew that my father didn't like Black people, and that meant that, of course, he thought Alex wasn't good-looking. My brother had more African features than I did. It took years, and my brother having more amazing Black Wong children, before Papi stopped saying these things. And I did remind Papi that he didn't marry a white woman when he married Mom. He married a light-skinned Black woman. He would bring whitening creams back for her when he'd visit his family in Hong Kong and Malaysia.

As I was starting back up a relationship with my father, now that he wasn't on the run, I was slowly cutting off my mother, deflecting her requests to come over and visit or meet up somewhere in the city. I was still fairly fragile from my divorce drama and unable to handle her presence. But she still called me on the phone. She rang one early evening as I was cleaning my apartment, prepping for one of my younger sisters to visit. I loved having them visit me in the city. If I was lucky, I'd get either a solo visit or multiples a couple of times a year and we'd go out to my favorite bar off of the Columbia campus, get stupid drunk, dance our asses off, and crash on the couch and floor of my apartment. Imagine a bunch of young women who look fairly alike, cute, pulling up to a bar at the same time. We would have a blast. Though one night, one of my sisters got into a screaming match with another sister in front of my building in the Heights. I forget what started the row, but I remember thinking, watching them escalate out of the corner of my eye as I paid the cabbie who was dropping us off, how this scene heartened me a bit. How very Dominican of them. Of us. It felt homey. (And I pulled the two of them apart, calmly.)

"Why are you cleaning for her?" Mom asked me, as I cradled the phone between my shoulder and cheek, sweeping up the bathroom floor.

"Because she's a visitor. And she's my sister."

"That's why she should be cleaning for you!"

"I'm going to have my sister visit me and clean my apartment? Why the heck would I do that? She doesn't live here," I said, incredulous. I always treated my sisters like guests, and just like those times back in New Hampshire when I'd take the girls out for McDonald's ice cream after school or to the beach, I looked forward to taking them to museums and stuffing them full of restaurant food. Treating them was my sibling love language and maybe a way to make up for much of the darkness of our childhood.

"Because that's what younger sisters should do. You took care of them when they were little, cleaning up after them. Now it's their turn to do that for you," Mom said.

"No. I'm not doing that, Mom."

As was the norm with Lupe, this disagreement led to another and another. So I hung up on her midsentence. I had never, ever dared to do something like that before. We all lived in fear of her, fear of disrespecting her. But now it was my turn to have had enough. As I put the phone down, my heart beat like a stereo bass and I started to sweat. I shocked myself with this act of defiance, hanging up the phone on a Latin mother. Might as well have signed my death warrant. As I finished up the bathroom and put the broom and cleansers away, I shook my head clear and felt my fear turn into pride. I stood up for myself. I wasn't going to take it anymore.

The phone rang again. I knew it was her, ready to yell at me for hanging up. I let the landline ring and ring and ring and go to my analog answering machine, where I heard her hang up after the beep. I wouldn't talk to my mother again for nearly two full years. I told myself that she felt like a tumor that needed to be cut out. I couldn't survive if I didn't exorcise it. It was strangling me, stifling me. I was drinking alcohol again, much too much, waking up some weekend mornings with tremors after a night out hitting the bars with friends until four A.M., unable to do anything the whole day but eat salty, greasy foods and drink water. I realized that if I wasn't careful, I could become a full-blown alcoholic. Plus, I was putting myself in some dangerous situations with men on those drunken nights. The friends I hung out with were in danger often too. Things were getting scary. Mom needed to go. I couldn't get on my feet psychologically with her around. Every time I'd try to stand up, she'd call, and I'd slip back down into darkness. I needed to save myself. I had to let her go. Over that time of no communication, sure, I missed her. Though I think I missed what I wanted and needed from her rather than her herself—love, support, and pride. Things she couldn't provide to me as she was. Things I might never get from her.

One afternoon, Alex and I went to one of our favorite spots, the

Chino-Latino diner La Caridad on the Upper West Side, where we could get our favorites from our childhood, lo mein and plantains.

"Mom went back to New Hampshire," he said to me. I couldn't believe it. She'd been living in New York maybe four or five months. He continued, "She divorced that guy."

"Divorced? Well, that lasted less time than *my* marriage!" We both chuckled. I asked him, "What happened? Not that I'm surprised."

"She says he was too controlling and didn't want her running around. He wanted her making him dinner and stuff."

"Ah. And she wasn't having that," I said.

"Nope."

"She comes back here, ready to get back to her people, but she ended up too American."

"Looks like it," he said.

"But Alex, what did she expect, huh? Look at who she married! Some ancient Latin guy who was probably just like her father. And she's lived in New Hampshire for what, over twenty years?"

"Yeah, yeah, I know," he said. Alex usually said that same phrase, "yeah, yeah, I know," to me three hundred times when it came to my complaining about Mom and Papi. We were continuously exasperated by them both, but Alex could not fully remove himself from either, like I had done with Mom. To be honest, I probably counted on him to do just that, stick with them. I counted on him—my sisters too—to tell me what was going on with Mom. And there ended up being a lot going on with Mom after the divorce, besides the travels with the retired ladies.

On one of our usual brother-sister check-in calls, usually a couple of times a week, or in times of need (for me), every other day, Alex had something big to tell me about our mother. This call coincided with a time that I was digging deep into my identity and asking questions.

Defending myself from attacks on my identity was my born duty for nearly three decades, my whole life at that point. From the schoolyard ("You're not Chinese. Oh yeah? Then say something in Chinese.") to my graduate internship at a Dominican American nonprofit in the Heights whose team was painfully standoffish with me, only to find out on my last day, from the head of the organization, that everyone—including him—thought I was Anglo, not Latina at all. Then there was the Chinese American receptionist at my doctor's office who exclaimed for the whole waiting room to hear, "Your father is not Chinese!" to which I answered, "I think I know who my father is!" In response, she let out a cackle and laughed and laughed as I turned red and walked away.

Some people's questions and comments pricked like a splinter, no blood lost but sticking under my skin. Others burned my chest so hard I could barely speak the rest of the day. I was never Latina enough, Dominican enough, American enough, Chinese enough. Even the fetishizing and backhanded compliments left bruises. "Chinese? Oh, that's where you get your cheekbones and your brains." "Sexy blend! Best of both worlds." "You're like a mutt—mutts are smarter and better than other dogs." Dogs. I can't tell you how many times white people thought they were complimenting me using references to dog breeding.

Identity shouldn't be such pain. It shouldn't be about playing an exhausting defense to simply exist on par with the majority culture. It means that the default—white—is best and you are less, always. I just wanted to live and feel good about who I was. All my parts.

In response to all the questioning, and maybe my own desire to connect more deeply with what I'd missed as a child, particularly in these post-divorce years, I delved back deep into Chinatown, visiting an herbalist to counter the shocking hair loss that struck me after my divorce. I bought my fish and vegetables from street vendors and my favorite black bean bao from the bakeries. I read all the Lao-tzu I could find. This former Catholic swooned over the Tao Te Ching and its philosophy, so contrary to the nuns of my childhood. You can't be Chinese by experiencing the culture, but I wasn't doing these things as a colonizer. I was looking for ties, for the connection, inclusion, that I had through my father to an extended cultural family. The family of a father I couldn't be close to because he was a hot stove.

I also wanted to exist as much as possible around the Latinness and Blackness I had lost living among a pale New England. I spent any extra money I had on more books, building a library of identity culture, from *Why Are All the Black Kids Sitting Together in the Cafeteria?* to the small number of books I could find covering the Latino ideas of marianismo (the mother/virgin role of women in Latin culture) and machismo. I read as much fiction by Latino, Asian, and Black authors as I could find, gorging on them as I'd gorged on books in the library as a child, all filled with white characters created by white authors simply because that's the way things were in the 1980s. But this time instead of only escape, I was looking for connection.

It also felt like reclamation. Maybe what my mom was after when she moved back to the city too briefly. But she discovered that she had become too suburban and feminist for old-school urban Latino culture. Looking back, I feel for her. I recognize the yearning, badly, to belong again like we had decades before on Claremont Avenue.

With all this self-discovery, plus the outside world's comments, I couldn't shake a feeling, a nudge deep in my gut that something was off. I was spending a lot of time digging into myself, the recesses of my identity that I'd not been able to touch, feel, or see until I was back home in the city and on my own. In all this excavation, I was searching for my origins as a person—wanting to get to the bottom of why I'd made so many mistakes. And there I dug up the feeling that I was nothing like my father, Papi. Not on the surface, my phenotype, but who I was growing into as a person. My temperament, my personality, my tendencies, my likes and dislikes. I compared myself with my brother, who clearly was very much like Papi in temperament. He was also super cheap like Papi (and I had no problem telling him so). He vacuumed up food into his mouth like Papi. Said the very Chinese hand-me-down expression "Ay-yaaa!" consistently (while I used my mother's "Ay-yi-yi"). Alex had very little Lupe in him. Did he just take after our father, and I took after our mother? Was it because I had spent fewer years living with Papi? But what about this nose I had? No one in Mom's family or Papi's family had my nose. Not one cousin, aunt, or uncle. Where did it come from? Questions like these buzzed like bees around my head, covered with the pollen of possibilities.

All of this, plus my deep feeling of being an outsider in both families—Papi's and Marty's—that I had carried since childhood was transforming into the sensation of something undiscovered. Something out of place. Of the six children my mother had, I was the one floating, orbiting the rest, one hand in the family while someone or something else held my other, or it was on its own. I dared not ask my mother for answers lest she accuse me of thinking such a "shameful" thing of her. It turns out I didn't have to ask.

"Mom has joined this church—I think it's Evangelical? Born-again, or something," Alex told me on the phone that day.

"Oh no. That's not good," I said, rolling my eyes to the back of my head. Yeah, that's what she needed, another religion. From giving to the grifters Jim and Tammy Faye Bakker to serving donuts at our Catholic parish to banning alcohol in the house, and now she'd gone full Holy Roller. This did not bode well for any reconciliation with me. During one of the last full-on screaming fights we had had, she yelled at me, "Psychology is your religion!" To which I responded, as I usually did when she'd criticize my more logical thinking, "God gave us a brain and it's a sin not to use it!"

I could tell that Alex was struggling with telling me what he'd called to tell me. He was spending time painting a picture of the scene, which is not his usual MO. "Yeah, so I was sitting there with her in the house. It was kinda dark because I got there late—"

"Yeah . . . ," I pressed.

"She told me that part of what she needed to do with this church is to come clean with her sins and confess them to people so she could be absolved."

"Sins?" This was taking a turn I did not expect. Alex was uncomfortable.

"So, she says that when she was young, she had some abortions." No wonder she was such a monster about me and sex. "She had three," Alex said. Three. I was shocked. "Two before you were born, after me, though, and one after you were born."

"Two before and . . . and one after . . ." My voice drifted with those numbers. "But that means that she had abortions before it was legal, right?"

"I . . . I guess so," Alex said.

I saw my mother as a young woman—twenty to twenty-four, getting backyard abortions, a wire hanger appearing in my mind, dirty instruments, pain and distress. This must have been awful for her to go through. And no, I didn't blame her 100 percent for not using birth control. Lupe had told me when I was in my early twenties that she couldn't handle the pill. She'd tried and gotten very sick. So the onus was on the man, and in the late 1960s, my mother still a fairly new immigrant, I don't know how much she would have felt she could protest if the man decided not to use protection. Thinking about it now, I realize too that a part of me also thought that maybe, just maybe, she had wanted to get pregnant. And the man didn't want it. But she was still married to Papi all this time, during these abortions.

"Alex, did she say whose these were? I mean, was it Papi or was it someone else?"

"I dunno. No, she didn't say."

Once I asked as many questions as I could then hung up the phone, I kept repeating to myself: Two before me, one after. Two before, one after.

Alex was born first when she was married to Papi. Then she had two abortions. Then I was born when she was still married to Papi. Then she had another abortion. Then my first sister was born when she was married to Marty.

The only explanation I could come up with was that she had been having an affair. But then that meant that I wasn't Papi's child. Whose child was I? Someone else could be my father, not Papi?

Could this all be true? Of course, I needed to know. But if I wasn't talking to my mother, how was I going to find out?

CHAPTER 9

. . . Because I Thought
We Had Time

W HEN YOU GROW UP AND BEGIN TO SEE YOUR PAR-
ents as separate, full human beings, it's jostling. And when your mother,
the warden of your virginity, discloses that she'd had multiple abortions
before you were born, well, it makes you question what else she's not
telling you and much of what you've already been told. Sure, maybe
she'd been too young and lonely, repented, then had an overcorrection, I
thought, her moral pendulum swinging in the other direction into hyper-
religiousness. This is how I reconciled her overprotectiveness of me, not
wanting her firstborn daughter to fall into the same traps she did early in
her life. But it wasn't just the swing of moral stance that was most surprising, it was the revelation of something so big and incongruent kept
quiet, secret. What else could she be hiding?

Concerns about my mother's past had to take a back seat for a while
as I focused on paying my bills and landing an actual career rather than
adding to my line of admin jobs. I went back to the magazine business.
Back to the same company that couldn't see me beyond an assistant. This
was because even though my quest to continue to a PhD had been fully
supported and endorsed by my supervising professors and a psychiatrist

at the hospital—one even telling me that he'd take me through in three years rather than four or more if I worked with him—I had to leave that path. In only a few months in the program, surviving on a barely eighteen-thousand-dollar annual salary, I saw newly minted PhDs make obscenely small and unsustainable amounts of money, maybe thirty-four thousand dollars a year, if that. And if you were lucky, maybe, just maybe you'd get to seventy thousand dollars many years later. Granted, had I continued, knowing myself, I would have spun that doctorate into gold like a Jungian striver, but I had zero patience or respect for a system that put you into tremendous debt only to spit you out more broke than ever. This meant that the field of psychology, and graduate school in 2000 (and traditionally), may not have been filled with only the brightest of the bunch, I'd think, but instead with ones who could afford and endure living that way because they had familial financial support.

I was over forty thousand dollars in student loan debt and paying all my own bills. I subsisted on $1.50 wonton soup from the corner Chinese restaurant for dinner, Cheerios for breakfast, and a Frappuccino lunch. I was about to turn thirty. This way of life was not acceptable to me anymore. This was not why my mother and I had worked so hard. And in case I forgot the backbreaking work that got me to that desk job point, my permanently herniated disk (at nineteen) from picking up overloaded trays of food and drinks during my waitressing job in college would remind me with a ding-dong of pain out of nowhere. The higher-ups at the hospital weren't happy their model minority was leaving. One professor said to a colleague: "How awful and ungrateful of her to quit. We all survived and have done just fine." This from a woman who lived with her parents on the Upper West Side while in graduate school, a rent-free advantage I did not have. The program was filled with people like her.

I called my former boss at the magazine and asked—in my rather persuasive way—to get back into Time & Life. It was a constant push to land the right position, worthy of all I'd put into my career and education, all I had to offer. After all, I had an Ivy League master's degree now. Sure, not in journalism, but it certainly meant something, and I wasn't going to let all that work and money spent go to waste. After waylays on the corporate executive floor, then another at *Fortune* magazine, then the start-up known as CNNMoney—where I was still treated like a lowly assistant by another white male boss, his microaggressions very aggressive—I ended up back at *Money* magazine, finally with a title and salary I could live with. This of course was due to the advocacy of a not-to-be-messed-with Black woman, a high-ranking editor at the magazine. Sheryl H. Tucker had come from being the editor in chief of *Black Enterprise,* and saw me for who I was and knew I had much to offer. It took a Black woman in HR to get me into the building in the first place and a Black woman top editor to get me the spot I deserved. This is not a coincidence. And then there were the ones who I had thought to be friends of mine, or friendly, saying to Sheryl, "But isn't she still just your assistant?" I was special projects editor—an editor who straddled and strategized both sides, editorial content and the business side of publishing. My brain was built for both so theoretically, it worked. For a while.

Coming back to the city late one evening from a promotional event for the magazine in Boston, I sat exhausted in a yellow cab pulling out of Penn Station. It was raining and I was feeling a bit motion sick from the train and now the cab ride. I tried to focus my gaze straight ahead, on lights in the distance. Then my cellphone rang. It was one of my sisters who didn't call me often or ever.

"What's going on?" I asked her.

"I'm in the hospital with Mom. She went to the emergency room earlier. She has cancer."

"Cancer?"

"It looks like it's colon cancer but there are tumors everywhere—"

"What do you mean everywhere . . ."

"All over her—her liver, her stomach. The doctor said that when the nurse lifted her gown to feel her stomach, she could see the tumors through her skin. They didn't even need to feel them. They're huge."

It was a strong visual. I felt sick. "Why . . . how—how did they get like this?"

"I dunno. I didn't see them. She didn't seem sick. But she's been wearing baggy clothes lately," my sister said.

"What brought her into the hospital, though?"

"Pain. She was in so much pain she couldn't stand it anymore."

A logjam formed in my mind. Fear, despair, anger, guilt, frustration all pushed at my temples. *Why didn't she go to the doctor? She was hiding it—why didn't anyone see it? Why didn't my sisters see it? Why didn't she tell anyone?*

I hadn't seen or spoken to Lupe in almost two years, counting on, assuming, that she'd be looked after or over, in a way, by my sisters, or even Alex, from afar. It was maybe a year since Alex told me about the abortions. I found out from Alex that she had joined the local Dominican American association, making new friends and finding ways to advocate within the community. After running back to the city to find her people again, Mom had turned back north and found that they'd come to her, moving out of cities to follow booming business and work opportunities in southern Massachusetts and New Hampshire. I flashed back to Abuela, wasting away in our living room. The pain she'd been in. Quietly suffering. The multiple medications taken at all hours of the day and night. How quickly she seemed to go. She was in her early sixties, but Mom, she was only in her late fifties.

Just because I couldn't manage having my mother in my life didn't mean I didn't love her or need her. My love tended toward protection and caretaking in general, so those forces locked into place that night for Lupe. I could hear the distress in my sister's voice. Lupe wasn't just my mother, she was the same for my four sisters and our brother, Alex being especially close to her. It was problem-solving time. What I do best. I was going to find out everything I could about her diagnosis and what treatments were available and ensure that even two-hundred-plus miles away I'd somehow increase her chances of surviving. The doctors gave her two months to live. The clock was ticking.

Within a few weeks, I had researched the newest colon cancer treatments in medical journals, still having access through my graduate program to get past paywalls. I got ahold of her oncologist in New Hampshire, nudging him with my city-professional voice and my media position. He was able to get Mom into a trial for a cancer drug not yet approved for colon cancer, which turned into one of the biggest cancer drug of all, Gleevec. Her tumors were inoperable, so we just had to wait and see if the drugs would work. I thought hard about making time to visit her. I figured pounding the pavement to get her the best care and treatment was the priority. She didn't need the stress of seeing me yet. And I needed a bit more time to steel myself up for my own.

The pressure to see her more quickly started with another surprise phone call, this one from Marty. This was strange in and of itself as Dad wasn't known to reach out and call anyone. We all had to call him.

"Dad? What's going on?" I asked as I pulled the phone cord into my kitchen, away from my date who was sitting on the couch.

"Well . . ." He sounded incredibly tense. "Uh, I need you to come see me."

"Come see you? Like, go to Rhode Island? Why?" I still wasn't flush with funds, so jumping onto a train or bus wasn't budgeted except for holidays and maybe once a summer.

"I need to tell you something."

"I don't understand, why can't you tell me on the phone?" I waved over to the guy—not someone worthwhile, as was my wont—gesturing that I'd get off in a minute.

Dad sighed. "I . . . I can't. I need to see you in person."

He was really struggling. I couldn't imagine what this could be. After the divorce and Mom's cancer, what else could possibly be so important? One of my sisters had told me that when Mom divorced short-term husband number three and came back to New Hampshire, she'd regretted divorcing Marty and had been trying to get him back, to no avail. He was having none of it. During one of our calls, he told me he was dating an administrator at my little sister's college in Rhode Island. But that's all I knew. He didn't talk about Lupe.

"Is this about your will or something?" was all I could come up with.

"Uh, yeah. Sure," he said.

I went to see him the following weekend. Marty had lifted himself up quite a bit from his first bachelor pad to owning a very nice cottage in a picturesque town in Rhode Island. It was up the road from a running and biking trail that ran from Newport to the capital, Providence, along the water. Dad had been a bit overweight at one point before the divorce, but now in his sixties he had taken up running to stave off a high blood pressure diagnosis, and this trail had become his church. (There was no more going to mass for him once he and Mom split.) The guy I was dating at the time had a car, so he offered to drive me up to see Dad. Meeting family was not something he was deserving of, but it seemed like a good idea at the time.

"Uh, can we have that talk now?" Marty asked after some small talk with me and this guy as we sat at Dad's kitchen table. I turned to my date and nicely asked him to step outside for a bit.

It was a round, carved dark wood table, very midwestern Americana, just like Dad liked. The hum of the refrigerator our score. The lights above us casting everything in a yellow glow, a bit sickly rather than golden. We were sweaty in the summer evening, air-conditioning not standard. I crossed my arms and leaned back.

"Okay. So, Dad. What was so important to tell me?"

Marty also leaned back from the table a bit, his face drawn and heavy. He kept his eyes focused on the wood surface in front of him, not on me.

"Peter is not your father," he said.

Shock. This was not anything I'd expected to hear, especially from Marty. Why was he telling me this? Was he doing me a service or something? He'd never liked Peter. Maybe this was late-in-life revenge? My vision sharpened as fight-or-flight instincts turned on, my chest pounding and my heart in my ears.

"Then who is?" I asked in a monotone, barely breathing.

Marty looked down at his hands, now folded in his lap. "I am," he said.

In a millisecond, memories with Marty tore through my mind. Me as a child chopping wood with him. Playing badminton in the yard on a hot summer day. The sound of his newspaper folding as he read the daily stock prices. The feel of his trench coat as we girls hugged him when he got home from work. The aroma of potato chips as we ate through a bag in minutes. The rocking feeling as he shifted the gears in his car, driving me to school in the morning. His voice telling me to look up a word in the dictionary when I didn't know what it meant.

I burst into tears. Childlike tears. I cried for that little girl who so badly wanted a father, this father, and he'd been there the whole time.

He sat there across from me, my dad, with his head hanging low. As I willed myself to snap out of it—so many questions, so many feelings—I first walked to his bathroom to get some tissues to hold the snot and tears pouring from my face. I came back to see him in the same position, unmoving. My hard hat came back on.

"You knew? You knew all this time?" I asked.

"Yeah," he whispered.

This angered me like nothing else. I had to say it again. "You knew. You knew, my whole life, and you didn't tell me?"

He nodded.

"So why now, huh? Why are you telling me this now?" I said as I wiped my face.

"Well. You know that lady I'm dating?" The college administrator. She was younger than him but seemed like a nice enough person. "She told me that I had to tell you before Lupe dies. That it wasn't right to keep it from you."

"You think?" How dare he. How dare they. Understanding was not going to come from me that day. To fool with my life like this. As if I wasn't a full human being like they were. As if the "secret" they'd given birth to would never grow up into an adult herself. And if Mom hadn't gotten sick? When would I ever find out? Ever? All I had was anger and pain, down to my tingling fingertips.

"I wanted to be your kid, Dad. All these years I wanted to be yours, just like the girls, and all this time . . . I was? And you knew?" My voice was all sorrow, disappointment, and ire.

He nodded again.

"Does Mom know you're telling me this?" I asked.

"No."

"Does anyone know?"

"No."

I must thank the woman Dad was dating at that time. I never really knew her, but she was the instrument of chaos that I needed. She coaxed and guilted the truth out into the light. She did me a tremendous favor and for that, I will always be grateful.

My sisters came to mind. I had always loved them in full and never once called them my half-sisters, and when others did, I would correct them. I needed to tell them, at least one, the oldest, the news. I didn't ask more questions of Dad. It felt like something of incredible value had been set on the table and I had to grab it and run before time slid backward and took it from me. I had to share this news right away too or else it wouldn't feel real. The revelation was also too heavy for me to carry by myself. Someone else in the family needed to know. I thought of my sisters first, my now "full" sisters.

"I'm going to make some calls," I said as I pushed away from the table and went into the ground-floor bedroom, converted into his office, and sat among all his piles of papers and computer equipment, replicating his space back in the family home. I picked up the landline and called the oldest of my sisters and told her what Dad had told me, that we were full sisters. She cried along with me as I sat in the dim light of Dad's tiny desk lamp. She was shocked, like me. Curious. I ranted a bit with anger, which she too understood.

Then I called Marty's sister, my dear, gentle Aunt C, whom I loved so much, to tell her the news. Aunt C, like Abuela, had always seemed to see me as a person. She'd visit with her professor husband, Uncle David, when I was a child and have long conversations with me about whatever I was into at the moment, whether my temporary obsession with the planets or creating elaborately decorated salads. She'd even write me the sweetest cards and letters. When I told her this new news, she cried too, then said to me, "You know, one time when Grandma came back from visiting you when you were little, she said to me: 'I wouldn't be surprised if she's Marty's.'" I didn't know how to feel about that. Adults talking about me, holding my identity in their hands and minds without sharing. But it was soothing to hear my aunt's birdlike voice.

My brother, Alex, I didn't want to call. I had to tell him in person. Because on my sisters' side, this was conjoining news. Even though none of them met it with enthusiasm, exactly. Our relationship was still uneven and fraught. It was every-man-for-himself at that point in our lives. I had hoped that maybe this would make us all closer, but suddenly sharing a father didn't repair the damage of my having to be their second mother growing up (as nasty as I could be generous because remember, I was a kid without the tools to handle being a parent). On Alex's and my side, I felt that this was a painful fissure. I couldn't even think of it that night. Couldn't face it. My big brother was my everything as a kid and my rock as an adult. The only person I had been raised with as full family. It was too much to lose him, even a bit.

When I finished the calls, I found my guy friend sitting at the table with Dad. They went quiet as I approached. My face was tearstained and puffy. I asked my trip mate to go outside with me so I could talk alone to him about what had just happened. Afterward, he and I slept on the sweltering ground floor, hoping it would be cooler than the upstairs bedrooms. That night, my tossing and turning was not so much a consequence of the heat wave but of my own stifling thoughts.

Pulling the same move as Marty, back in the city I called Alex and asked him to come see me as soon as possible because I had something to tell him that was very important.

We both sat on my couch a few days later, leaning forward, resting our arms on our legs like twins. I told him what had happened. The tears fell more quietly for me this time. I didn't like crying in front of him. I wanted to seem as strong as he seemed.

Alex stared straight ahead, away from me. "Do me a favor, okay?" he asked. "Don't tell Peter."

"Don't tell Papi? Aren't we sick of the lies here? I mean—"

"No, no, see, we are all he has. It's just you and me. He has no family here. He's old. What's it going to do to him?" I sat silent. I needed to hear him out. After all, this was his father now, not mine. "Look, it may make you feel good to get the truth out there but it'll do nothing but give him pain. It does nothing for him."

Knotting up wet tissues, I let this sink in.

"Just promise me, okay?"

"Okay. Okay," I said. I have kept this promise and always will.

I STARED AT THE framed silk screen faux-antique portrait of a beautiful Chinese woman on my wall.

How do you stop being Chinese?

Do you shed thirty-one years of your life like a skin? Do you erase every day of your past like from a whiteboard? Where does your Chineseness go? Do I pull it out of me with tweezers or brush it out of me like knots? Your community, your people, where do they go? Do you say goodbye even if it's the last thing you want to do? How do you sever a lifelong identity, a tie?

I stared and stared at her, so beautiful. My tears, ugly.

Letting go was not an option. I didn't want it to go. I didn't want being Chinese to go. My identity excised forcibly one night at a kitchen table, not of my doing. But it had all been a lie. An important part of my ethnicity, my legacy, and cultural and racial heritage, a lie. Does that make it all not real? Am I fake? A racial fake now?

What was real was my upbringing with the man I called my papi as my biological father. This problematic man my brother and I shared as a parent. The memories we held of Chinatown, stepping onto gold-and-red daisies, presented proudly as Peter Wong's daughter. His rolls of crisp bills, his prodding in restaurants to "Eat the fish brain! Makes you swim! Eat the eye! Makes you see underwater!" as he plopped both into his mouth with his chopsticks. And what about my cousins, our fellow Chino-Latino family, whom I loved so much? Bad enough we moved up north and they stayed in the city for a while longer. Now there'd be another gulf between us.

How do you stop being Chinese?

Would it ever morph into something else, maybe no less precious and prideful? That would take time. In the meantime, I mourned the loss of a piece of me. I puzzled over how to manage my "new" identity. How to manage having lived so long in someone else's lie. My anger grew. All those years as a child I wanted nothing more than to be one of the "G Girls," Marty's girls. Growing up, living in that house in New Hampshire, living with and around my stepdad all while he was my biological father? What went through his head as he passed me in the hallway or in the kitchen? Or when I brought home great grades? Was he thinking *Oh, that's my daughter, all right*? Is that why he spent so much time talking to me about money and business and movies and news? Investing time and energy into me because I was his firstborn?

The lies. The lie I was born into. *Fuck*. (No wonder Mom smirked when the nuns said I was so smart because I was Chinese.)

I was at least a bit happy to be full sisters with my sisters, though something still wasn't sitting right. Just as with Alex, I wasn't very much like my sisters either. The four of them fit together. Each with obvious characteristics of both Mom and Dad. Being their full sibling felt like a much-too-big sweater. Gaps and space. And Italian? I was now Dominican Italian? I guess. This didn't fit right with me either. Maybe it's not true? Take my Asian identity, and all I felt inside of me was Latina. Marty's part didn't fit where Papi's was removed.

The Italian American side I knew well too. Grandma and Grandpa G came to visit a couple of times from their home in Southfield, Michigan. They were tiny people, both no taller than five foot three or four, and slim. Grandpa was a smoker and, I remember, had hairy ears. Grandma made the most decadent Italian wedding cookies; their white powdered sugar pleasantly covered your lips no matter how carefully you tried to bite them. She'd send care packages to us and little notes to me. Aunt C did the same. I loved this family very much. But I never thought that they were mine. I wonder how much safer and more supported I would have felt if I had known.

Only one person could know what the truth was.

"Can I ask you to please come with me to talk to Mom?" I asked my sister, the oldest of the four, when I called her once I got back home. I needed intermediaries and support not only to see my mother, now riddled with stage 4 cancer, for the first time in two years but to confront her with this revelation. I knew it was not going to be pretty. My sisters knew it too. Both the oldest and youngest agreed to go with me in support. They were curious too. This affected them and their ideas about Mom and Dad as well. They deserved answers. We all did.

ALL THREE OF US pulled into the parking lot of our mother's apartment complex. It was a brick development that we used to pass by regularly while driving around town in years past. My stomach was a mess. I asked the girls to sit in the car with me for a moment as I worked up the courage to go in.

"Oh my god. There she is," I said. Lupe had walked outside and was standing at the entrance to the building. She must have seen us pull up. From my seat in the car, she looked small and frail. Her torso and face thin, waning, the rest of her a bit wider and hidden under baggy clothes. She wasn't dressing sassy anymore in tight jeans and heels as she'd been back in the city. She'd gone back to her conservative ways. I imagined the tumors that sat beneath her loose clothing.

My sisters got out and approached her first and gave her hugs. I anxiously awaited my turn behind them. The push-pull inside of wanting my mami so badly while holding her at a psychological arm's length so she couldn't hurt me anymore.

"Hi, Mom," I said as she looked at me with watery eyes behind her thick glasses. Mine welled up too as I struggled to be stoic. I hugged her little frame as she cried, hard, holding me tight. I couldn't remember the last time we embraced. It felt foreign. But there was love there. Sadness and longing. Even if my walls remained up.

"Okay, okay, let's go inside, people," I teased as I pulled away gently. She felt like she could break, she was so thin. Lupe held tightly to my hand as we went inside. It was a foreign feeling to me, my mother's hand holding mine. Both the alienness of the sensation and the need for her to not let me go stung in my chest.

The apartment was clean and well put together but dark, much of the furniture too big for the space. Mom had furnished her small one-bedroom with the furnishings from our old home, furniture for a large four-bedroom house with eight people. Ornate, carved, dark-stained dining chairs, painted with flowers and curly details, that had been parked in the recesses of our living room / Mom's future hoarding room, never used, were set up with the dining table we'd always had, its deep, carved scratches and water stains forming their own abstract patterns in contrast. The table made me feel warm. The chairs, cold. The table carried memories, good and bad. The chairs, empty for years.

The four of us sat down. I took the head of the table, positioning myself at the head of this truth-finding session.

I asked Lupe how she was feeling, about any updates from her doctor. How she was managing the drugs. I noticed she'd lost hair, her ubiquitous ponytail tiny and thinned out. Mom answered questions almost demurely, fiddling with the tissues in her hand. It was hard to tell, as always, if this was a genuine result of being humbled by her diagnosis, or by my withdrawing from her, or if this was a display to get the reaction she wanted from me.

"Mom. Dad called me over to his place to tell me something." Lupe looked down at her tissues and nodded, waiting. "I needed to come here and check it with you."

"Okay," she said.

I took a moment. There was a brief impulse of wanting to pretend that this was all not happening. That maybe I should let the charade run on. I loved being Chinese and Dominican. I appreciated having a fucked-up drug-running gambling-addict entertaining Asian father whom I saw only once in a while. The contrast between who I supposedly was as a product of Papi and my life with Marty was interesting. Maybe I didn't want to be Marty's kid after all. Part of my personality was my multiple cultural, racial identities. It was my story. Plus it seemed that Marty didn't want me enough to claim me. That he would rather have kept things copasetic with my mother than stand up and say I was his. Was I not worthy enough? If Marty had not thought so, why acknowledge this new (for me) reality now? Did he deserve to call me his daughter at all, then?

Mom used to say to me when I came home in grade school complaining of feeling less than the other girls, mostly because I wasn't white like them, "There will always be someone prettier, smarter, more talented than you. But there will never, ever be another you. Carmen. Rita. Wong." She would make a point to say my full name, enunciate every syllable, pinching her fingers together to make the point. I had attached myself to my name and identity and all it implied. I didn't want to let it go. But I needed to know the why. Why had they done this to me?

"Mom. Dad told me that Peter is not my father. That he—that Marty—is my father."

Mom's face lit with a sad anger. "How dare he? How dare he tell you! That was not for him to tell!" She raised her voice.

I raised mine. "Well, when were you going to tell me? I'm thirty-one years old!" I was angry that this was her first reaction. Of course. Of course, it was all about the two of them. Not about me. Always and forever about them.

My sisters sat in silence. One looking at me with sympathy. The other holding it together.

Lupe started crying harder. I waited her out a bit. She blew her nose and wiped her eyes. I glared down my nose at her.

"Why did you do it?" I asked.

"Your father—"

"Which one?"

"Peter. Peter was your father. Marty didn't want you."

My eyes narrowed. Here was the story. Mom was good at telling stories. Obviously. But as I found out in a life-changing way, I couldn't trust them. "What do you mean?"

"I had an abortion—two abortions—before you, and then I was pregnant with you and Peter found out that I was going with my sister to get another abortion—we were in the car to go there! But Peter said, 'No! No! This one is mine! I'll take care of this one.' So I didn't do it. Peter saved your life!" She was implying that Marty had gotten her pregnant several times and paid for illegal abortions (not legal in New York until the year I was born, 1971) and that Peter also knew about it. Lots to dig into but I didn't have my newsroom hat on in the moment. I wasn't about confirming those tumultuous facts just then. I was all about finding out why the lie. Why the secrets. How could they have done this to me?

"Well. No, not really because I didn't exist yet." Remember, I was the teenager with an abortion fund who argued with the nuns about the "mortal sin" of birth control. Even Lupe had once said to me when I was in college that the greatest invention ever was birth control. I now deeply understood, despite her (supposed) religiosity, why she'd say such a thing.

Mom waved off my defanging of her dramatic delivery. In retrospect this was maybe a cornerstone for living the lie as a Wong. The story had to be that my "life was saved" and that I was on the brink of being, well, disposed of. But then Peter, Papi, saved me. Saved my life. This foundational tenet was paramount to keeping everyone in their place, playing their roles. Without this gem, the lies would have had no righteousness to stand on. And Mom (and maybe Marty too) needed moral ground to justify such a grand, obscene falsehood. She needed to hold it over Dad's head.

"This is why I did it. Marty wanted you aborted. Peter didn't. And from then on I swore that you were Peter's child and that Marty would have no hand in supporting you." So she punished Dad for wanting me aborted by having him live with me, help raise me, but never allowing him to claim me as his child, which she's saying, and he's saying, I always was. Messy and vengeful. Peter thought he was my father, and Marty knew he was my father. But Mom made sure both men were missing a piece of me. Peter, the truth (claiming a daughter that secretly wasn't his). And Marty, a lie (raising a stepdaughter who he knew was his daughter).

"So that's why I didn't get any money from him like the girls did. Because he didn't want me." Insensitive comparison, maybe, in my sisters' presence, but a very important point that shaped my life. It's why I worked so much. It's why I always felt unmoored, unsupported, under pressure to sustain myself. "And I wanted so bad to be his child— remember how I begged for him to adopt me when I was little?" I asked.

"Yes. But he didn't deserve you! He didn't want you, like he didn't want the others, so . . . ," she said, sniffling.

"But then you had another abortion after me, right? Was that his too?"

"Yes." Mom hung her head.

My anger toward her, a heavy, humid phantom, withdrew a bit. I imagined my mother, so young, twenty-six, trapped in an abusive marriage to Papi, with no support, and only more abuse from her father at home. Plus little Alex, my brother. I thought back on all the times I had been scared in my teens and twenties of being pregnant. Scared too of being trapped. Always wanting and fighting for a way out. Mine had been school, education. She gave me those options by raising me how she did. What were her options then? Another man? What was her realistic recourse? She was an immigrant with an education that had stopped before high school graduation. She was a Black Hispanic twenty-six-year-old mother with a heavy accent.

"I couldn't escape your father!" She passionately straightened up.

"Peter?"

"No, Marty. I couldn't! I tried to leave him when you were born—took you as a newborn baby to the Dominican Republic"—first I was hearing of this—"I needed some space, but he sent me these letters . . . I still have them! These letters so filled with love; you should see—"

"No. Nope, that's okay. I don't need to see them." In retrospect, I should have seen them or at least made copies.

"But wait, Ma," I said, "you came back to the city but then you had another abortion?" If Marty had been so in love, why do it again?

"Yes. But finally, with Nina"—the oldest of the four sisters, sitting to my right—"I said I wasn't going to do it again."

"So, he married you. Finally."

"Yes. I got a fast divorce from Peter, and then we got married."

"This was in the cabin in the woods, right? In Vermont? Alex and I were there?"

"Yes."

Mom needed time to talk and tell her side of things. Defend herself and her decisions. My sisters remained quiet. I appreciated their presence. And I sat and listened, nudging Mom along when I spotted a hole in the story that needed filler. But there were so many holes, and many of her own creation, surely intentionally. How can you trust someone—your own mother—who kept and enforced such a lie? How can you trust a father who would go along with it? The answers run deeper than any place I'd known within myself. All I could do in this conversation was try my best to find out what I could while simultaneously managing a tornado of emotions inside me.

The scene felt like an interrogation, which it was in many ways. As I sat at the head of the table, the backs of our chairs rising dramatically several inches above our heads, it had the feel of a Gothic tableau. All we were missing were dark robes. There, a sobbing, dying mother to my left. Two sisters silently, patiently, if not painfully, bearing witness. Me, interrogator, jaw tight. Voice firm. Four women affected by Mom's choices decades ago. By her and our father's complicity.

Should I have been happy? That finally, after a childhood pining to be included in Mom's second family with Marty, to be a legitimate, full sibling to my baby sisters? To share a last name and family history? I was the furthest thing from happy. This revelation didn't untie and retie bonds three decades old. It didn't satisfy that little girl pining to be included in a new family. I had been denied it before I'd been born. It didn't solve any problems about who I was. I still had my name. I still had my history, my memories. I felt nothing new inside of me but betrayal.

When she went to the emergency room, Mom was told she had two months to live. With the drug trial, she was on her way to go well past that. I felt a twinge of guilt for causing her additional stress during a time when she needed all her strength. But then I reminded myself that she and Marty had had plenty of time to set things right with me. Three decades. Thirty years. My whole life at that point.

As my sisters and I left Mom's apartment, all of us emotionally worn, riding along the edges of my righteous anger at both parents, but more Marty than Mom, was the nagging idea of, again, not being seen. I felt like a ghost trying to push a spoon off a table, useless to change or influence the reality before me. Did they think of me? What this would do to me? How did they justify what they did? The answer was right there: I didn't matter. And maybe, just maybe Mom was ready to take the truth of who my father was to her grave. If Marty hadn't had a kind (sane!) girlfriend to push him into revealing it, when would I ever have known?

And why didn't Marty want to claim me? I had been a good kid, a solid kid. I thought he loved me and thought highly of me. Why wouldn't he want me to be his? Why didn't he fight Mom on this? Wasn't I worth it? Was it because he wanted me aborted, like the others? He didn't think it was his place? When Lupe was pregnant, I was an idea. Cells. But to deny your own child while living with her and her mother, then making more children and a family along the way? Knowing how much that little girl wanted to become yours. And he didn't fight for me.

My mother was dying. I lost a biological father and his race and culture. Found out my upbringing was a lie. I was a divorcée with a biological clock ticking. I was still thought of as less-than at the office no matter how great my work was. Nothing but turmoil.

When I was a teenager, I remember Mom telling me about the Chinese curse "May you lead an interesting life." Unfortunately, it seemed my "curse" was just getting started.

CHAPTER 10

... Because It Was Too Late

I T WAS 2005 AND I WAS SITTING IN THE GREENROOM OF A local news station. Despite the colorful industry name for the space, the room was gray, musty, dusty, tight, and dark, with a dirty window that looked into the building next door. I was there to have my first television appearance ("hit," as it's called in the business) to promote my new money advice book.

"Carmen?" A young producer popped his head in. "We'll come get you in five minutes. And oh—you'll be on with Geraldo today."

Isn't that nice! A new kid on TV named Geraldo. Mom would love this. She'd be so proud that there's another Latino on air. When I was growing up, Mom loved Geraldo Rivera, the macho, mustachioed New York City Puerto Rican. He had made it all the way up to the national news before falling into a network doghouse for questionable judgment while reporting in Iraq and Afghanistan. I hadn't seen him on air in ages and this was the local news so this must be a new guy, I thought. *They're about to have two Latinos on air. Wild.*

"Okay—ready to go?" The same producer came back to fetch me. I remember feeling an odd sangfroid about going live on air for the first time but also sizzling with nerves. My attitude was, simply, I was just doing my job. Promoting my book. Instead of anxiety coming out of my pores, I buzzed with excitement because this appearance was a big win and part of my overall plan for all that was about to come with my newest venture. A venture that had to work, as I'd been laid off from *Money* magazine months before and I'd put all my eggs into a freelance-business basket. All bets were on me. So, I was blinders on, full steam ahead, gates open. Failure was not an option.

Holy shit. If only Mom was here to see this.

I nailed that interview (despite Geraldo—yes, the OG Geraldo Rivera!—throwing me unplanned questions that sounded more like he was asking me for money advice for himself than the audience, or he was trying to trip me up—but failed). Mom couldn't see me on a TV screen. She'd passed away the year prior, just shy of her sixtieth birthday, two years after her colon cancer diagnosis. She didn't get to watch her investment pay off in person. All those hours over the years, watching TV news with her, as a family, every single day, mornings and evenings. Her admonishments to me to speak like Dan Rather or Peter Jennings (except for the words he pronounced in his native Canadian accent). And then there was the time she switched the channel in the mornings from *Good Morning America* to *Today* with the addition of the first national Black morning show cohost, Bryant Gumbel. "Mira! He looks like a cousin! Oh, I love him," she'd say. "So handsome."

I wish Lupe had gotten to see both my name on a book and me on television at least once, especially with her 1980s crush, Geraldo, before she passed away. To have a mother bear witness, no matter how strained our relationship, is powerful. Especially an immigrant mother. Accomplishments that I know she would have found some way to find some fault with per usual, but also, she would have been so proud even if she didn't tell me so.

Before she passed, she did get to see one life-changing circumstance for me. She met the man who was to become my husband number two, a new work colleague at the magazine, whom I'll call Ted. The red flags on this one flew directly at my face from the beginning. Nay, the flagpoles bonked me on the head a few times, but I had no power to extricate myself from getting sucked into this situation. Ted was Marty, Dad. But tall instead of small and with dyed platinum hair. A white guy from the Detroit suburbs just like Dad, the magazine's new "car guy," who loved to talk about anything, on the surface, just like Dad. Cars, politics, movies, books, music, you name it.

The big difference was that this was not the white-savior trope of my mother. Our dynamics went more the other way. He was the wide-eyed import to NYC, and I was the savvy, established city gal. I was higher ranking on staff and much more ambitious and serious. He was the rebellious, comfortable, quirky one with a rock 'n' roll 'do. I was the proverbial suit and tie.

It wasn't only that I was drawn to him because he mirrored Marty, just as my first husband had mirrored Lupe (we try to master what we couldn't master in childhood, so shoot me), but that this man's timing was also right. I was in my early thirties and my baby-having clock was clanging in my head. Before Ted showed up, I was looking into building an adoption fund just as I'd built an abortion fund fifteen years earlier. I didn't necessarily want to go it on my own as a parent, but if I had to, I would, to be a mother by forty. My desire for a child was bigger than my desire to get married again. But I wasn't only allergic to the idea of having a baby unmarried, I was anaphylactic. Racial, cultural stereotypes can be so dangerous that they can lead to bad decisions in order to defy the ideas others have about us. It makes your own life about *them*.

No matter how successful I got, there was still much too much working against me to add another reason for bosses—and white people in general—to see me as "just another" Hispanic, not built for the big jobs, doesn't fit into the office "culture," is not competent enough to get ahead (because only white equals an assumption of competence). The looks of disdain white men and women in the office would give me when I would mispronounce a word I had only read, not heard pronounced out loud, or the disgust when I plopped a whole edamame, pod and all, into my mouth at a business lunch, having never had one before. Now, if they reacted like that when I pronounced "biopic" like "myopic," imagine what they'd think if I got pregnant without a ring.

It wasn't the right way for me to be, to care so much about what others thought. But I'm far from the first non-white woman, first American kid from an immigrant family, to fall into the trap of white patriarchy and attempt to play the game of life on their terms. That was—and in places still is—the power of white gatekeepers, to shape the choices in our lives in ways unsuitable for our mental and emotional health, not to mention careers. Adding stress to the matter was that I didn't have a community of like-minded non-white people around me, having my back, supporting me, nor did I have money from my parents (any of the three of them). One misstep on my part meant falling back down again into the abyss of financial and professional distress, alone. So, a guy like my dad shows up at work, I tell myself it's fate, true love, and I marry him.

We got engaged when my mother was declining rapidly. She had managed to be mobile and able to work for twenty months or so after her diagnosis, much longer than she'd been initially given to live. I had visited her in New Hampshire two or three times during that period, keeping up with her oncologist on her treatment via phone, and staying in contact with my younger sisters, who were visiting her more often, the youngest pretty much moving in with her. Alex and Belinda were expecting—unexpectedly—a set of twin girls, so their ability to make the many-hour drive from suburban New York to New Hampshire was limited. But one morning at the office, Mom's healthcare aide, who was seeing her daily, called me and advised me to get in touch with everyone in the family and encourage them to visit as soon as possible. She said that Mom had told her to call me when it came to that. Mom knew I could put on my captain hat and manage the situation, handing out the difficult, dire news. Marty, Dad, was in a far orbit. I was still managing my anger at him for the deception. I had gone fairly radio silent. Peter, Papi, was somewhere, calling Mom occasionally, saying he wanted to see her, but she'd beg off. I didn't ask why she didn't want to see him. But I was grateful she didn't. Selfishly, we kids were managing enough, let alone a reunion with someone I now knew was not my father, who hadn't been to New Hampshire in maybe two decades.

When I arrived at Mom's apartment with my new partner, bringing him to Lupe's bedside, I knew she'd be pleased once she saw him. "Ay, cielito!" she managed to whisper as she took his hands in hers. She was weak but the enthusiasm was there. Mom's eyes lit up looking him up and down.

Later, Ted asked me, "What did she call me?"

"Cielito," I said. "Little piece of the sky. Because you're white with blue eyes." Mom may have been a champion of all people, like defending my brother marrying my Black sister-in-law, but old colorism habits die hard. She was thrilled he was a white American man. And yes, I was happy she was happy. The desire to please our parents runs so deep, even as deep as pleasing their racism.

During the same visit, my aunt Maria, my mother's younger sister, sat at Mom's dining table along with me, two of my sisters, the oldest and youngest of the four, and my mother's half-brother, Alberto, whom I never remembered meeting before. He was a child of Abuelo's wife, the "legitimate" side of the family, as opposed to my mother and Maria and Uncle Lou being from our abuela. Maria was telling us horrifying childhood stories in her tight, accented English while Alberto, a large, imposing brown man with a salesman look, nodded in agreement. My sisters and I had wide eyes at her stories. Mom was resting in her bedroom on the hospital bed that hospice care had installed for her and Ted was out running an errand.

Maria would pause after dropping a bomb of shared traumatic history with Mom and we'd all sit in silence for a moment. The horrible images she'd conjure up would loll about in my mind, trying to find a place to fit. *Do I create a whole new filing category for this new information that transforms my ideas about and feelings toward my mother? Where am I supposed to put all this?*

My imagination worked too well with what Maria was telling us. My mind had me see through the dark of night, through my mother's childhood eyes, watching her father force himself on her mother. I felt paralyzed with shock, with sorrow, but at the forefront was anger. I wondered if my mother had felt the same thing in that moment when she was a too-young witness. If trauma like this was what formed the anger in her that could split worlds. I could feel it moving around in me like an inherited parasite.

We hadn't seen our aunt Maria in at least a decade. She was an extraordinarily pretty woman. She hadn't spoken to my mother for many years after they fought over something in Abuela's estate after she passed away. I remember hearing an argument on the phone and my mother bitching to me about how her sister "didn't send flowers" and then something about Maria being upset with how Mom sold the apartment on Claremont and split the proceeds. That Mom cheated her. (Considering the dollar bills missing from my drawer, I didn't see this as a stretch.) Either way, these sisters didn't speak for at least ten years. During that time, Maria had managed her own stage 3 colon cancer diagnosis, unknown to any of us. After surgery and chemo, she survived and was sitting across from us. She looked so good, with that pile of thick gorgeous hair on her head, you'd never know she had been sick. I was a bit envious on my mother's behalf.

Maria's brutal stories of their shared childhood started the deep and long dig to build a well of forgiveness in me for my mother—her lying about who my father was and her abuse of me and my siblings. How could anyone survive all she did intact? Then to come to this country, knowing no one or the language. Married off to a Chinese gangster at nineteen. To this day I can't comprehend this life my mother had. I can only try to imagine. I can only empathize. When there was a lull in Maria's dining table revelations, I got up to go to the kitchen, closed my eyes for a moment, and thought, *Mami. I'm so sorry you went through that.*

The saying is "hurt people hurt people," but that's not something that's easy to think about when you're the one being hurt, especially as a child. Yet it seemed this saying held very true for Mom. I was beginning to understand the odds against her more and more. To feel more for her than against her, even if I was late to the table.

Maria, Alberto, my sisters, and I spent the next hour disagreeing with each other on expected roles for the women in the family. We Lupe

girls—raised with tales of American meritocracy and independence—
were happily living on our own, college educated and then some. Alberto was horrified that the oldest of my sisters wasn't married yet as she
approached thirty. Even more so when she declared that she probably
wouldn't have children. The looks on Maria's and Alberto's faces were
priceless. I think the three of us girls enjoyed shocking them (in return)
with the way we lived and our attitudes of self-direction. I later found
out that Alberto told the extended family that we were full of ourselves
and way too "gringo." Ah well. Thus hath Lupe engendered.

Our mom, the creator of our egoistic-gringa selves, lay still in her
bedroom. She was resting, but eagerly waiting to meet my brother's
newborn twins, who had just arrived. Born small and early, they were
tiny, alien girls with thin limbs who had made the five-plus-hour trip
with their mom, dad, and big sister. It was the first time we all met them
too, at only about ten weeks old. (They'd grow up healthy and gorgeous.)
With their arrival, the apartment felt like a living allegory, the cycle of
life from birth to death.

We each took turns spending alone time with Mom by her bedside.
She had withered, her tendons and bones visible under her crepe-like
olive-brown skin, tinged yellow with jaundice from a liver overtaken
with tumors. The veins on her right hand were lined with the burn tracks
of the chemo that had run through her bloodstream. She managed to
open her eyes from time to time, to move her fingers onto one of our
hands, squeeze, and smile a bit. Ted and I had brought a bottle of wine
with us from home. My mother, who hadn't let a drop of alcohol or even
the suggestion of it in the house ever, asked for a glass. She took a tiny sip
and smiled.

The respectful quiet we all tried to maintain the day after Maria and
Alberto left and my brother and his family arrived was broken by the arrival of two women from Mom's newest church, the evangelicals. This
was the church that had her initially confessing her abortions to my
brother. The congregation was mostly Latino, many Brazilians, and was
growing along with the numbers of Latinos overall moving north. I saw
this congregation as preying on a new community looking for belong-

ing, taking their money to line pockets. Mom always loved TV preachers. She was a prime candidate.

Alex opened the door to them, a pair of tiny brown middle-aged women with the insincere smiles of missionaries. I hated them already. They asked Alex to see Mom. I stood up and said I'd take them to her. There was no way that I was going to leave them in a room alone with her. I sat myself on a chair toward the back of Mom's room, facing the foot of her bed, and folded my arms. The two women sat at her bedside and held her hand. She seemed happy to see them, and for a moment I felt a bit guilty for my harsh judgment. Until they started to pray over her.

First, it was the usual prayers, recited in tempo in Spanish, asking God for grace and forgiveness. Mom's eyes were closed, and her mouth moved along with the women's words. The one who appeared to be the leader of the two, her hair dyed magenta, paused for a moment as they all bowed their heads in silence. Then came part two. The women started speaking more loudly and forcefully, the magenta one standing up, swaying, waving her hands over Mom, raising her voice in Spanish into a chant: "Get out, devil! Devil, get out of her body! Release her! Devil! Devil! (Diablo! Diablo!)" My mother contorted her face and started crying and mumbling. They were performing an exorcism.

"Okay. Está bien. Time to go." I stood up and said, "You're getting her upset. She needs her rest." I herded the surprised women out the door of Mom's room after they whispered their last prayers to her, kissing her hands. I closed it behind them, leaving me alone with Lupe. *Let Alex deal with that goodbye.*

"Mom, are you okay?" I asked her. She nodded, her eyes still closed. I took a tissue and wiped the tears off her face. "I'm sorry, Mom, but they were getting you upset, okay? You need peace. Peace and quiet." I sat next to her holding her hand as she nodded, smiled at me, and seemed to fall asleep. Did she need peace and quiet or did I? Was she getting upset or was I? Who was I to police her religious ritual? She seemed caught up in the theater and maybe she had needed it. Sure, I knew it wasn't the devil possessing her that made her so sick. And I knew that at that point she had maybe a few days left. There was no miracle that was going to heal a body barely hanging on to life. I detested those women for giving Mom false hope. But I realize now that I should have asked my mother before shooing them away. Maybe Lupe found peace in their shooing the devil out of her as I shooed the women out of the room. Who's to say he was any less real in her mind than my discomfort was in mine? Who was I to say—the former child with an altar who used to talk to spirits in her walls?

Two days later, Mom still hanging on though she'd lost consciousness, I asked my siblings to be left alone with her again. She wasn't letting go. No one could tell Lupe what to do—including Death trying to tell her it was her time—and she was going to fight it as long as she could. Before she fell asleep one last time the day before, she'd woken up struggling, crying "No-no-no!" to the air above her, as if railing against God. I wanted to let her know that we'd be okay, and that relief was on the other side. I told her those things. That she'd done good things. That we were all grown now. She could be proud. And that we'd carry on the legacy of all her hard work. "It's okay, Mom. You can go now. We love you. And always will." I laid my head down on her arm, holding her hand, just listening to her shallow, sporadic breaths. After a while, Belinda came into the room and sat at my mother's other side. My sister-in-law held Mom's other hand, and in minutes, we both watched her take her last breath. In that moment I felt relief for her. The expression on her face changed. From pain to peace. But before I could go into eldest-sister mode—wrangling funeral arrangements, shopping for the clothes she'd wear in the casket and a bra with padding (as her body had shrunk and that chest she'd always been so proud to have had caved)—I kept her hand in mine and softly wailed. No matter how contentious our relationship, no matter the resentment I carried, this was my mother. My creator. I will never stop mourning the loss of her.

A SMALL GROUP OF us, family and a handful of local friends Mom had made in her last years, stood and watched as our mother's coffin was lowered into her grave in a cemetery in the large town next door, in southern New Hampshire. It was a place we'd all driven by regularly over the years, its silent occupants all strangers then. Our mother, this Dominican immigrant woman, who started her American life in New York City, wanted very much to be buried in her adopted home of New Hampshire, among the green and trees. Despite the painful and lonely reception this place had given her and us when we arrived from Manhattan, Mom had loved it here. She'd found in her last years that more Dominicans, more Latinos of all backgrounds, had been moving north, into nearby towns. She was able to work her way up in New Hampshire to become a bigger fish in a small pond in the community. As for the city, just as I'd moved back only to find myself alone, no immediate family left, unable to re-create what I had missed so much, she'd found an empty house too. We once had a home there, in NYC, loud and brown and full of perfume and plantains, but when we both went back, the home and its people were gone. It would have to be built back up from scratch and memories. Maybe Mom was too tired. Why do that when she could start back up in the community in a place now familiar to her? And yes, more welcoming than when she'd first arrived, rolos and all.

Marty, Dad, was there in an old suit. Mom must have filled her cousins' and sister's ears about him because none of them greeted him warmly, some not at all. He stood respectfully toward the back. I had given him a hug at some point. But that day I had to place him and our new story to the back of my mind.

As the pulley withdrew from the casket, now deep and out of our sight, my mother's sister, Maria, let out a wail and ran to the edge of the empty pit, positioning herself to fall on top of Mom's casket, into the grave. Belinda's mother, Stella, a true Guyanese South American matriarch who had seen this happen a few times in her life, jumped up as fast as her knees let her and held our aunt back in a tackle hold. "No, no, you're not going with her," we could all hear her say between Maria's moans of "It should have been me!" My mother's younger sister—who didn't talk to Mom for at least ten years—was putting up quite a fight. My brother and I looked at each other in astonishment, and as our eyes met, we couldn't help but both chuckle sadly. *Fucking crazy*. It was madness, and we were not about to get involved. This was some old-school Caribbean shit, completely foreign to us. I also think that we grown kids either were ready to let Maria try to jump into that abyss or saw her performance for what it was: a performance, nothing more. No one moved a toe to stop her except Grandma Stella. I was hoping Stella would succeed in getting Maria to sit down soon because as the seconds passed by, I was starting to get angry. Causing a scene at your sister's funeral is not the I-love-you-so-much flex you think it is. It was narcissistic theater.

Finally, Stella too had had enough of this grown woman's drama. She raised her voice, "That's it! You stop this right now! This isn't about you—today isn't about you!" With her hefty arms wrapped around Maria's waist, she picked her up off the ground and moved her away from the grave, not letting go until she knew Maria was not going to fight her anymore. Stella stayed close by her, ready to be a grave bouncer again if need be, until the service was over. We six grown children of Lupe all just looked at one another and shook our heads. What a family.

CHAPTER 11

. . . Because I Didn't Know the Truth Could Ever Be Found

IN A SPAN OF EIGHTEEN MONTHS, I HAD LOST MY MOTHER, my father, a whole racial and ethnic community, identity, and heritage. Both my fiancé and I were laid off from the magazine as the print business continued to contract, a victim of the internet. I rolled all this upheaval into a ball of motivation. I promoted the shit out of my book on every medium, launched a lucrative freelance business, started my television career, and, somewhere in there, the greatest thing happened, I gave birth to a magical—and surprisingly blond, blue-eyed—baby girl. These were eighteen months of my life that I'd never want to live through again.

IT WAS LATE IN the evening, and I had just come off of hosting and coproducing the premiere of my national one-hour prime-time news show. I was slouched in the back of my ride home, the smell of the black town car making me nauseous, helped along by my curse of motion sickness. I pushed the feeling to the back of my pounding head, as I was too thrilled by what I had just done. Before I called my brother, who was always my first go-to, this time I called my dad, Marty. I wouldn't say that there was a clear reconciliation in terms of my anger at him for hold-ing on to the secret of my paternity, more like a sublimation of my feel-ings in order to keep the peace in the family, to not lose my sisters, who were much closer to him. And because it was more important to me that my daughter have a grandfather. So, we'd spoken occasionally, me calling him of course. My anger was my business, I felt. Expressing it to him wasn't going to be helpful or satisfying. The family MO was to shut down when confronted on anything. Or fight. I had neither the energy nor the desire for either. So, I kept in touch with Dad. Papi called me once in a while too, but I leaned on Alex to keep me posted on him for the most part. It was hard to tamp down all the things I wanted to say to both men, my fathers. And it was natural that what I would love to hear was their praise for what was a hard-earned, difficult accomplishment on a national stage.

"Hi, Dad! Did you watch? What'd you think?"

"Oh yeah, yeah, I did. I didn't know you could do that!" he said, genuinely surprised.

"Well, uh, yeah! I did that." I felt confused for a moment. That didn't feel like a compliment. Why didn't he know I could do that? Was his opinion of me so low that he couldn't even imagine it? I threw my praise-fishing lure out again. "So what'd you think, though?"

"Ya know, I don't know if I can watch it . . . ," he trailed off.

"What? What do you mean you can't watch it?"

"It's too depressing," he said. I knew in the back of my mind that as he'd gone through financial distress himself, it could be hard to watch people talking about their own. But I was his daughter. I wanted my par-ent to be proud of me. Someone who could put their own shit aside for a moment and see what their child had done and what she needed.

My CNBC show, *On the Money,* premiered the summer of the begin-ning of the Great Recession, riding NBC network promos along with the Olympics in 2008. My TV appearances to promote my book had led to more TV appearances and soon I had beat out over one hundred (ac-cording to the executive producer at the time) auditioning hosts in a mass casting call for what was to be a tentpole show for the start of a new network spin-off channel that would focus on lifestyle and money. Certainly, the network did not have any idea of the market crash that was about to destroy all their newness just as it started. I certainly didn't, though I did know that I was the proverbial black sheep in the building. I covered personal finance, not day-trading. I was Main Street, not Wall Street. I was also the only solo host who wasn't white.

"Why don't you use maracas? Or wear a sombrero or something!" The top producers on my show wanted me to pump up my Latinness to nab some ratings and bring new viewers to the network. We were all sitting in our windowless conference room where we hashed out the show every day. "Throw in some Spanish words! Use an accent sometimes—why not?"

"How about this: How about we build like a graphic of a fortune cookie and put your name on it—Wong—like 'Wong Wisdom' or 'Wong's World,' and then it cracks open and there's a gong—" This was from the number two producer on the show. Both white women. I shook my head and put them off with humor. That's all I could do.

Had the recession not happened and the network not lost half its advertisers, who knows how long I would have been on the air. My show was beating the highest-rated evening show on the network at the time at least twice a week—solid for a newbie. I was also the first host on the network to use social media to drum up interest and viewers. I was filming promos that aired along with the popular game show with the briefcases and girls in little dresses, a tiny me waving at viewers, superimposed on the screen, with my time slot to tune in. There was a full-page ad of me in USA Today. A giant poster of me in the magazine kiosk at LaGuardia Airport. The division head was talking about my own Times Square electronic billboard and an old-fashioned billboard along the West Side Highway, on my daily commute. It was exciting, but I didn't have a moment to enjoy it. I was beyond exhausted.

I look back at clips from my time hosting that show and say something similar to what Marty said to me: "How the hell did I do that?" Well, I had to do that because my home life was falling apart and I knew that soon enough, I'd end up a single parent, possibly paying alimony. I was not going to fail and not give my child financial stability. But also, hosting and coproducing that show was the only job I've ever had where every single bit of me was utilized. All my skills and smarts running on all cylinders. It was a state of flow, and intoxicating for that one hour. And the male guests, damn, they fueled my competitive spirit no end. I fed off their low expectations like a surf and turf dinner. Of course, their dismissal of me wasn't only because I was a woman.

Gratefully, a few months into the show, I ended up with a young, bright Canadian executive producer who was totally up on all the bullshit that came my way. I started a "drinking game" with him. Guests on the set were asking me so often if I was "Hispanic" or "Spanish" that when they did, we'd all pretend to down a tequila shot. It's helpful to have a great team. I miss working with them.

The network demanded that I essentially run a full marathon every day. (And they asked me to wear tighter dresses, to lose weight, to smile more, and all the things you can imagine come the way of a woman on air not that long ago.) When I came down hard with massive food poisoning, they called the nearest hospital to get me in, pumped me up with meds and fluids, and had me editing that day's show from my hospital bed. Two hours after the IV was taken out of my arm, I was out of the makeup chair and ready to go. No one watching knew the difference. Trust me, I asked.

I missed my baby girl so hard it tore a hole in my chest every day, but I couldn't stop. I knew my marriage was over. That it was just a matter of time. And then what? I was the main breadwinner. I didn't think I had a choice. I had turned into the "dad" who worked too much. And yes, I did want to succeed in my work and was proud of where I ended up, but I needed it to take less from me so I could give more to my girl.

A bottle of pink Pepto occupied a permanent spot on my executive producer's desk—this was the boss of the whole division, not my sensible Canadian. I kept my eyes on the bottle, noting its level was getting low, as I sat down in front of her, called to her office for an unscheduled meeting.

"Whazzup?" I asked.

"Um, so . . . ," she said. I could see the dissonance in her head play itself out on her face. "I wanted to tell you before it hit the papers in the morning."

"Okaaaaay," I said.

"I mean, I dunno who leaked it but it's out there, so . . . ," she said as I just stared at her, thinking, *You leaked it, whatever it is.* She finished her thought, "We've ended the show."

"What."

"Done. We're done. Look, we had a good run, but ya know, we just couldn't do it."

I took a breath. "So, the show we just wrapped, that was the last one? No goodbyes or anything?"

"Uh, nope. Yup. That was it."

Why am I smiling? Don't smile! It wasn't just a smile forcing its way onto my face, it was a full-blown grin. *Fuck. My show is canceled. Failure, right? Then why do I feel so goddamn happy and relieved?*

"Well. Okay, then," I said, taking in a deep breath, still smiling.

My boss looked at me like I was nuts. Then she told me how my contract was for another year so I was going to remain at the network, popping up here and there to do interstitials, local news segments, etc. All I could think about was my B, my golden-haired little girl, whom I could possibly now spend time with. It had been only a year with this insane workload. Maybe it wasn't too late. Maybe I could have at least one day off a week now. Maybe this was a good thing.

It was and it wasn't. I did get to go home and hug and smooch my little girl, take her to the Bronx Zoo the next day, recoup some sleep. But with the end of my marriage looming, I couldn't stay still for too long.

I kept doing TV to the point where I was on air (again) seven days a week with one stretch of work lasting forty-seven straight days. But despite invitations to be on a full hour of *Oprah* (only to be canceled the night before I was to fly to Chicago because someone else insisted on doing my show, ahem), appearances on *The View*—Barbara Walters asking me in her famous accent in front of the live audience, "Oh, Carmen, what aaaaare you?"—a pilot test with Paula Deen (no comment needed here), short contracts at CBS and CNN, and a few more pilots that flopped, going back to TV full-time was not to be. And about that, I was okay. I had built a business with multiple income streams; TV turned into my personal public relations siphon rather than my bread and butter. I was booking five-figure speaking engagements, taking on consulting gigs from banks that paid ridiculously well. Within the first year after my TV network contract ended, I was making double what I'd made hosting my prime-time television show. And in some ways, I'm sure that despite the extreme prejudice of many people in the business, my color and "ethnic" name assuaged their guilt and gave the media I was on a diversity halo that advertisers liked. Checked many boxes. But I just did what I always did. Kept at it, blinders on, using what I had how I could, just as Lupe taught me. *There is no competition but you.*

Most important of all, I saw my child. Outside of the few days each month that I'd travel to speak, and the hour or two I'd spend going into the city from Brooklyn to do a TV hit, I was home. Working from home, dropping my girl off and picking her up from the kindergarten two blocks up the street, making breakfasts and dinners, bath time, reading before bed, then I'd work at night after she was asleep, after we held each other together, tight, before she drifted off. Because though I gained my professional autonomy back, and my time and focus, it was now just her and me at home, and our new rescue pup. All three of us girls holding one another together. The mêlée of the previous two years included both my biggest professional highs and my absolute personal lows. As goes life.

Again, the thought gnawed at me: I thought I did everything right. I worked so hard. How did I end up here? Divorce number two. The betrayals worse than number one, plus a child, made this the most painful period of my life. Too deep, too much, and not yet far enough in my rearview mirror to share. It brought both my daughter and me to years of therapy.

Maybe ten years after the premiere of my show, only a few years ago, I was in therapy and recounted for my therapist that time when I called my dad from the car ride home after my first show and what I felt was his painful response to my work and achievement: "It's too depressing."

"So I don't factor into this assessment? His daughter? He couldn't watch the show to support me? To cheer me on? Compliment me or something?" I was crying. "My sisters didn't even watch the show nor cared, my mother wasn't around, Papi was certainly not watching it, and only Alex watched—he's my biggest fan." I sniffed. "He watched and taped every single one. My last show aired right before his Super Bowl party and he put it up on his big screen where everybody was while I was there, which was tooootally embarrassing." I rolled my eyes. "But it was nice. He was proud of me."

I remembered Alex's face lit up as he pointed to the screen with the remote, my blown-out hair and heavily made-up face looming over the gathering, "Hey guys—my sister! That's her show!"

Abruptly, the connections in my head lit up and my back straightened.

"Wait. What if . . . What if—my dad . . . He used to watch that network in particular all the time, every day, and he read the magazines where I used to work all the time. . . . What if I so wanted to be seen by him—*seen*—that I put myself into the pages he read and then on the screens he watched? So that he'd *see* me?"

My therapist, one of the wisest men I've ever known, nodded vigorously.

"But," I said, "he still changed the channel."

I PUT MY DAUGHTER FIRST, which meant prioritizing family for her, visiting Alex, Belinda, and their girls often, making the drive back and forth between the city and Maryland a regular jaunt, just as Mom had made the drive up and down the Northeast from New Hampshire to the city when we were kids. For decades I have wished and hoped that family, my brother and his, or my sisters, would live near me. But I was the only one who chose to return to the city, our first home, my birthplace.

So, like my mother, I drove a lot. But unlike her, I had distanced myself from them of my own accord, my roots in the city too strong to pull out and start over. My love for my home so tight it was a fabric woven into my skin.

B and I, a little two-person family, was nontraditional enough, but there was also the issue of race. When she was a baby, the fact that I was brown and she appeared white meant being held by immigration at the airport until they could google me, making sure I wasn't kidnapping my own (blond) child; or, it was nannies in the park thinking I was a nanny, or au pairs thinking I was an au pair, or all the moms at pick-up and drop-off thinking I was an au pair or nanny. Now that she was older, my girl started to notice that the family and world around her was a different shade. She had a brown mama and our brown family, my sisters, her Black cousins, plus her Auntie Belinda and Grandma Stella. And, oh yes, her Chinese grandfather, Papi, whom we'd see a couple of times a year. Sometimes she'd cry because we didn't "match" or because she wanted to be Black like her cousins and "Obama and Beyoncé!" She and I grew up on the flip sides of a racial mirror. I wanted to be a girl like her growing up and she wanted to be like me.

I had long talks with B about how she came out with porcelain skin, blue eyes, and light hair even though her genes carried African ancestry. Her phenotype (physical expression of genes) did not reflect her genotype (genetic code) and the outside world responds only to one, the outside. We spoke about how Latina is not a race. We talked about how her cousins, who were darker-skinned like their mother, ended up in the same boat of phenotype trippin'. They had the same Chinese grandfather that their big sister did, a big sister who looked clearly "Blasian" (Black and Asian) like her dad, Alex, and they all had Spanish/European heritage too but looked not a drop Asian or European. Alex and I would mull over our kids and discuss their racial identities, experiences, and worlds often. When you're this mixed, talk about race and identity is inescapable.

One long weekend when Alex and his three daughters came to visit, we all took Papi out for dinner in Chinatown. I hadn't seen him in a while, had been keeping my distance, as I didn't want to answer questions about my divorce. He'd known my ex-husband, as I made sure to see Papi at least a couple of times a year. I'd talk to him on the phone often, though. He'd call at least once a week, asking how the baby was doing and when would I see him. My feelings regarding the secret I knew didn't factor much anymore as I was filled up so much with the pile of life on my plate, no chaser. I still felt a claim for him as my father. He was my father still, in a way. My B needed to know that.

I had done TV earlier that day of the dinner, so my hair was blown out and my makeup still on. We asked the server to take our photo on our way out, and every time I look at that picture, I shake my head—it's incredible. Even though I wasn't Chinese biologically—and no, I haven't told Papi; I kept my word to Alex and always will—we were all still related. Yet most people would look at that photo and not see one family but a hodgepodge of what looks like unrelated people of all different races. But we were family and are. Unlike our childhoods, Alex and I were raising daughters who had the privilege of being upper-middle-class with highly educated parents, while his girls and my girl were at opposite ends of the spectrum when it came to what their races mean in this country. My brother with his Black girls and his sister, me, with a white one.

Because my brother and I grew up as we did, and now even more with our children appearing so different, Alex and I were fascinated by genetic testing early on. We shared an apprehension, though, for the storage and use of our genetic material, while I was more worried about the financial implications of what insurance companies could do if they could know what your genes held in your future, health-wise. But I took the leap first into genetic testing, my curiosity too strong. Ancestry.com was rudimentary early on as the data was built off respondents, so the data couldn't be deep and clear until a larger number of people took the test. Initially, the site couldn't tell me much. I was of southern European and African descent. But no specificity in Europe, where I was hoping to see Marty's Italian history. It did however make clear that I wasn't Chinese. And I saw no surprise relatives. The results for me were unfulfilling. But with time, the technology grew, and a new site promised deeper digs.

Just before the winter holidays in 2018, my brother, on our usual near-daily call, said, "Did you know that 23andMe is having a holiday sale? I'm gonna get a kit for me and C." He and I loved nerding out on tech or science. It was like his Asimov novels and *Omni* magazine coming to fruition. He was especially excited to take the test with his eldest daughter, C, a budding scientist at MIT who was majoring in bioengineering.

"Well, shit, sign me up!" I said. I couldn't resist. My genetic heritage had shaped my life much too much to ignore. Plus I did want to know all that medical stuff. I was a planner and all about prevention. After my mother's death, I was the first in the family to sign up for a colonoscopy, which is now an annual preventive appointment in my calendar after polyps were found four years ago. If I was to learn that I had a faulty gene for something, maybe I could get ahead of it somehow.

Alex got his results first. He was thrilled to report to me that he was a descendant of Genghis Khan (as are one in two hundred men of Asian descent). I had a few more days to wait for my reveal. My expectations in terms of family history were that I would see, in printed letters on a screen, that I was truly not Chinese but half Italian. The knowledge that this was coming to me renewed my feelings of melancholy at again losing my genetic ties to the Wong family and my dear brother. Trying to think of the bright side, I told Alex, "Oh, well. I guess now I'll see that I'm full siblings with all the girls." But that made me sad too. My tie with my brother was tighter and stronger than the one I had with anyone in the family. I wasn't looking forward to seeing more confirmation of the Wonder Twins' half-sibling status.

It had never sat right in my gut that I was Marty's biological child. I chalked the feeling up to too many years being Papi's kid, even though I had wanted to be Marty's child. For me and Papi, it was three decades of a bond with family, culture, and a people. You can't turn that off. My feelings of confusion and skepticism about my stepfather being my "real" father were three layers below a feeling of inevitability in the results that were coming to me, and just under that, deep disappointment that my parents had lied to me for the first thirty-one years of my life. Sadness that what was about to be confirmed was the lie that they'd raised me with, one they surely didn't think through. Not only a lie about who my father was but a lie about my race.

As I popped down the stairs leading to the entrance of the gym in my building, I refreshed the emails on my phone. My 23andMe results were in. I stopped at the waiting area just before the gym entrance, sat on the couch, quickly logged in, and opened the results.

Strange.

I scrolled and scrolled through the report. *Where's the Italian?* My heart began to thud in my ears.

It was clear that I was not Chinese, and I saw and clicked on Alex's request to connect, which would then compare our results and state our genetic relationship. I scrolled through the results again, a bit surprised too at how African I was (25 percent), the map showing a big blob of descent all over the Caribbean, but what should have been a full 50 percent or close to it of Italian (Amalfi Coast was where Marty's family had emigrated from) was almost all Portuguese. *Portuguese?* What the hell. I started to panic and speed-dialed my brother.

"Portuguese? Well, isn't Italy close to Portugal?" Alex said, trying to calm me somehow but knowing full well that that was incorrect. "One of the girls [our sisters] needs to take the test and see, and then you can link up too and see what happens."

He was right. So I called up the oldest of the four, anxiously told her what happened, and asked if she'd take the test and link up with me. She was happy to. My head was spinning and I couldn't focus in the gym. I went back up to my apartment and tried to get on with my day and the next couple of weeks of my life with a heavy question mark making itself at home in my head.

AT CHRISTMAS AND NEW YEAR'S holiday break, my B and I started our family travels by driving north to New Hampshire to see the family there, including Marty, who would drive up from Rhode Island. As conflicted as my feelings have been, I very much wanted my B to have a solid relationship with him. As she was only with me so much, she needed her Tio Alex and her Grandpa. I'd love to say that I forgave and moved on from my anger at my dad, but instead I'll say this: I grew myself into a wiser woman who could see him as a human being, faults and all. And yes, privileges and all. Privileges of maleness and whiteness that my mother didn't have. Still, though, a flawed human being that I loved very much. I made sure B and I saw him at a minimum twice a year, once during the holidays and then during the summer, and B did grow to love him very much as well. I watched her learn how to play chess with him when she was six years old, a skill that I never had the patience to focus on, and Dad enjoyed playing with her. He gifted her a folding wooden chess set she has to this day.

Later, we'd head down to Maryland to spend holiday time with the Wongs, my brother and his family. The evening before we were to head down, the Wong family FaceTimed me and B. They were all sitting down to eat dinner, their phone propped up so we could see nearly all the table and who was seated or milling about. B and I were on to eating dessert, so we chatted together, Alex, Belinda, their three daughters, and Grandma Stella, as if we were all in the same room. The conversation was lively and loving. We were all excited to see each other the next day. Then Alex brought up our 23andMe results.

"Did you see all the African countries we have?" I asked. Twelve in total for me and Alex, our mother's Dominican history a product of the slave trade across continents. We listed them off for the girls: "Nigeria, Angola, Congo, Benin . . ."

I logged in to my 23andMe profile to make sure to get the countries right.

"Oh!" I yelped. "Nina accepted my connection . . . let me see . . ."

WHAT.

My hands flew to cover my whole face—eyes, nose, mouth, everything.

B, concerned, said, "Mom! What? What happened?"

Everyone on the other side of the camera also got quiet and looked at me.

On my computer screen, in black-and-white and in capital letters, as clear as day, the relationship between me and my sister said HALF-SISTER. No. *No, no, no.*

My heart shrunk backward into my chest. How was this possible?

"Tia. Tia, what?" my nieces asked. Alex leaned down into the camera to get a better look at me.

Through my fingers I whispered, "I can't believe it. I can't believe it." The word "half-sister" grew larger and darker in my vision. I kept staring at it, thinking it would change. B sat next to me and looked at my screen.

"Half-sister?" my daughter said.

Everyone who heard on the other side of the screen sucked in their breath.

"What?" Belinda said.

"Half-sister?" Alex repeated.

I finally was able to speak. "It says 'half-sister.'"

My child and the teenage twins let out an adolescent "Ooooooo!" in unison.

"Alex! How can this be?" I knew the answer, but I had to ask my brother, the person who always came to my aid, who reassured me that everything was going to be okay, whether it was another divorce or Mom screaming at me as a teenager. "This means that there's *another father*! That I don't share a father with *anyone*!"

"You have another father? Wow, Mom. Your life *is* like a telenovela!" my child said. (I loved her wide-eyed wonder at our nutty family history.)

"Let me see," Alex said. "I'll log in and connect with her too." He left the table to get his laptop.

The voice of Grandma Stella, Belinda's mother, rang out from her usual spot at the far head of the dining table. "What did she say?" she asked the kids. "What's going on?"

"Grannie, she said——" one of the twins started but was interrupted by Belinda.

"She has another father—a different one than Marty or Peter." I could hear the unsaid "incredible" from my sister-in-law in the tone of her voice, her face off-screen.

"Another father? So what!" Grandma exclaimed.

"So what?" Belinda and I responded. The kids laughed. Alex was quiet, back at the table logging in to his account.

I still had my head in my hands. I was blocking out the world. It was too much. Much too much. But with the kids all watching, I had to make sure to keep it as light as I could. This was ridiculous, after all. It felt absolutely ridiculous. My mother was dead, and not only did she lie about who my father was, she lied *two times* over! And she got Marty to think that he was my father my whole life. And Papi to think that *he* was my father my whole life. Passing me off to *both* men as their daughter? But I am not related at all to *either* of them. And she took it to her grave. Damn. *Mom*.

The question of why I'd always felt so different from my siblings was answered. Why I felt like I was floating out of orbit from them all, tethered only to my mother and Alex. But goddamn, I was shaken by not knowing who the hell my father was and that Lupe dared to die with the truth.

B AND I SAT in an alcove, leaning into each other, playing a game on her phone, in what used to be Oscar de la Renta's home in colonial Santo Domingo, the capital of the Dominican Republic. It was the former residence of my abuela's once jefe, boss. It was February 2019, just a few weeks after the news the genetic test revealed: that I was the one kid in the family who didn't know her biological father. The air was warm and humid like a familiar blanket that always warmed my heart. This annual mother-daughter Presidents' Day trip for me and B started out lovely and like a dream. I took my daughter on a city tour to see places like the capitol building, the malecón (boardwalk), Columbus's mausoleum (weighty and macabre for us, as we suffered no romantic notions about the island's history). We ate an early dinner outside in the cobblestone public square a short walk from the bed-and-breakfast where we were staying. I saw my daughter fall in love with the music and colors and the chicharrón that tasted somehow magical in my mother's homeland. "Mom, can we come here all the time? I could totally live here," she said as we walked the neighborhood, careful not to trip over the many centuries-old stones of the sidewalk. Of course, B was seeing the rarefied and moneyed side of this city. Not the D.R. my mother grew up in. This one was lined with hot-pink azaleas, peaceful within its boundaries. I saw it all through B's eyes, but I also saw it through my mother's and heard and felt the footsteps of the thousands who came before us, of their own volition and not, our ancestors.

"Oh, B. Auntie Belinda is calling me. I wonder why." My cellphone rang. I always picked up if Belinda or Alex called. We were sitting in the courtyard of our hotel, having a nibble and cool drink.

"Hi, B!" I said happily. Belinda was the original "B." "The OG B," as I called her.

She was crying.

"We're at the hospital. Alex was admitted. They ran some tests. He has fluid around his lungs—remember that cough he couldn't get rid of?"

"Yes," I said.

"It's cancer," she said, and sobbed.

A force punched into my chest, gripped my heart, and squeezed until I couldn't breathe. I couldn't breathe. Not Alex.

"Belinda. Belinda" was all I could say through tears.

I flashed back to teasing Alex at his family dinner table about what I thought was a tic (because we both had tics once in a while) recently, the clearing of his throat. *It was cancer.* I flashed back to him coughing and looking pale as we all sat on the beach just a few months before on vacation together with our girls. *Cancer.* His doctor had told him it was allergies. Belinda and I pressed him a bit to get it taken care of somehow, medications or something. But he had been so busy. He loved being busy. Loved working hard.

I told Belinda that we were going to cut our trip short and fly back the next morning to pick up our things and drive down to them and to the hospital to see him. My B was holding my hand and telling me as I cried, "Mom, Mom, it's gonna be okay."

TWO DAYS LATER, B and I were in the hospital in Washington, D.C., with Alex, Belinda, and his girls. I waited until our next visit, after he was discharged, to start talking theories as to who my father could be. Together, as he started chemotherapy and recovery, we became amateur sleuths, sitting at his desk in his finished basement in Maryland talking through scenarios and family stories, searching the internet for clues from places Mom may have worked, where she may have had dalliances, like an optometrist's on Delancey Street I'd heard about from Pimpa, my godmother.

During one weekend afternoon detective session, Alex had an idea. "You know who may know? Epi, Cookie's mom, down in Florida."

"Epi? But why?" I asked.

Epi was Alex's godmother. She and her daughter, Cookie, were related to us through our grandmother's, Abuela's side. They had come to Maryland a few years earlier when I threw both Alex and Belinda a fiftieth birthday party. But Epi had had a stroke and was limited in mobility.

"She was Mom's best friend—outside of Pimpa. Plus she was closer in age. I bet she knows," he said.

"In Florida?" I looked up at him, his head now bald from chemo. He nodded. "Okay then!" I said. "We're going to Florida!"

Everything becomes so much more doable when there's the urgency of someone being sick, a clock ticking loudly, as cancer does. He and I and Belinda planned travel dates and made our Florida trip happen. Alex and I stayed in Miami with our daughters while Belinda stayed in Maryland to watch over her mother. How far we'd come from the last time we had been in Florida together, two kids melting outside in the heat in the parking lot of the greyhound racetrack, waiting for our father to stop gambling. But the best outcome of the trip was watching our daughters happily enjoying Cookie's saltwater swimming pool and her husband grilling us the most insanely delicious meal. My girl and Alex's twins giddy together: "Oh, when can we come back? We love it! I wanna live here!" they'd say.

Unfortunately, Epi had no idea who my biological father could be. None.

After we left, Cookie promised to try to jog her mother's memory as best she could. But I wasn't too hopeful because as Epi told me herself as we held hands, "Your mother was very private."

That was one way to put it.

It was time to ask the only other person who was close to Lupe then: Dad.

CHAPTER 12

. . . Because You Know Who You Are

T HE WILD THING ABOUT DNA TECHNOLOGY—AND SCI-ence in general—is that it keeps getting more precise. Over the months since the discovery of the third father in the family, mine, I had developed a new daily routine: refreshing the 23andMe app on my cellphone. For months I thought that maybe, just maybe, this would be the day that a sibling or first cousin or even a second cousin on my mystery father's side would appear in the New Relatives section. I refreshed and refreshed and refreshed every day in what felt like The Game of Life. *Roll again— you have a father!* But instead of the answers I was looking for, or should I say the people I was looking for, all I got was a growing legion of hundreds of third, fourth, and fifth cousins. None close enough in relation for me to connect to this man's identity.

This mystery ate at me from the inside out. Every day. I was looking in the mirror at my nose again, wanting to see it in another face, my father's face. I thought about my brother, in a dire state from an aggressive cancer now too common in Asians, particularly Chinese, a genetic code he inherited from Papi's side. Time was precious and pressured. I needed to know. I needed to know who I came from. Who made me with my mother. Even if it was from something horrible like violence or coercion. Or something beautiful, if only for a day. To call my former (I guess?) father, Marty, to ask him if he knew who his wife had cheated on him with (even though he, himself, had been a cheatee with this married woman) churned my stomach. *Gee, Dad, do you know who Mom was screwing while you were screwing her while she was married to someone else?* This was all awkward, to say the least. Parental infidelity is not a topic of discussion anyone wants to have with a parent, let alone infidelities found decades later by the human being you helped raise who was the product of it.

One late weekday afternoon, sitting at my desk in my home office, I had had enough of my painful procrastination. The answer could be right there. I just had to be brave enough to call Marty. Fed up with myself— *Stop being a chickenshit, this is your information to know*—I picked up my cell and dialed, my chest tight with anxiety. This wasn't just about me, of course. Asking my dad what he knew meant first telling him that I was not his daughter. I had no idea how he'd react. Would he be furious? Furious at Mom? Would he cry and be sad at losing me? I steeled myself for consoling him or talking him down. I looked out the window in front of me, the view lined with shiny glass city buildings, and said to myself: *Deep breath.*

"Dad? So, um. So, back during the holidays, me, Alex, and Nina took a DNA test, an ancestry thing."

"Oh. Oh, yeah? What'd ya find?" he asked.

"Uh, Dad, I have another father." The words had barely left my mouth before I fell into full-on sobbing. I was the one crushed. I had just orphaned myself.

By telling Marty that he too was not my father, my mother now dead for years, I made myself an orphan with one phone call. As long as someone thought they were my father, I still had a live parent. No longer.

Through my wet sobs, Dad ended up consoling me. "Oh, now, now. You know I'm still your dad. No one's gonna take that away." (This spoke to my heart that needed a father, but the echo of it felt more a bit "I'll have my cake and eat it too"—I hid that I was your father your whole life but I still get to claim it now.)

"I know. I know." I sniffed. "It's just so sad."

"Oh, well, your mother, I tell ya." He sighed. It sounded like a shrug of the shoulders. The same "That's Lupe" that had him lying about my paternity to keep the peace. I knew that shrug too well.

"I'm sorry," I said, wrongly apologizing for my emotions.

"It's okay. This doesn't change things. Doesn't change all these years," he said, sounding very calm.

"But"—I blew my nose and wiped my eyes and face—"who could it be? I mean, do you have any idea? Of who Mom could have been with then?"

"Hmmm. There was this Cuban doctor at the clinic your mom used to work at. I used to pick up her and her sister after work from there. I never liked him."

Oh my god. A rival? Her boss? Or colleague?

"Dad, any chance you remember his name? Or the clinic?" I asked.

"Nope. Not the name . . . but the clinic . . . I don't remember the name, but it was just off the Cross Bronx parkway there. I remember that because of the drive."

That's all Dad had for me. But it felt like a lot because I hoped beyond hope that I could trust this was somehow the truth coming from him. My biological father was maybe a Cuban doctor. Well, Madame Accomplishment that I am, you know I was happy to hear I was spawned—possibly—by an MD.

I called Alex right after I hung up with Marty. "So I guess I'm an orphan now," I said through more tears.

The feelings I'd grown up with of floating just beyond my family, being outside of them, on my own and disconnected, entrenched in a new, more tragic way. There was no rule book or guide for how to manage these discoveries. I had offered advice for years in my columns and on air. This was all too specific. Where would I find "When You've Orphaned Yourself with a Phone Call"? Or "Your Parents Have Been Lying to You All Along: A Guide to Parental Deception" (maybe that one exists)? I could have used "You Thought You Knew Your Father? How to Father Yourself." Or "What to Do When You Were Raised the Wrong

Race." And then for extra credit, "Oreos, Bananas, and Coconuts: Managing the Whiteness Inside."

Loneliness cut in a different way that day. Would I ever find my other family? And would they want anything to do with me? Or would I want to have anything to do with them?

I plopped down some bucks and hired a genealogist team. They had all my accounts, from Ancestry.com and 23andMe to GEDmatch, the national database that pulls all the ancestry DNA sites together (and is known for solving cold-case murders via DNA). I joined Facebook genealogy groups and The DNA Detectives, posting pleas for information and guidance. I got some comments that I knew were going to come my way: "Your father is the one that raised you. That's all you need." No shit. As if I hadn't thought of that. But that wasn't good enough and also wasn't the point. It was that mentality that got me into this mess after all. The don't-ask-just-do-as-I-say condescending school of parenting.

Hours and sleepless weeks went by as I became my own amateur detective. I managed to track down what I thought could be the clinic that Mom could have worked at in the Bronx, Lincoln Hospital. (There were news clippings on the hospital in 1970, as it was the site of a takeover by the Young Lords, "a militant Puerto Rican" group, per *The New York Times*. They were looking to improve conditions and worker pay in a place they called a "butcher shop" of a hospital.) I spent Saturday mornings when B was sleeping scouring troves of reports and photos online, trying to see if I could find a doctor's name that matched names in my list of relatives. One photo halted me. It was a black-and-white picture documenting the doctor coalition that negotiated with the Young Lords at Lincoln Hospital during the takeover. In the line of doctors, side by side, was a younger man, handsome, a full shock of thick black hair. We had similar eyes and nearly the same long nose. He was looking into the camera. *Is it you?*

ALL THIS LOOKING FOR my father, and I was losing my brother. The day before the first anniversary of my brother's cancer diagnosis, I was sitting by Alex's side, crying, in the hospital. He was unconscious and close to dying. Days before, he had been awake but in pain. His daughters, Belinda, my daughter, and I had all been with him, scrunched into his small private room for hours, keeping him company, trying to make him laugh. (I attempted to give him a shave with an electric razor—that was a hoot and a mess.) The hospice counselor felt that having so many of us in the room with him was making him agitated so she asked us to keep it to only two people at a time. We took turns sitting with him, holding his frail hands, all tendons and yellow, just like Mom's had been before she passed. His breath beleaguered, his lungs near tapping out. We knew the end was very near, so we took turns spending time alone with him. Marty was there too, along with our sisters. We took up two waiting rooms in the hospice center. The six of us kids back together again with Dad. Not in the way we'd ever want to imagine. One of us was dying.

It was my turn for alone time with him. After telling my big brother how mad I was that he was leaving me, how unfair of the universe it was to take him, and how much I'd miss him, to my soul, I gave him a mission: "Alex, you do me a favor, okay?" I cupped his hand in mine and spoke out loud. "When you get up there and you see Mom, you find out who my father is, okay? You tell her she's got to tell you." I knew that hearing was the last sense to go so I hoped he was hearing me. "And you find out and then you find a way to tell me, okay? I mean it. You go up there and get her to tell you." I paused. "Goddamn her, Alex." My brother sympathized with me in this plight. He knew better than anyone what all this who's-my-daddy business was doing to me. How much it hurt me that Mom took this to her grave and left it up to the rest of us— mostly me—to clean up and deal with the mess she'd left behind. He knew how lonely it made me feel within our own family.

My big brother, my Wonder Twin, passed away the next morning, one year to the day of that heartbreaking call from Belinda while we were in the Dominican Republic: 2/22/2020. There are not enough words to communicate the devastation I felt in my soul. And it's too new to do the pain justice with words. Too new and too deep. I don't think

I'll ever feel less grief about losing my first, my best friend, my brother and closest family member. The man in my daughter's life who showed up and showed her love. The man who showed up for me. We grow around the grief. It doesn't get smaller.

What I didn't expect to feel was a particular anger. Sure, Kübler-Ross's stages of grief lists anger as a stage, but this felt much darker. My ire was specifically toward whatever god was out there who took him away from us and his family, so young, before taking someone like Papi. The continued existence of Peter "Papi" Wong on this earth at eighty-eight years old, a man who did not run his life as my brother did—with a focus on being a father to his children, a legitimate co-provider and a present husband to his wife. Why take Alex and not him? This was proof to me that the universe is so far from fair that to expect that we have any control in tipping the scales in our favor for any reason is to be delusional.

Later that summer, during the near lull in the pandemic, Belinda came to see us with the twins so we could all visit Papi in Brooklyn.

"Papi, I'm here now, aren't I?" I tried to keep it light and not yell.

"No, no, you always say that." Papi was trying to amble from his chair to his desk in his tiny one-room studio apartment in Catholic Charities housing that Alex was able to move him to years prior after five years on a waiting list. His pants were tied around his waist with shoelaces as he'd lost too much weight to keep any pants up and refused to wear pants that I'd buy him. He'd been suffering from recurring prostate cancer for over twenty years and late-stage kidney cancer for nearly five. Yet he outlived his son.

Alex hadn't wanted Papi to know he was so sick. He knew that his father would want to go live with them in Maryland to help take care of him. But though they had an extra bedroom and bathroom in their finished basement, Papi would be much too much of a demanding disruption for everyone, so Alex asked us all to keep up the ruse that he had some kind of lung problem but not that it was cancer. (Deception, truly a family tradition.) This walk around the truth rather than simply confronting the man with a boundary, saying "No. You can't come see me and I don't want to see you right now." But that was not their relationship. Peter verbally abused Alex, consistently. And when Alex was a child, physically. Yet my brother did his "duty" and took care of his father. I hated it. I hated that he put up with it. I told him time and time again that it was his right to say "Enough!" And mean it. But I also accepted that this was Alex's choice. And it was easier for me to say as this was no longer my father too, and Peter was never abusive to me. Alex was the "bad son," and I was a bit too absent for his liking, but all he did was complain "Why you no call me? Why you no call your Papi?" And I'd answer: "But I'm talking to you now, right?" And he'd take that as a cue to stop.

But once Alex passed away, Papi turned his bile toward me.

The Wong twins and my B, all teenagers now, thin and lanky, sat together in the one lounge chair in the studio apartment, a bulky, beat-up maroon pleather. Belinda and I stood. Papi's place was a run-down, low-ceiling space, linoleum floors peeling, everything a shade of sandy brown either on purpose or from use. A small flat-screen TV I had bought him sat dark and barely used on a large folding card table behind us, next to piles of paperwork and old sales documents from his sometimes-legitimate work. (A few years back after we'd taken him to a doctor's appointment, he told Alex and me how he'd do "monkey business" with the way his home attendants got paid so they both could pocket cash from the government program. Once a con man, always . . .) Between his two windows Papi hung his Chinese newspaper clippings, stories on politics and pop stars. This was a collage he rotated in and out, arts and crafts like my tween hobby of hanging up ripped-out pages of my favorite bands from teen magazines.

"Listen to me." Papi pointed at me, his tone one he had never used toward anyone but Alex. "You listen to me now! You no care about Papi! How many years, huh? How many years you no visit me? You no call me?"

The girls hung their heads, uncomfortable with the tension in the air. Though I had witnessed their grandfather in this mood, they had never heard him raise his voice like this.

"I'm here now!" I said sternly. This time that didn't work. He just kept at me.

"No! You don't talk!" he yelled at me. It hurt.

Belinda stepped in to defend me. It calmed him down for only a moment.

Now I knew why it was easier to just take it and move on. When I'd stand my ground, he'd get nastier, in my face. Was it worth it? Certainly not in front of our kids. No. I was not going to let that happen. We stuck around for only a little longer once he'd relaxed a bit. All five of us walked out onto the sidewalk, deflated from the experience. The girls seemed rattled.

"I guess I'm the bad guy now," I said to Belinda. "Now that Alex is gone."

"Yeah," she agreed. "I guess so."

But now he would be my responsibility. I am the last Wong of my generation. He's a father to me but no longer my father. A criminal father, an abusive father, a charming, chatty, funny father. A giver of money and a taker of joy. The origin of my Chinese self. My brother's father and grandfather to his children, our children. I will one day bury him too. But I will never inter my memories of being Asian.

WORD GOT AROUND MY mother's extended Dominican family that I was looking for my biological father. Or, should I say, the chisme (gossip) was that Guadalupe, Cita, as she was known as a kid, had pulled the ultimate escándalo (scandal). This worked in my favor, or so I thought. A cousin that I hadn't seen or heard from since Abuela's funeral back in the early nineties messaged me on Facebook. He wanted to hop on the phone.

"So, I was talking with my mother about Cita, your mom, and how you're looking for your father, and she said that the gossip was that it was your godmother's brother," he said.

"Pimpa's brother? Hmm. He lived down the hall so that'd make sense. I think I remember a brother." I flipped through the files of all my memories of Claremont that had to do with hanging out with Pimpa and her mother and other neighbors and cousins. I found an image in my mind of a thin, dark-haired, narrow-faced young man maybe even younger than my mom was at that time.

This felt like the best lead I'd had, maybe ever. It set me on fire. I spent a full workday and through the night doing my detective work online through public information sites to find names and photos. I reached out to Pimpa, who was taken aback by this suggestion. She actually had two brothers. I thought it was one, she thought it was the other.

"Wouldn't that be so nice, to be actual, real family?" she said.

(Let's not get ahead of ourselves.)

One brother, the one she thought could be my father, was a doctor in Atlanta. Well, that was one check mark, but I looked at photos and didn't feel that thing in my gut that I thought I needed to feel. That I knew I'd feel—or hoped I would—when I saw the right man. Thanks to social media again, I found his young son who looked so much like he could be my son or brother, it was uncanny.

The other brother, though. Tall, fit, and handsome, in his seventies. Like the doctor in the black-and-white news photo. Tan skin and full head of neat, straight white hair. Glistening teeth. He could have been a politician. He was the president of a tech and engineering company down in Orlando, Florida, with a degree in engineering. *A fellow nerd.* I found his email address and his LinkedIn profile. Again, I gathered the mental strength to make the move to ask a man a very awkward and heavy question: *Are you my father?*

In the email I sent that day to him, I gave my cell number. The next morning, I woke up to a voicemail he'd left after I fell asleep and missed his call, sounding pleasant as could be but adamant that he was not my father. The message made me sad, but I was heartened by his offer to help in any way and to call him back if I'd like to. So I did call and reached him midday. His tone was very different from the one on his message. Any awkwardness gone. It was replaced by vim and vigor.

"Carmen! Holy shit! When I saw your picture online, I said, that's Lupe reincarnated!" He sounded giddy. It made me smile. I asked him what he remembered about Mom, and he asked me about my brother and sisters, and we talked happily for over an hour. Only toward the end did I mention 23andMe, to which he said, "Oh! I did 23andMe." My stomach fell. This canceled him out as a possibility of being my father, or any relation at all to him or his brother.

"Oh, we would have been connected—we would have shown up to each other if we were related." I sighed. This had felt so right. He was chatty and smart and successful (a former special agent too!), and handsome and warm. All things anyone would want in a father. It was wonderful to connect with him, especially after losing about thirty-six hours of my life with little sleep in anticipation.

Before we got off the phone, promising to meet up with each other once we were in the same city, he said, "If Lupe felt compelled to have a tryst, it was because she was extremely lonely and frustrated, and now you're here! You're the product of that —you won the genetic lottery!"

"Yeah," I said. "Thank you. Thank you for talking to me and thank you for spending the time."

"You bet. And you know what? I wish I was your father."

I wish you were too.

Ghost Dad, I call him now. The myth, the idea, the concept I have of a missing father in my head. I didn't realize how much I had built him up, from my initial searches of Lower East Side opticians, to the Bronx hospital news clippings, to Pimpa's brother, the once-young man who lived down the hall from us. I fell in paternal love with a ghost, a father I made up in my head. Hours, days, months, immersing myself in internet searches, intent on finding the truth. And yes, I hoped one day to do just that. But maybe, just maybe, I thought, he'll stay a ghost. Like Mom. And Alex. And one day, me.

Epilogue

ND WITH A CLICK ON MY KEYBOARD, I FOUND HIM.

One week in the summer of 2021 as I was writing this book, without genealogists or research or phone calls, abruptly my biological father became a ghost dad no more. All it took was refreshing the perpetually open webpage of my Ancestry account.

What had been a nearly religious habit of checking for new relatives on my genetic heritage accounts had become a lapsed practice over time. My search had been slowed by the pandemic as my team of hired genealogists had hit walls in finding records with libraries shut down. Add to this managing my daughter's serious long-haul Covid complications—not to mention the pandemic as a whole and the loss of my brother—and my energy was focused on what was real rather than what may be. But after nearly two months of open DNA tabs unrefreshed, I felt a tug that August day to check those webpages yet again.

In a blink, she appeared. On my list of DNA matches, high up, there was a new lovely, feminine name, listed as sharing 11 percent of my genetics, a possible niece or first cousin. I instantly emailed my genealogists and they confirmed that she would be not a cousin but my half-niece, the daughter of a biological half-sister.

It took a day for me to foment the bravery to message her, first gathering words of support from Belinda and a few friends. My niece messaged back the day after that. She wrote that her mother, my sister, was excited to meet me. But my father, our father, had been dead for nineteen years. I read that news over and over through tears. I cried the full day. I had missed the opportunity to meet and know my father.

"He loved art—he made a studio where he painted and he loved to read, collected books. Self-taught, though, because his education stopped very young." I was sitting outside at a café with my new biological half-sister, whose youngest daughter was the mystery niece who had popped up in my account. We didn't look alike, my half-sister and I, but we *felt* alike. She was tall, blond with blue eyes, like my daughter. Her mother, his wife at the time I was conceived, was tall and blond, hence my sister's looks. At one point during our lunch as I spoke with my usual energetic gesticulation, she burst into tears. She saw him for a moment. Our father. Our father who had passed away nineteen years ago, two years before Mom, our father, who was to me a stranger, but to her a lifelong parent who was gone. She showed me photos of him at her wedding, bearded and gaunt. He'd had his first heart attack in his forties and passed from emphysema in his sixties, a lifelong pack-and-a-half-a-day smoker. My first thought was that he looked so much like Marty, it was uncanny. Short statured, similar complexion and build, beard and hair. They could have been brothers. Easy to see how the deceit was pulled off.

His name was Florencio but he went by Frank. When he knew my mother, he lived with his wife, my sister's mother, just up the street on Claremont, where he was the building manager at the New York Theological Seminary. He was a Lothario, my sister tells me. And a hard man. One of eleven siblings, all from the Canary Islands. By our definition in the United States, they are Hispanic, not Latino, like their famous native actor Javier Bardem. I was the daughter of a Canario, a man from a land geographically North Africa but colonized concurrently with Latin America in the 1500s by the Spanish. Christopher Columbus stopped in the Canary Islands just before landing his genocidal self in Hispaniola, aka the current Dominican Republic. Two stops for him, each at the origin of one of my biological parents. Frank was the only one in his family who'd made it to the United States.

"Did you know about me?" I asked my new older sister.

"When I was twenty-one, my Tia Carmen—she's the youngest—told me that my father had had a daughter with a married woman in the neighborhood," she said. I was shocked to have a Tia Carmen. Another connection. Was I named after her? Or my godmother? Or both?

My sister and I FaceTimed Tia Carmen in Tenerife, in the Canary Islands, during our lunch. My cheeks hurt from smiling so broadly. Her warmth radiated through the phone. We all connected via social media and the old photos started pouring in. Tia Carmen sent me a photo of my father from the year that I came about, 1971. The resemblance is clear. It's a typically blurry old picture. His head is bowed down with a slight smile. Sitting next to him, looking right at the camera, is my sister, who was nine years old when I was born. Frank's skin was lighter than mine, but the shape of his head, hairline, brow, and features were all too familiar. It helped that my haircut was similar to his in the picture, short and shaped. I showed the photo to my teenage daughter. "Bah!" she laughed. Without his mustache and with a tan, she said, "that's you, Mom!"

A long-preserved memory surfaced from that photo. I was maybe three years old, and I remember that my mother and I were alone, which was rare, in our apartment on Claremont. She had dressed me up as if we were going to Sunday mass, hair done too, but we weren't. The doorbell rang. Mom let a man in the door, and I ran and hid under the kitchen table, bashful for some reason. I heard Lupe bring the man over to the kitchen. She said to me, "Come out here, m'ija. Let him take a look at you."

I peeked out from under the table to see his face. He was small and pale with black hair, a black mustache, and big dark eyes. *Frank?*

I called Marty to tell him that I had found my biological father.

"I know this isn't nice to hear, but . . ." I recounted that he had been a married man who lived just up the street, and how much they looked alike.

He sighed. "You know. I look back now and see things differently.

She was so crazy jealous, accusing me of things, but this whole time . . ." His thoughts drifted.

That scene where she drove to his coworker's house in a rage came to both our minds. Justified or not, I may not ever know and frankly, it doesn't matter to me who had been in the right or wrong that night. A parent betraying a child is much worse.

Dad continued, "It was a few really hard years there at the end. I really regret that." He was talking about those last few years before their split when the house was such an angry, painful place for everyone, the two of them taking all the air and turning it into soot. But I was only a visitor to the house then, grown and out. My littlest sisters bore the brunt of it, and I can only imagine their stories.

"Yeah, Dad. It was brutal, but especially for the girls." I needed to say that out loud to him. I needed him to hear that.

"So now I'm thinking," Marty said, "back to when we got married, up there in Brattleboro, Vermont, and how hard she was crying——I mean, she was wailing! But now I see it as maybe she was crying so much because it was the end of something, not just the beginning. There was a whole side of her I didn't know."

He was talking as if I wasn't on the line anymore. As if this call wasn't about me at all, just them. I had to focus him on questions I still needed answered. "Dad," I said, "I never asked you: Why did you keep it a secret, that Peter wasn't my father, that you were?"

"You know, I intended to adopt both of you [Alex and me], and I kept trying but it would just lead to arguments, so I stopped."

"But even then, why didn't you tell me?" I pressed.

"I was trying to keep the peace," he said.

That's what we all were always trying to do. Lupe as an entity, her existence, required all those around her to work hard to keep the peace, her peace. To not anger her, question her, stand up to her. Feel anything different from her. My upbringing by Lupe didn't start this way. It soured over time, catching my younger sisters in the crosshairs. We ended up raised with only two states of being: saccharine (pretending) or sour (defending). Nothing in between. Either we were posturing to keep the peace or reacting with bitterness. Combative or conciliatory. And caring about both Mom's and Dad's feelings was front and center. Not our own or each other's.

"Well, all this, it doesn't change the fifty years that've gone by," Dad said.

"Oh, it does," I said. "Just like you're seeing your past with Mom differently, I've had to do the same thing with both of you—Mom and you—thinking back about all the ways I was treated differently, signs that something was up. And finding out after thirty years that I'm not Chinese is a very big deal."

"Maybe if we'd all known the truth from the beginning, from day one, things would have been better," Dad said.

"Well. I don't know about that," I said. "But once I grew up, once I became an adult, or even eighteen, I should have known."

"Yeah," he said.

I don't know if I'm still waiting for an apology. I've learned as the daughter of people who never apologized in their lives that waiting for apologies, expecting even one, is moot. And I shouldn't have to ask. But I'd certainly welcome one. A recognition of responsibility. Of the pain they caused protecting their secrets.

Four people, one mother and three fathers, all served their own interests rather than the human being they brought into this world.

Peter thought he'd get to keep his wife by claiming me as his own.

Marty got his wife, more kids, and kept the peace by not.

Frank got his illicit romance and kept his marriage.

Mom, she had three men thinking that I was their child. Three. Impressive.

And for me, Papi provided a name, cultural identity, the hustle, plus legitimacy as a child born in wedlock. Marty provided sisters, an introduction to white America, traditional fatherhood, and a presence. And Frank, the "sauce." The genes that helped make me me.

I have three fathers but not one whole one.

"Yes. I recognize him." Pimpa, my godmother, wrote to me in response to seeing the photo of Frank with my sister around when I was born. "He was a very talented person according to what your mom would tell me—she had some of his written work. She wrote poetry and he wrote as well."

WHY DIDN'T MOM TELL ME? What did she have to lose, in the end? Therein lies the answer, I think. She didn't tell me ever because of what she'd have to lose. She would have lost maybe all the financial support of her first husband, Papi. She would have possibly lost her second husband, Marty, the father of her subsequent four children, her white knight. She could have lost any standing she had in the church, her families, both our Dominican family and Marty's family. But then why, after she and Marty divorced, and his and her parents had passed, friendships and the church long gone too, would she continue to not tell the truth? Once I was grown?

Because she would have lost who she was to me and who she was to everyone else. The idea of herself she wanted me to have, all of us kids to have of her. That she had done things by the book. The matriarch who did no wrong. An idea tied to ego. But I'm a person. One greatly shaped and affected by the maintenance—careful, tenuous maintenance—of a deception.

Mom's gone. She took her answers and her stories with her. But I've settled in with what may have been. And in so many ways, I'm grateful to her. I should be glad for these men in my life, each a father in their own way. It all could have been better, but I turned out okay.

Lupe ended up pouring a solid foundation for me despite all the things working against her, an Afro-Latina immigrant woman in the twentieth century. She made sure I didn't become trapped in the ideas of being lesser-than. Ideas that surrounded her at home and in the worlds around us. How can I not forgive her? Of course, it's easier to forgive once someone is gone. And easier to love.

Now I have dozens of new cousins, a few aunts, a sister, nieces, all waiting to live lives with me in them. Photos sent to me by my new family in the Canary Islands give hope to my heart. I see warm, smiling people with faces that resemble mine, standing together, holding each other over paella, cervezas, and wine. One day I'll go there with my birth sister and my daughter and discover a new inheritance. I'll learn a new history, build new memories and ties.

Leave few questions unanswered.

ACKNOWLEDGMENTS

I AM FOREVER GRATEFUL TO MY HEART, MY WISE, TALENTED, brave daughter, B. Always with gratitude to my big brother, Alex, and my big sister, Belinda, thank you. To friend and family Sheryl Tucker, you have changed my life for the best. To my ancestors who have held me up, have my back, and nudge me forward, gracias por siempre.

Thank you, Johanna Castillo, for championing my story and so many others that need to be told. Madhulika Sikka, my fantastic editor, I am grateful for your vision and heart. Dear friend and first reader, Suzanne Rust, thank you.

To my Yoda, Dr. Bill Murray, thank you for years of wisdom and guidance. I feel the force. Friend and ally, Mary Pender, I appreciate you always. To my first writing champion, Adam Sexton, I did it! To Angela Mayack, family and support for me and B, we are forever grateful for you.

Amazing Catherine Burns, thank you for honoring me with your Moth stage and your grace to first bring this story to light. Trailblazer, dear amiga, and inspiration, Veronica Chambers, gracias always. Beloved friend and former board colleague, Aimee Cunningham, you are a treasure.

And to the crew of women who have been there so hard for me over the years, I wish blessings upon you, always. #CRDUBSDR50

Why
Didn't You
Tell Me?

—

CARMEN RITA
WONG

A BOOK CLUB GUIDE

Questions and Topics
for Discussion

1. What does knowing our origins do for us and how might not knowing our true origins affect us? Why do you think we place so much importance on family history?

2. Describe the author's feelings upon learning the truth. How does this change her relationship with the man who raised her? How would you have felt in her position?

3. Did the book give you insight into your own family dynamics? How does your family's culture or race influence those dynamics?

4. "In a span of eighteen months, I had lost my mother, my father, a whole racial and ethnic community, identity, and heritage." There are still more seismic changes to come for Carmen. How does she handle these? How have you handled major changes in your life?

5. How does Carmen's experience affect her relationship with her own daughter?

6. Referring to the book's title, why do you think Carmen's mother didn't tell her the truth?

7. Every family has secrets. If family secrets are so universal, why do we still keep them?

8. What does *Why Didn't You Tell Me?* ultimately say about family and identity? What did you take away from this reading experience?

9. How does this book make you think about your relationship with your own mother? Are there things about her that you don't know or may never know?

CARMEN RITA WONG is a writer, producer, and nonprofit board leader, including the boards of The Moth and the Planned Parenthood Federation of America. She is the former co-creator and television host of *On the Money* on CNBC, a former professor, and was a national advice columnist for *Glamour, Latina, Essence, Men's Health,* and *Good Housekeeping.* Carmen is the author of a series of novels and two best-selling advice books. She is the founder and CEO of Malecon Productions, LLC, where she develops woman-focused media and entertainment. She lives in Manhattan with her daughter.

Carmenritawong.com

ABOUT THE TYPE

This book was set in Bembo, a typeface based on an old-style Roman face that was used for Cardinal Pietro Bembo's tract *De Aetna* in 1495. Bembo was cut by Francesco Griffo (1450–1518) in the early sixteenth century for Italian Renaissance printer and publisher Aldus Manutius (1449–1515). The Lanston Monotype Company of Philadelphia brought the well-proportioned letterforms of Bembo to the United States in the 1930s.